# Microsoft® Office PowerPoint® 2007

## ILLUSTRATED

**INTRODUCTORY**

David Beskeen

COURSE TECHNOLOGY
CENGAGE Learning™

Australia • Brazil • Japan • Korea • Mexico • Singapore • Spain • United Kingdom • United States

COURSE TECHNOLOGY
CENGAGE Learning™

## Microsoft® Office PowerPoint® 2007—Illustrated Introductory

### David Beskeen

Senior Acquisitions Editor: Marjorie Hunt

Senior Product Manager: Christina Kling Garrett

Associate Product Manager: Rebecca Padrick

Editorial Assistant: Michelle Camisa

Senior Marketing Manager: Joy Stark

Marketing Coordinator: Jennifer Hankin

Contributing Author: Elizabeth Eisner Reding

Developmental Editor: Rachel Biheller Bunin

Production Editor: Summer Hughes

Copy Editor: Harold Johnson

QA Manuscript Reviewers:

Jeff Schwartz, Danielle Shaw, Teresa Storch,
    Susan Whalen

Cover Designers: Elizabeth Paquin, Kathleen Fivel

Cover Artist: Mark Hunt

Composition: GEX Publishing Services

Proofreader: Cecile Kaufman

Indexer: Alexandra Nickerson

For product information and technology assistance, contact us at
**Cengage Learning Academic Resource Center, 1-800-423-0563**
For permission to use material from this text or product, submit all requests online at
**www.cengage.com/permissions**.
Further permissions questions can be e-mailed to
**permissionrequest@cengage.com**

ISBN-13: 978-1-4239-0524-0

ISBN-10: 1-4239-0524-5

**Course Technology Cengage Learning**
25 Thomson Place
Boston, MA 02210
USA

Cengage Learning products are represented in Canada by Nelson Education, Ltd.

For your course and learning solutions, visit **academic.cengage.com**

Trademarks:

Some of the product names and company names used in this book have been used for identification purposes only and may be trademarks or registered trademarks of their respective manufacturers and sellers.

Microsoft and the Office logo are either registered trademarks or trademarks of Microsoft Corporation in the United States and/or other countries. Course Technology is an independent entity from Microsoft Corporation, and not affiliated with Microsoft in any manner. Microsoft product screen shot(s) reprinted with permission from Microsoft Corporation.

Credit List

| Figure | Credit Line |
| --- | --- |
| C-6 | Courtesy of Jennifer L. Beskeen |
| C-12 | Courtesy of Barbara Clemens |
| D-5 | Courtesy of Christopher Garrett |
| G-6 | Courtesy of Karen Beskeen |
| G-13 | Courtesy of Karen Beskeen |
| G-15 | Courtesy of Karen Beskeen |
| H-18 | Courtesy of MT Cozzola |
| H-19 | Courtesy of MT Cozzola |
| H-22 | Courtesy of Karen Beskeen |

Other photos provided by Barbara Clemens

Printed in the United States of America
3 4 5 6 7 13 12 11 10 09 08

# About This Book

Welcome to *Microsoft Office PowerPoint 2007—Illustrated Introductory*! Since the first book in the Illustrated Series was published in 1994, millions of students have used various Illustrated texts to master software skills and learn computer concepts. We are proud to bring you this new Illustrated book on the most exciting version of Microsoft Office ever to release.

As you probably have heard by now, Microsoft completely redesigned this latest version of Office from the ground up. No more menus! No more toolbars! The software changes Microsoft made were based on years of research during which they studied users' needs and work habits. The result is a phenomenal and powerful new version of the software that will make you and your students more productive and help you get better results faster.

Before we started working on this new edition, we also conducted our own research. We reached out to nearly 100 instructors like you who have used previous editions of this book and our Microsoft Office texts. Some of you responded to one of our surveys; others of you generously spent time with us on the phone, telling us your thoughts. Seven of you agreed to serve on our Advisory Board and guided our decisions.

As a result of all the feedback you gave us, we have preserved the features that you love, and made improvements that you suggested and requested. And of course we have covered all the key features of the new software. (For more details on what's new in this edition, please read the Preface.) We are confident that this book and all its available resources will help your students master Microsoft Office PowerPoint 2007.

## Advisory Board

We thank our Advisory Board who enthusiastically gave us their opinions and guided our every decision on content and design from beginning to end. They are:

Kristen Callahan, Mercer County Community College

Paulette Comet, Assistant Professor, Community College of Baltimore County

Barbara Comfort, J. Sargeant Reynolds Community College

Margaret Cooksey, Tallahassee Community College

Rachelle Hall, Glendale Community College

Hazel Kates, Miami Dade College

Charles Lupico, Thomas Nelson Community College

## Author Acknowledgments

**David Beskeen** Experience, dedication, hard work, and attention-to-detail with a little humor thrown in are the qualities of a great editor and Rachel Biheller Bunin is truly a great editor—thank you so much! To all of the professionals at Course Technology, led by Christina Kling Garrett, thanks for your hard work. I would also like to especially thank Marjorie Hunt, who fifteen years ago, gave me my first opportunity to use my knowledge of PowerPoint to help others learn. Finally, a special thanks to my wife, Karen, and the "J's", for always being there.

# Preface

Welcome to *Microsoft Office PowerPoint 2007—Illustrated Introductory*. If this is your first experience with the Illustrated series, you'll see that this book has a unique design: each skill is presented on two facing pages, with steps on the left and screens on the right. The layout makes it easy to digest a skill without having to read a lot of text and flip pages to see an illustration.

This book is an ideal learning tool for a wide range of learners—the rookies will find the clean design easy to follow and focused with only essential information presented, and the hot-shots will appreciate being able to move quickly through the lessons to find the information they need without reading a lot of text. The design also makes this a great reference after the course is over! See the illustration on the right to learn more about the pedagogical and design elements of a typical lesson.

## What's New in This Edition

We've made many changes and enhancements to this edition to make it the best ever. Here are some highlights of what's new:

- **New Getting Started with Microsoft Office 2007 Unit**—This unit begins the book and gets students up to speed on features of Office 2007 that are common to all the applications, such as the Ribbon, the Office button, and the Quick Access toolbar.

- **Real Life Independent Challenge**—The new Real Life Independent Challenge exercises offer students the opportunity to create projects that are meaningful to their lives, such as a personal letterhead, a database to track personal expenses, or a budget for buying a house.

- **New Case Study**—A new case study featuring Quest Specialty Travel provides a practical and fun scenario that students can relate to as they learn skills. This

Each two-page spread focuses on a single skill.

Concise text introduces the basic principles in the lesson and integrates a real-world case study.

---

**UNIT D**
**PowerPoint 2007**

# Using Slide Show Commands

With PowerPoint, you can show a presentation on any compatible computer using Slide Show view. As you've seen, Slide Show view fills your computer screen with the slides of the presentation, showing them one at a time. Once the presentation is in Slide Show view, you can use a number of slide show options to tailor the show to meet your needs. For example, you can draw, or **annotate**, on slides or jump to different slides in other parts of the presentation. Ellen wants you to learn how to run a slide show and use the slide show options so you can help her when she gives the presentation. You run the slide show of the presentation and practice using some of the custom slide show options.

## STEPS

1. **Click the** View **tab on the Ribbon, then click the** Slide Show **button in the Presentation Views group**
   The first slide of the presentation fills the screen.

2. **Press [Spacebar]**
   Slide 2 appears on the screen. Pressing [Spacebar] or clicking the left mouse button is the easiest way to move through a slide show. See Table D-2 for other Slide Show view key commands. You can also use the Slide Show shortcut menu for on-screen navigation during a slide show.

3. **Right-click anywhere on the screen, point to** Go to Slide **on the shortcut menu, then click** 8 Mediterranean Islands Bike Tour
   The slide show jumps to Slide 8. You can highlight or emphasize major points in your presentation by annotating the slide during a slide show using one of PowerPoint's annotation tools.

   > **TROUBLE**
   > The Slide Show toolbar buttons are semitransparent and will blend in with the background color on the slide.

4. **Move the pointer to the bottom left corner of the screen to display the Slide Show toolbar, click the** Pen Options menu button ✎**, then click** Highlighter
   The pointer changes to the highlighter pointer.

5. **Drag to highlight the text below the picture**
   Compare your screen to Figure D-5. While the annotation tool is visible, mouse clicks do not advance the slide show; however, you can still move to the next slide by pressing [Spacebar] or [Enter].

   > **QUICK TIP**
   > You have the option of saving undeleted annotations you create while in Slide Show view when you end or quit the slide show.

6. **Click the** Pen Options menu button ✎ **on the Slide Show toolbar, click** Erase All Ink on Slide**, then press [Ctrl][A]**
   The annotations on Slide 8 are erased and the pointer returns to when you press [Ctrl][A].

7. **Click the** Slide Show menu button ▣ **on the Slide Show toolbar, point to** Go to Slide, **then click** 10 Adventure Series **on the menu**
   Slide 10 appears.

   > **QUICK TIP**
   > If you know the slide number of a slide you want to jump to during a slide show, type the number, then press [Enter].

8. **Press [Home], then press [Enter] to advance through the slide show, then when you see the black slide at the end of the slide show, press [Spacebar]**
   You are returned to Normal view. The black slide indicates the end of the slide show.

**PowerPoint 78**     Finishing a Presentation

---

Hints as well as troubleshooting advice, right where you need it—next to the step itself.

Every lesson features large, full-color representations of what the screen should look like as students complete the numbered steps.

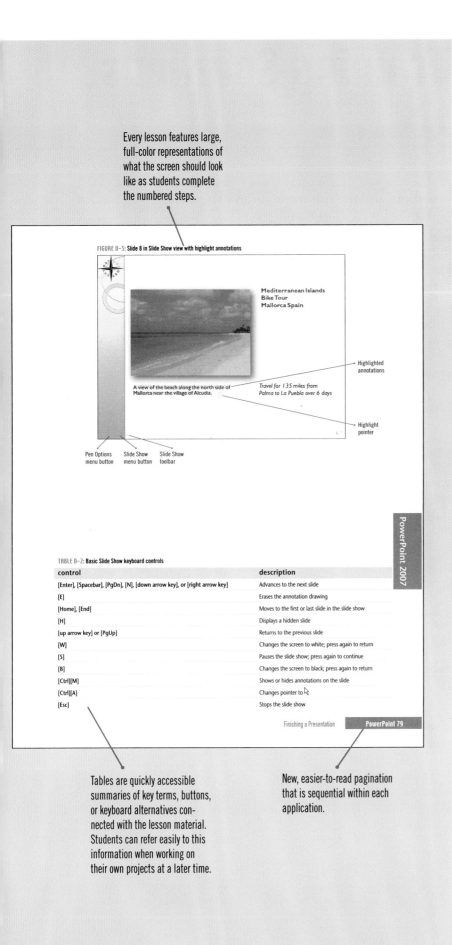

FIGURE D-5: Slide 8 in Slide Show view with highlight annotations

Mediterranean Islands
Bike Tour
Mallorca Spain

Highlighted annotations

A view of the beach along the north side of Mallorca near the village of Alcudia.

Travel for 135 miles from Palma to La Puebla over 6 days

Highlight pointer

Pen Options menu button     Slide Show menu button     Slide Show toolbar

TABLE D-2: Basic Slide Show keyboard controls

| control | description |
| --- | --- |
| [Enter], [Spacebar], [PgDn], [N], [down arrow key], or [right arrow key] | Advances to the next slide |
| [E] | Erases the annotation drawing |
| [Home], [End] | Moves to the first or last slide in the slide show |
| [H] | Displays a hidden slide |
| [up arrow key] or [PgUp] | Returns to the previous slide |
| [W] | Changes the screen to white; press again to return |
| [S] | Pauses the slide show; press again to continue |
| [B] | Changes the screen to black; press again to return |
| [Ctrl][M] | Shows or hides annotations on the slide |
| [Ctrl][A] | Changes pointer to ↖ |
| [Esc] | Stops the slide show |

Finishing a Presentation     **PowerPoint 79**

Tables are quickly accessible summaries of key terms, buttons, or keyboard alternatives connected with the lesson material. Students can refer easily to this information when working on their own projects at a later time.

New, easier-to-read pagination that is sequential within each application.

fictional company offers a wide variety of tours around the world.

- Content Improvements—All of the content in the book has been updated to cover Office 2007 and also to address instructor feedback. See the instructor resource CD for details on specific content changes for PowerPoint.

## Assignments

The lessons use Quest Specialty Travel, a fictional adventure travel company, as the case study. The assignments on the light purple pages at the end of each unit increase in difficulty. Data files and case studies provide a variety of interesting and relevant business applications. Assignments include:

- **Concepts Reviews** consist of multiple choice, matching, and screen identification questions.
- **Skills Reviews** provide additional hands-on, step-by-step reinforcement.
- **Independent Challenges** are case projects requiring critical thinking and application of the unit skills. The Independent Challenges increase in difficulty, with the first one in each unit being the easiest. Independent Challenges 2 and 3 become increasingly open-ended, requiring more independent problem solving.
- **Real Life Independent Challenges** are practical exercises in which students create documents to help them with their every day lives.
- **Advanced Challenge Exercises** set within the Independent Challenges provide optional steps for more advanced students.
- **Visual Workshops** are practical, self-graded capstone projects that require independent problem solving.

# Assessment & Training Solutions

## SAM 2007

SAM 2007 helps bridge the gap between the classroom and the real world by allowing students to train and test on important computer skills in an active, hands-on environment.

SAM 2007's easy-to-use system includes powerful interactive exams, training or projects on critical applications such as Word, Excel, Access, PowerPoint, Outlook, Windows, the Internet, and much more. SAM simulates the application environment, allowing students to demonstrate their knowledge and think through the skills by performing real-world tasks.

Designed to be used with the Illustrated series, SAM 2007 includes built-in page references so students can print helpful study guides that match the Illustrated textbooks used in class. Powerful administrative options allow instructors to schedule exams and assignments, secure tests, and run reports with almost limitless flexibility.

## Student Edition Labs

Our Web-based interactive labs help students master hundreds of computer concepts, including input and output devices, file management and desktop applications, computer ethics, virus protection, and much more. Featuring up-to-the-minute content, eye-popping graphics, and rich animation, the highly interactive Student Edition Labs offer students an alternative way to learn through dynamic observation, step-by-step practice, and challenging review questions. Also available on CD at an additional cost.

## Online Content    Blackboard

Blackboard is the leading distance learning solution provider and class-management platform today. Course Technology has partnered with Blackboard to bring you premium online content. Instructors: Content for use with *Microsoft Office PowerPoint 2007—Illustrated Introductory* is available in a Blackboard Course Cartridge and may include topic reviews, case projects, review questions, test banks, practice tests, custom syllabi, and more.

Course Technology also has solutions for several other learning management systems. Please visit *www.course.com* today to see what's available for this title.

# Instructor Resources

The Instructor Resources CD is Course Technology's way of putting the resources and information needed to teach and learn effectively into your hands. With an integrated array of teaching and learning tools that offers you and your students a broad range of technology-based instructional options, we believe this CD represents the highest quality and most cutting edge resources available to instructors today. Many of these resources are available at *www.course.com*. The resources available with this book are:

- **Instructor's Manual**—Available as an electronic file, the Instructor's Manual includes detailed lecture topics with teaching tips for each unit.

- **Sample Syllabus**—Prepare and customize your course easily using this sample course outline.

- **PowerPoint Presentations**—Each unit has a corresponding PowerPoint presentation that you can use in lecture, distribute to your students, or customize to suit your course.

- **Figure Files**—The figures in the text are provided on the Instructor Resources CD to help you illustrate key topics or concepts. You can create traditional overhead transparencies by printing the figure files. Or you can create electronic slide shows by using the figures in a presentation program such as PowerPoint.

- **Solutions to Exercises**—Solutions to Exercises contains every file students are asked to create or modify in the lessons and end-of-unit material. Also provided in this section, there is a document outlining the solutions for the end-of-unit Concepts Review, Skills Review, and Independent Challenges. An Annotated Solution File and Grading Rubric accompany each file and can be used together for quick and easy grading.

- **Data Files for Students**—To complete most of the units in this book, your students will need Data Files. You can post the Data Files on a file server for students to copy. The Data Files are available on the Instructor Resources CD-ROM, the Review Pack, and can also be downloaded from www.course.com. In this edition, we have included a lesson on downloading the Data Files for this book, see page xvi.

Instruct students to use the Data Files List included on the Review Pack and the Instructor Resources CD. This list gives instructions on copying and organizing files.

- **ExamView**—ExamView is a powerful testing software package that allows you to create and administer printed, computer (LAN-based), and Internet exams. ExamView includes hundreds of questions that correspond to the topics covered in this text, enabling students to generate detailed study guides that include page references for further review. The computer-based and Internet testing components allow students to take exams at their computers, and also saves you time by grading each exam automatically.

## CourseCasts—Learning on the Go. Always available...always relevant.

Want to keep up with the latest technology trends relevant to you? Visit our site to find a library of podcasts, CourseCasts, featuring a "CourseCast of the Week," and download them to your mp3 player at *http://coursecasts.course.com*.

Our fast-paced world is driven by technology. You know because you're an active participant—always on the go, always keeping up with technological trends, and always learning new ways to embrace technology to power your life.

Ken Baldauf, a faculty member of the Florida State University Computer Science Department, is responsible for teaching technology classes to thousands of FSU students each year. He knows what you know; he knows what you want to learn. He's also an expert in the latest technology and will sort through and aggregate the most pertinent news and information so you can spend your time enjoying technology, rather than trying to figure it out.

Visit us at *http://coursecasts.course.com* to learn on the go!

# Brief Contents

Preface                                                                                          iv

OFFICE 2007          Unit A: Getting Started with Microsoft Office 2007                            1

POWERPOINT 2007      Unit A: Creating a Presentation in PowerPoint 2007                            1

POWERPOINT 2007      Unit B: Modifying a Presentation                                             25

POWERPOINT 2007      Unit C: Inserting Objects into a Presentation                                49

POWERPOINT 2007      Unit D: Finishing a Presentation                                             73

POWERPOINT 2007      Unit E: Working with Advanced Tools and Masters                              97

POWERPOINT 2007      Unit F: Enhancing Charts                                                    121

POWERPOINT 2007      Unit G: Inserting Illustrations, Objects, and Media Clips                   145

POWERPOINT 2007      Unit H: Using Advanced Features                                             169

Appendix                                                                                         1

Glossary                                                                                         9

Index                                                                                           13

# Contents

Preface ...........................................................................................................................iv

---

**OFFICE 2007**

## Unit A: Getting Started with Microsoft Office 2007      1

Understanding the Office 2007 Suite.......................................................................2
    Deciding which program to use
Starting and Exiting an Office Program .................................................................4
    Using shortcut keys to move between Office programs
Viewing the Office 2007 User Interface ..................................................................6
    Customizing the Quick Access toolbar
Creating and Saving a File ......................................................................................8
    Using the Office Clipboard
Opening a File and Saving it with a New Name ...................................................10
    Exploring File Open options
    Working in Compatibility mode
Viewing and Printing Your Work...........................................................................12
    Using the Print Screen feature to create a screen capture
Getting Help and Closing a File.............................................................................14
    Recovering a document
Concepts Review ...................................................................................................16
Independent Challenges .......................................................................................16

---

**POWERPOINT 2007**

## Unit A: Creating a Presentation in PowerPoint 2007      1

Defining Presentation Software ..............................................................................2
Planning an Effective Presentation ........................................................................4
    Understanding copyright
Examining the PowerPoint Window .......................................................................6
    Viewing your presentation in grayscale or black and white
Entering Slide Text .................................................................................................8
    Saving fonts with your presentation
Adding a New Slide................................................................................................10
Applying a Design Theme ......................................................................................12
    Customizing themes
Comparing Presentation Views .............................................................................14
Printing a PowerPoint Presentation ......................................................................16
    Animating in PowerPoint
Concepts Review....................................................................................................18
Skills Review .........................................................................................................19
Independent Challenges ........................................................................................21
Visual Workshop....................................................................................................24

---

**POWERPOINT 2007**

## Unit B: Modifying a Presentation      25

Entering Text in the Outline Tab ..........................................................................26
    Setting permissions
Formatting Text .....................................................................................................28
    Replacing text and fonts

Converting Text to SmartArt ..................................................................................30
   Choosing SmartArt graphics
Inserting and Modifying Shapes ...............................................................................32
   Changing the size and position of shapes
Editing and Duplicating Shapes...............................................................................34
   Understanding PowerPoint objects
Aligning and Grouping Objects ...............................................................................36
   Distributing objects
Adding Slide Headers and Footers ...........................................................................38
   Entering and printing notes
Checking Spelling in a Presentation .........................................................................40
   Checking spelling as you type
Concepts Review.....................................................................................................42
Skills Review .........................................................................................................43
Independent Challenges .........................................................................................45
Visual Workshop....................................................................................................48

**POWERPOINT 2007**      **Unit C: Inserting Objects into a Presentation**     **49**

Inserting Text from Microsoft Word .........................................................................50
   Inserting slides from other presentations
Inserting Clip Art ..................................................................................................52
   Finding more clips online
Inserting and Styling a Picture................................................................................54
   Picture compression
Inserting a Text Box ..............................................................................................56
   Sending a presentation using e-mail
Inserting a Chart....................................................................................................58
Entering and Editing Chart Data .............................................................................60
   Series in rows vs. series in columns
Inserting a Table ...................................................................................................62
   Saving slides as graphics
Insert and Format WordArt .....................................................................................64
   Using content templates from the Web
Concepts Review.....................................................................................................66
Skills Review .........................................................................................................67
Independent Challenges .........................................................................................69
Visual Workshop....................................................................................................72

**POWERPOINT 2007**      **Unit D: Finishing a Presentation**     **73**

Understanding Masters.............................................................................................74
   Create custom slide layouts
Customizing the Background Style ...........................................................................76
Using Slide Show Commands ..................................................................................78
Setting Slide Show Transitions and Timings .............................................................80
   Rehearsing slide show timings
Setting Slide Animation Effects ...............................................................................82
   Presentation checklist
Inspecting a Presentation ........................................................................................84
   Digitally sign a presentation
Evaluating a Presentation........................................................................................86
Creating a Design Template ....................................................................................88
   Applying a theme from another presentation

Concepts Review...................................................................................................90
Skills Review .......................................................................................................91
Independent Challenges .......................................................................................93
Visual Workshop..................................................................................................96

**POWERPOINT 2007**    **Unit E: Working with Advanced Tools and Masters**    **97**

Drawing and Formatting Connectors ...................................................................98
    Drawing a freeform shape
Using Advanced Formatting Tools......................................................................100
    Creating columns in a text box
Customizing Animation Effects...........................................................................102
    Understanding animation timings
Creating Custom Slide Layouts ..........................................................................104
    Restoring the Slide Master layout
Formatting Master Text ......................................................................................106
    Exceptions to the Slide Master
Changing Master Text Indents.............................................................................108
Adjusting Text Objects .......................................................................................110
    More on text spacing
Customizing Handout and Notes Masters ...........................................................112
    Creating handouts in Microsoft Office Word
Concepts Review.................................................................................................114
Skills Review .....................................................................................................115
Independent Challenges .....................................................................................117
Visual Workshop................................................................................................120

**POWERPOINT 2007**    **Unit F: Enhancing Charts**    **121**

Working with Charts in PowerPoint ....................................................................122
    Data series and data series mark
Changing Chart Design and Style .......................................................................124
    Save a chart as a template
Customizing a Chart Layout ...............................................................................126
    Using the Research task pane
Formatting Chart Elements .................................................................................128
    Saving in PDF and XPS file formats
Animating a Chart ..............................................................................................130
    Adding voice narrations
Embedding an Excel Chart..................................................................................132
    Embedding a worksheet
Linking an Excel Worksheet................................................................................134
Updating a Linked Excel Worksheet ...................................................................136
    Using Paste Special
Concepts Review.................................................................................................138
Skills Review .....................................................................................................139
Independent Challenges .....................................................................................141
Visual Workshop................................................................................................144

Creating Custom Tables ............................................................................146
   Drawing tables

Designing a SmartArt Graphic ....................................................................148
   Creating organizational charts

Formatting a SmartArt Graphic ..................................................................150
   Changing page setup and slide orientation

Inserting an Animation ..............................................................................152
   Inserting movies

Inserting a Sound ......................................................................................154
   Playing music from a CD

Using Macros .............................................................................................156
   Macro security

Adding Action Buttons................................................................................158
   The compatibility checker

Inserting a Hyperlink ................................................................................160
   Changing PowerPoint options

Concepts Review.........................................................................................162

Skills Review ..............................................................................................163

Independent Challenges .............................................................................165

Visual Workshop.........................................................................................168

Using Templates and Adding Comments ....................................................170
   Creating a document workspace

Sending and Reviewing a Presentation ......................................................172
   Using PowerPoint's proofing tools

Using Advanced Slide Show Options...........................................................174
   Using Presenter view

Creating a Custom Show ............................................................................176
   Link to a custom slide show

Preparing a Presentation for Distribution ..................................................178
   Creating a strong password

Saving a Presentation for the Web.............................................................180
   Publish slides to a Slide Library

Packaging a Presentation ...........................................................................182
   Using the Microsoft PowerPoint Viewer

Creating a Photo Album.............................................................................184

Concepts Review.........................................................................................186

Skills Review ..............................................................................................187

Independent Challenges .............................................................................189

Visual Workshop.........................................................................................192

Appendix   **1**

Glossary   **9**

Index   **13**

# Read This Before You Begin

## Frequently Asked Questions

### What are Data Files?

A Data File is a partially completed PowerPoint presentation or another type of file that you use to complete the steps in the units and exercises to create the final document that you submit to your instructor. Each unit opener page lists the Data Files that you need for that unit.

### Where are the Data Files?

Your instructor will provide the Data Files to you or direct you to a location on a network drive from which you can download them. Alternatively, you can follow the instructions on the next page to download the Data Files from this book's Web page.

### What software was used to write and test this book?

This book was written and tested using a typical installation of Microsoft Office 2007 on a computer with a typical installation of Windows Vista.

The browser used for any steps that require a browser is Internet Explorer 7. If you are using this book on Windows XP, please see the next page, Important Notes for Windows XP Users. If you are using this book on Windows Vista, please see the Appendix.

### Do I need to be connected to the Internet to complete the steps and exercises in this book?

Some of the exercises in this book assume that your computer is connected to the Internet. If you are not connected to the Internet, see your instructor for information on how to complete the exercises.

### What do I do if my screen is different from the figures shown in this book?

This book was written and tested on computers with monitors set at a resolution of 1024 × 768. If your screen shows more or less information than the figures in the book, your monitor is probably set at a higher or lower resolution. If you don't see something on your screen, you might have to scroll down or up to see the object identified in the figures.

The Ribbon (the blue area at the top of the screen) in Microsoft Office 2007 adapts to different resolutions. If your monitor is set at a lower resolution than 1024 × 768, you might not see all of the buttons shown in the figures. The groups of buttons will always appear, but the entire group might be condensed into a single button that you need to click to access the buttons described in the instructions. For example, the figures and steps in this book assume that the Editing group on the Home tab in Word looks like the following:

## 1024 × 768 Editing Group

Editing Group on the
Home Tab of the
Ribbon at 1024 × 768

If your resolution is set to 800 × 600, the Ribbon in Word will look like the following figure, and you will need to click the Editing button to access the buttons that are visible in the Editing group.

## 800 × 600 Editing Group

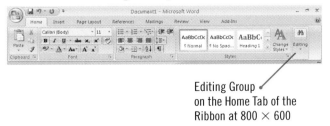

Editing Group
on the Home Tab of the
Ribbon at 800 × 600

## 800 × 600 Editing Group Clicked

Editing Group on the Home Tab of the Ribbon at
800 × 600 is selected to show available buttons

# Important Notes for Windows XP Users

The screenshots in this book show Microsoft Office 2007 running on Windows Vista. However, if you are using Microsoft Windows XP, you can still use this book because Office 2007 runs virtually the same on both platforms. There are a few differences that you will encounter if you are using Windows XP. Read this section to understand the differences.

## Dialog boxes

If you are a Windows XP user, dialog boxes shown in this book will look slightly different than what you see on your screen. Dialog boxes for Windows XP have a blue title bar, instead of a gray title bar. However, beyond this superficial difference in appearance, the options in the dialog boxes across platforms are the same. For instance, the screen shots below show the Font dialog box running on Windows XP and the Font dialog box running on Windows Vista.

**FIGURE 1: Dialog box in Windows XP**

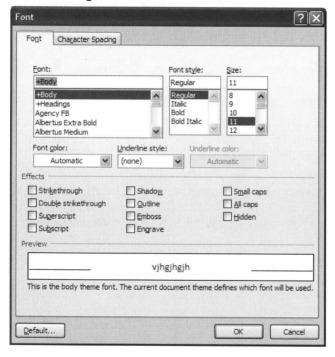

**FIGURE 2: Dialog box in Windows Vista**

## Alternate Steps for Windows XP Users

Nearly all of the steps in this book work exactly the same for Windows XP users. However, there are a few tasks that will require you to complete slightly different steps. This section provides alternate steps for a few specific skills.

## Starting a program

1.  Click the Start button on the taskbar
2.  Point to All Programs, point to Microsoft Office, then click the application you want to use

FIGURE 3: Starting a program

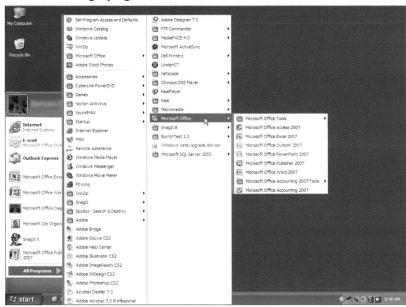

## Saving a file for the first time

1.  Click the Office button, then click Save As
2.  Type a name for your file in the File Name text box
3.  Click the Save in list arrow, then navigate to the drive and folder where you store your Data Files
4.  Click Save

FIGURE 4: Save As dialog box

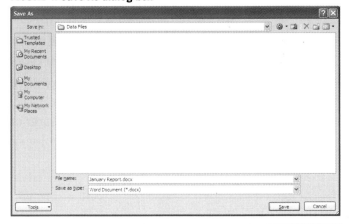

## Opening a file

1.  Click the Office button, then click Open
2.  Click the Look in list arrow, then navigate to the drive and folder where you store your Data Files
3.  Click the file you want to open
4.  Click Open

FIGURE 5: Open dialog box

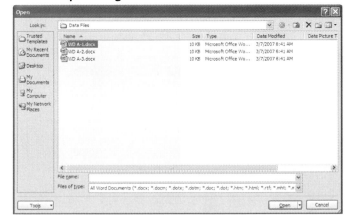

# Downloading Data Files for This Book

In order to complete many of the lesson steps and exercises in this book, you are asked to open and save Data Files. A **Data File** is a partially completed PowerPoint presentation or another type of file that you use as a starting point to complete the steps in the units and exercises. The benefit of using a Data File is that it saves you the time and effort needed to create a file; you can simply open a Data File, save it with a new name (so the original file remains intact), then make changes to it to complete lesson steps or an exercise. Your instructor will provide the Data Files to you or direct you to a location on a network drive from which you can download them. Alternatively, you can follow the instructions in this lesson to download the Data Files from this book's Web page.

1. Start Internet Explorer, type www.course.com in the address bar, then press [Enter]

2. When the Course.com Web site opens, click the Student Downloads link

3. On the Student Downloads page, click in the Search text box, type 9781423905240, then click Go

4. When the page opens for this textbook, in the left navigation bar, click the Download Student Files link, then, on the Student Downloads page, click the Data Files link

5. If the File Download – Security Warning dialog box opens, click Save. (If no dialog box appears, skip this step and go to Step 6)

6. If the Save As dialog box opens, click the Save in list arrow at the top of the dialog box, select a folder on your USB drive or hard disk to download the file to, then click Save

7. Close Internet Explorer and then open My Computer or Windows Explorer and display the contents of the drive and folder to which you downloaded the file

8. Double-click the file 905240.exe in the drive or folder, then, if the Open File – Security Warning dialog box opens, click Run

9. In the WinZip Self-Extractor window, navigate to the drive and folder where you want to unzip the files to, then click Unzip

10. When the WinZip Self-Extractor displays a dialog box listing the number of files that have unzipped successfully, click OK , click Close in the WinZip Self-Extractor dialog box, then close Windows Explorer or My Computer

You are now ready to open the required files.

**QUICK TIP**
You can also click Student Downloads on the right side of the product page.

**TROUBLE**
If a dialog box opens telling you that the download is complete, click Close.

**QUICK TIP**
By default, the files will extract to C:\CourseTechnology\905240

# Getting Started with Microsoft Office 2007

Microsoft Office 2007 is a group of software programs designed to help you create documents, collaborate with co-workers, and track and analyze information. Each program is designed so you can work quickly and efficiently to create professional-looking results. You use different Office programs to accomplish specific tasks, such as writing a letter or producing a sales presentation, yet all the programs have a similar look and feel. Once you become familiar with one program, you'll find it easy to transfer your knowledge to the others.  This unit introduces you to the most frequently used programs in Office, as well as common features they all share.

**OBJECTIVES**

Understand the Office 2007 Suite

Start and exit an Office program

View the Office 2007 user interface

Create and save a file

Open a file and save it with a
new name

View and print your work

Get Help and close a file

# Understanding the Office 2007 Suite

Microsoft Office 2007 features an intuitive, context-sensitive user interface, so you can get up to speed faster and use advanced features with greater ease. The programs in Office are bundled together in a group called a **suite** (although you can also purchase them separately). The Office suite is available in several configurations, but all include Word and Excel. Other configurations include PowerPoint, Access, Outlook, Publisher, and/or others.  Each program in Office is best suited for completing specific types of tasks, though there is some overlap in terms of their capabilities.

**DETAILS**

### The Office programs covered in this book include:

- **Microsoft Office Word 2007**

  When you need to create any kind of text-based document, such as memos, newsletters, or multi-page reports, Word is the program to use. You can easily make your documents look great by inserting eye-catching graphics and using formatting tools such as themes. **Themes** are predesigned combinations of color and formatting attributes you can apply, and are available in most Office programs. The Word document shown in Figure A-1 was formatted with the Solstice theme.

- **Microsoft Office Excel 2007**

  Excel is the perfect solution when you need to work with numeric values and make calculations. It puts the power of formulas, functions, charts, and other analytical tools into the hands of every user, so you can analyze sales projections, figure out loan payments, and present your findings in style. The Excel worksheet shown in Figure A-1 tracks personal expenses. Because Excel automatically recalculates results whenever a value changes, the information is always up-to-date. A chart illustrates how the monthly expenses are broken down.

- **Microsoft Office PowerPoint 2007**

  Using PowerPoint, it's easy to create powerful presentations complete with graphics, transitions, and even a soundtrack. Using professionally designed themes and clip art, you can quickly and easily create dynamic slideshows such as the one shown in Figure A-1.

- **Microsoft Office Access 2007**

  Access helps you keep track of large amounts of quantitative data, such as product inventories or employee records. The form shown in Figure A-1 was created for a grocery store inventory database. Employees use the form to enter data about each item. Using Access enables employees to quickly find specific information such as price and quantity, without hunting through store shelves and stockrooms.

### Microsoft Office has benefits beyond the power of each program, including:

- **Common user interface: Improving business processes**

  Because the Office suite programs have a similar **interface**, or look and feel, your experience using one program's tools makes it easy to learn those in the other programs. Office documents are **compatible** with one another, meaning that you can easily incorporate, or **integrate**, an Excel chart into a PowerPoint slide, or an Access table into a Word document.

- **Collaboration: Simplifying how people work together**

  Office recognizes the way people do business today, and supports the emphasis on communication and knowledge-sharing within companies and across the globe. All Office programs include the capability to incorporate feedback—called **online collaboration**—across the Internet or a company network.

Word document

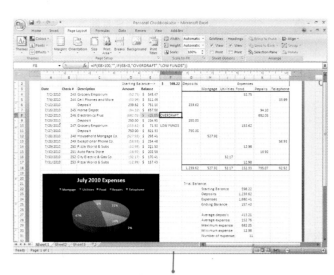

Excel worksheet

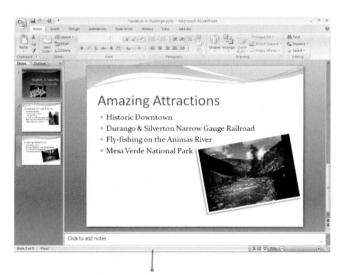

PowerPoint presentation

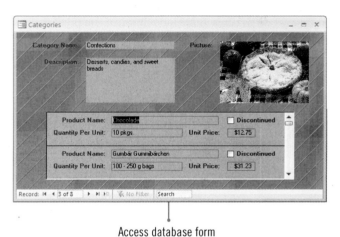

Access database form

## Deciding which program to use

Every Office program includes tools that go far beyond what you might expect. For example, although Excel is primarily designed for making calculations, you can use it to create a database. So when you're planning a project, how do you decide which Office program to use? The general rule of thumb is to use the program best suited for your intended task, and make use of supporting tools in the program if you need them. Word is best for creating text-based documents, Excel is best for making mathematical calculations, PowerPoint is best for preparing presentations, and Access is best for managing quantitative data. Although the capabilities of Office are so vast that you *could* create an inventory in Excel or a budget in Word, you'll find greater flexibility and efficiency by using the program designed for the task. And remember, you can always create a file in one program, and then insert it in a document in another program when you need to, such as including sales projections (Excel) in a memo (Word).

# Starting and Exiting an Office Program

The first step in using an Office program is of course to open, or **launch**, it on your computer. You have a few choices for how to launch a program, but the easiest way is to click the Start button on the Windows taskbar, or to double-click an icon on your desktop. You can have multiple programs open on your computer simultaneously, and you can move between open programs by clicking the desired program or document button on the taskbar or by using the [Alt][Tab] keyboard shortcut combination. When working, you'll often want to open multiple programs in Office, and switch among them throughout the day. Begin by launching a few Office programs now.

## STEPS

1. **Click the Start button 🪟 on the taskbar**

   The Start menu opens, as shown in Figure A-2. If the taskbar is hidden, you can display it by pointing to the bottom of the screen. Depending on your taskbar property settings, the taskbar may be displayed at all times, or only when you point to that area of the screen. For more information, or to change your taskbar properties, consult your instructor or technical support person.

2. **Point to All Programs, click Microsoft Office, then click Microsoft Office Word 2007**

   Microsoft Office Word 2007 starts and the program window opens on your screen.

3. **Click 🪟 on the taskbar, point to All Programs, click Microsoft Office, then click Microsoft Office Excel 2007**

   Microsoft Office Excel 2007 starts and the program window opens, as shown in Figure A-3. Word is no longer visible, but it remains open. The taskbar displays a button for each open program and document. Because this Excel document is **active**, or in front and available, the Microsoft Excel – Book1 button on the taskbar appears in a darker shade.

4. **Click Document1 – Microsoft Word on the taskbar**

   Clicking a button on the taskbar activates that program and document. The Word program window is now in front, and the Document1 – Microsoft Word taskbar button appears shaded.

5. **Click 🪟 on the taskbar, point to All Programs, click Microsoft Office, then click Microsoft Office PowerPoint 2007**

   Microsoft Office PowerPoint 2007 starts, and becomes the active program.

6. **Click Microsoft Excel – Book1 on the taskbar**

   Excel is now the active program.

7. **Click 🪟 on the taskbar, point to All Programs, click Microsoft Office, then click Microsoft Office Access 2007**

   Microsoft Office Access 2007 starts, and becomes the active program.

8. **Point to the taskbar to display it, if necessary**

   Four Office programs are open simultaneously.

9. **Click the Office button 🔘, then click Exit Access, as shown in Figure A-4**

   Access closes, leaving Excel active and Word and PowerPoint open.

**FIGURE A-2:** Start menu

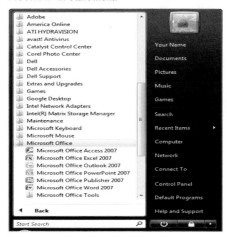

**FIGURE A-3:** Excel program window and Windows taskbar

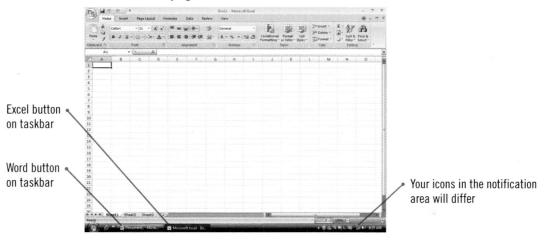

Excel button
on taskbar

Word button
on taskbar

Your icons in the notification
area will differ

**FIGURE A-4:** Exiting Microsoft Office Access

Microsoft
Office button

Exit Access
button

Mouse pointer

## Using shortcut keys to move between Office programs

As an alternative to the Windows taskbar, you can use a keyboard shortcut to move among open Office programs. The [Alt][Tab] keyboard combination lets you either switch quickly to the next open program, or choose one from a palette. To switch immediately to the next open program, press [Alt][Tab]. To choose from all open programs, press and hold [Alt], then press and release [Tab] without releasing [Alt]. A palette opens on screen, displaying the icon and filename of each open program and file. Each time you press [Tab] while holding [Alt], the selection cycles to the next open file. Release [Alt] when the program/file you want to activate is selected.

# Viewing the Office 2007 User Interface

One of the benefits of using Office is that the programs have much in common, making them easy to learn and making it simple to move from one to another. Individual Office programs have always shared many features, but the innovations in the Office 2007 user interface mean even greater similarity among them all. That means you can also use your knowledge of one program to get up to speed in another. A **user interface** is a collective term for all the ways you interact with a software program. The user interface in Office 2007 includes a more intuitive way of choosing commands, working with files, and navigating in the program window. Familiarize yourself with some of the common interface elements in Office by examining the PowerPoint program window.

## STEPS

1. **Click Microsoft PowerPoint – [Presentation1] on the taskbar**

   PowerPoint becomes the active program. Refer to Figure A-5 to identify common elements of the Office user interface. The **document window** occupies most of the screen. In PowerPoint, a blank slide appears in the document window, so you can build your slide show. At the top of every Office program window is a **title bar**, which displays the document and program name. Below the title bar is the **Ribbon**, which displays commands you're likely to need for the current task. Commands are organized into **tabs**. The tab names appear at the top of the Ribbon, and the active tab appears in front with its name highlighted. The Ribbon in every Office program includes tabs specific to the program, but all include a Home tab on the far left, for the most popular tasks in that program.

2. **Click the Office button**

   The Office menu opens. This menu contains commands common to most Office programs, such as opening a file, saving a file, and closing the current program. Next to the Office button is the **Quick Access toolbar**, which includes buttons for common Office commands.

3. **Click again to close it, then point to the Save button on the Quick Access toolbar, *but do not click it***

   You can point to any button in Office to see a description; this is a good way to learn the available choices.

4. **Click the Design tab on the Ribbon**

   To display a different tab, you click its name on the Ribbon. Each tab arranges related commands into **groups** to make features easy to find. The Themes group displays available themes in a **gallery**, or palette of choices you can browse. Many groups contain a **dialog box launcher**, an icon you can click to open a dialog box or task pane for the current group, which offers an alternative way to choose commands.

5. **Move the mouse pointer over the Aspect theme in the Themes group as shown in Figure A-6, *but do not click the mouse button***

   Because you have not clicked the theme, you have not actually made any changes to the slide. With the **Live Preview** feature, you can point to a choice, see the results right in the document, and then decide whether you want to make the change.

6. **Move away from the Ribbon and towards the slide**

   If you clicked the Aspect theme, it would be applied to this slide. Instead, the slide remains unchanged.

7. **Point to the Zoom slider on the status bar, then drag to the right until the Zoom percentage reads 166%**

   The slide display is enlarged. Zoom tools are located on the status bar. You can drag the slider or click the plus and minus buttons to zoom in/out on an area of interest. The percentage tells you the zoom effect.

8. **Drag the Zoom slider on the status bar to the left until the Zoom percentage reads 73%**

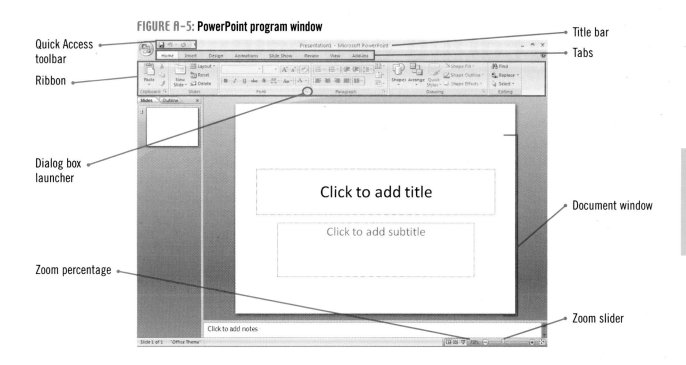

**FIGURE A-5: PowerPoint program window**

Quick Access toolbar
Ribbon
Dialog box launcher
Zoom percentage
Title bar
Tabs
Document window
Zoom slider

Click to add title

Click to add subtitle

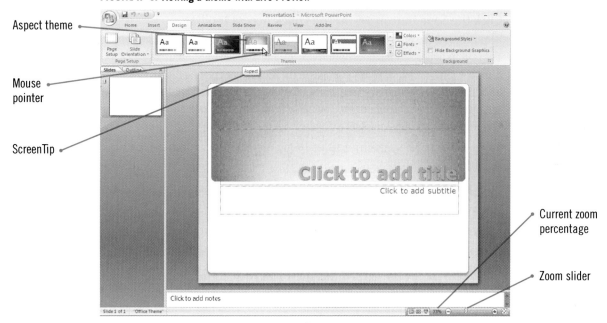

**FIGURE A-6: Viewing a theme with Live Preview**

Aspect theme
Mouse pointer
ScreenTip
Current zoom percentage
Zoom slider

Click to add title

Click to add subtitle

## Customizing the Quick Access toolbar

You can customize the Quick Access toolbar to display your favorite commands. To do so, click the Customize Quick Access Toolbar button ⬇ in the title bar, then click the command you want to add. If you don't see the command in the list, click More Commands to open the Customize tab of the Options dialog box. In the Options dialog box, use the Choose commands from list to choose a category, click the desired command in the list on the left, click Add to add it to the Quick Access toolbar, then click OK. To remove a button from the toolbar, click the name in the list on the right, then click Remove. To add a command to the Quick Access toolbar on the fly, simply right-click the button on the Ribbon, then click Add to Quick Access Toolbar on the shortcut menu. You can also use the Customize Quick Access Toolbar button to move the toolbar below the ribbon, by clicking Show Below the Ribbon, or to minimize the Ribbon so it takes up less space onscreen. If you click Minimize the Ribbon, the Ribbon is minimized to display only the tabs. When you click a tab, the Ribbon opens so you can choose a command; once you choose a command, the Ribbon closes again, and only the tabs are visible.

# Creating and Saving a File

When working in a program, one of the first things you need to do is to create and save a file. A **file** is a stored collection of data. Saving a file enables you to work on a project now, then put it away and work on it again later. In some Office programs, including Word, Excel, and PowerPoint, a new file is automatically created when you start the program, so all you have to do is enter some data and save it. In Access, you must expressly create a file before you enter any data. You should give your files meaningful names and save them in an appropriate location, so they're easy to find.  Use Microsoft Word to familiarize yourself with the process of creating and saving a document. First you'll type some notes about a possible location for a corporate meeting, then you'll save the information for later use.

## STEPS

1. **Click** Document1 – Microsoft Word **on the taskbar**

2. **Type** Locations for Corporate Meeting, **then press [Enter] twice**

    The text appears in the document window, and a cursor blinks on a new blank line. The cursor indicates where the next typed text will appear.

3. **Type** Las Vegas, NV, **press [Enter], type** Orlando, FL, **press [Enter], type** Chicago, IL, **press [Enter] twice, then type your name**

    Compare your document to Figure A-7.

> **QUICK TIP**
>
> A filename can be up to 255 characters, including a file extension, and can include upper- or lowercase characters and spaces, but not ?, ", /, \, <, >, *, |, or :.

4. **Click the** Save button 🖫 **on the Quick Access toolbar**

    Because this is the first time you are saving this document, the Save As dialog box opens, as shown in Figure A-8. The Save As dialog box includes options for assigning a filename and storage location. Once you save a file for the first time, clicking 🖫 saves any changes to the file *without* opening the Save As dialog box, because no additional information is needed. In the Address bar, Office displays the default location for where to save the file, but you can change to any location. In the File name field, Office displays a suggested name for the document based on text in the file, but you can enter a different name.

> **QUICK TIP**
>
> You can create a desktop icon that you can double-click to both launch a program and open a document, by saving it to the desktop.

5. **Type** Potential Corporate Meeting Locations

    The text you type replaces the highlighted text.

6. **In the Save As dialog box, use the Address bar or Navigation pane to navigate to the drive and folder where you store your Data Files**

    Many students store files on a flash drive or Zip drive, but you can also store files on your computer, a network drive, or any storage device indicated by your instructor or technical support person.

> **QUICK TIP**
>
> To create a new blank file when a file is open, click the Office button, click New, then click Create.

7. **Click** Save

    The Save As dialog box closes, the new file is saved to the location you specified, then the name of the document appears in the title bar, as shown in Figure A-9. (You may or may not see a file extension.) See Table A-1 for a description of the different types of files you create in Office, and the file extensions associated with each. You can save a file in an earlier version of a program by choosing from the list of choices in the Save as type list arrow in the Save As dialog box.

**TABLE A-1:** Common filenames and default file extensions

| File created in | is called a | and has the default extension |
| --- | --- | --- |
| Excel | workbook | .xlsx |
| Word | document | .docx |
| Access | database | .accdb |
| PowerPoint | presentation | .pptx |

FIGURE A-7: **Creating a document in Word**

Save button

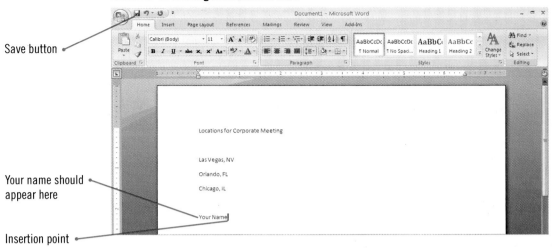

Your name should
appear here

Insertion point

FIGURE A-8: **Save As dialog box**

Address bar

Navigation
pane; your
links and
Folders setting
may differ

File name
field; your computer
may not be set to
display file extensions

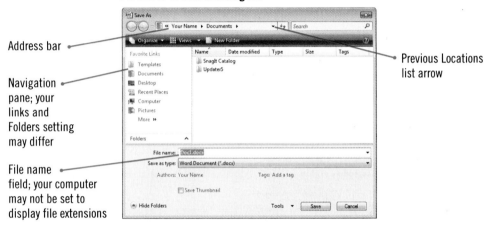

Previous Locations
list arrow

FIGURE A-9: **Named Word document**

Name appears
in title bar

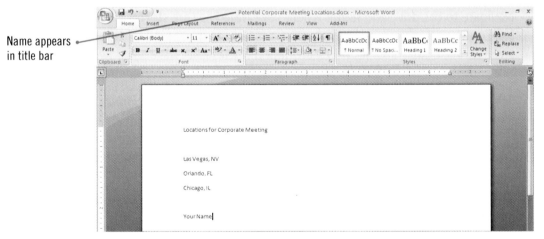

## Using the Office Clipboard

You can use the Office Clipboard to cut and copy items from one Office program and paste them into others. The Clipboard can store a maximum of 24 items. To access it, open the Office Clipboard task pane by clicking the launcher in the Clipboard group in the Home tab. Each time you copy a selection, it is saved in the Office Clipboard. Each entry in the Office Clipboard includes an icon that tells you the program in which it was created. To paste an entry, click in the document where you want it to appear, then click the item in the Office Clipboard. To delete an item from the Office Clipboard, right-click the item, then click Delete.

# Opening a File and Saving it with a New Name

In many cases as you work in Office, you start with a blank document, but often you need to use an existing file. It might be a file you or a co-worker created earlier as a work-in-progress, or it could be a complete document that you want to use as the basis for another. For example, you might want to create a budget for this year using the budget you created last year; you could type in all the categories and information from scratch, or you could open last year's budget, save it with a new name, and just make changes to update it for the current year. By opening the existing file and saving it with the Save As command, you create a duplicate that you can modify to your heart's content, while the original file remains intact.  Use Excel to open an existing workbook file, and save it with a new name so the original remains unchanged.

## STEPS

1. **Click Microsoft Excel – Book1 on the taskbar, click the Office button 🏢, then click Open**
   The Open dialog box opens, where you can navigate to any drive or folder location accessible to your computer to locate a file.

2. **In the Open dialog box, navigate to the drive and folder where you store your Data Files**
   The files available in the current folder are listed, as shown in Figure A-10. This folder contains one file.

3. **Click OFFICE A-1.xlsx, then click Open**
   The dialog box closes and the file opens in Excel. An Excel file is an electronic spreadsheet, so it looks different from a Word document or a PowerPoint slide.

4. **Click 🏢, then click Save As**
   The Save As dialog box opens, and the current filename is highlighted in the File name text box. Using the Save As command enables you to create a copy of the current, existing file with a new name. This action preserves the original file, and creates a new file that you can modify.

5. **Navigate to the drive and folder where your Data Files are stored if necessary, type Budget for Corporate Meeting in the File name text box, as shown in Figure A-11, then click Save**
   A copy of the existing document is created with the new name. The original file, Office A-1.xlsx, closes automatically.

6. **Click cell A19, type your name, then press [Enter], as shown in Figure A-12**
   In Excel, you enter data in cells, which are formed by the intersection of a row and a column. Cell A19 is at the intersection of column A and row 19. When you press [Enter], the cell pointer moves to cell A20.

7. **Click the Save button 🖫 on the Quick Access toolbar**
   Your name appears in the worksheet, and your changes to the file are saved.

### Exploring File Open options

You might have noticed that the Open button on the Open dialog box includes an arrow. In a dialog box, if a button includes an arrow you can click the button to invoke the command, or you can click the arrow to choose from a list of related commands. The Open button list arrow includes several related commands, including Open Read-Only and Open as Copy. Clicking Open Read-Only opens a file that you can only save by saving it with a new name; you cannot save changes to the original file. Clicking Open as Copy creates a copy of the file already saved and named with the word "Copy" in the title. Like the Save As command, these commands provide additional ways to use copies of existing files while ensuring that original files do not get inadvertently changed.

FIGURE A-10: Open dialog box

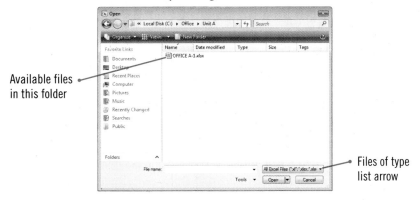

Available files in this folder

Files of type list arrow

FIGURE A-11: Save As dialog box

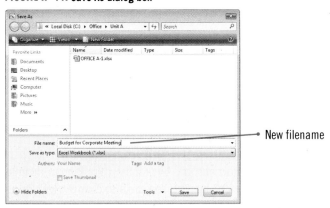

New filename

FIGURE A-12: Adding your name to the worksheet

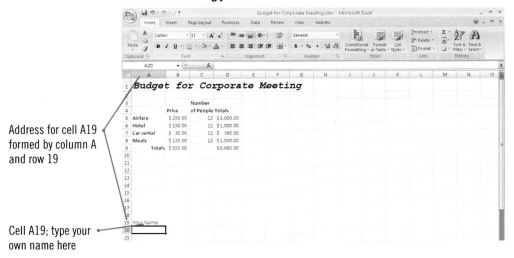

Address for cell A19 formed by column A and row 19

Cell A19; type your own name here

## Working in Compatibility mode

Not everyone upgrades to the newest version of Office. As a general rule, new software versions are **backward-compatible**, meaning that documents saved by an older version can be read by newer software. The reverse is not always true, so Office 2007 includes a feature called Compatibility mode. When you open a file created in an earlier version of Office, "Compatibility Mode" appears in the title bar, letting you know the file was created in an earlier, but usable version of the program. If you are working with someone who may not be using the newest version of the software, you can avoid possible incompatibility problems by saving your file in another, earlier format. To do this, click the Office button, point to the Save As command, then click a choice on the Save As submenu. For example, if you're working in Excel, click Excel 97-2003 Workbook format. When the Save As dialog box opens, you'll notice that the Save as type box reads "Excel 97-2003 Workbook" instead of the default "Excel Workbook." To see more file format choices, such as Excel 97-2003 Template or Microsoft Excel 5.0/95 Workbook, click Other Formats on the Save As submenu. In the Save As dialog box, click the Save as type button, click the choice you think matches what your co-worker is using, then click Save.

# Viewing and Printing Your Work

If your computer is connected to a printer or a print server, you can easily print any Office document. Printing can be as simple as clicking a button, or as involved as customizing the print job by printing only selected pages or making other choices, and/or **previewing** the document to see exactly what a document will look like when it is printed. (In order for printing and previewing to work, a printer must be installed.) In addition to using Print Preview, each Microsoft Office program lets you switch among various **views** of the document window, to show more or fewer details or a different combination of elements that make it easier to complete certain tasks, such as formatting or reading text. You can also increase or decrease your view of a document, so you can see more or less of it on the screen at once. Changing your view of a document does not affect the file in any way, it affects only the way it looks on screen. ▨▨▨ Experiment with changing your view of a Word document, and then preview and print your work.

## STEPS

1. **Click** Potential Corporate Meeting Locations – Microsoft Word **on the taskbar**

   Word becomes the active program, and the document fills the screen.

2. **Click the** View tab **on the Ribbon**

   In most Office programs, the View tab on the Ribbon includes groups and commands for changing your view of the current document. You can also change views using the View buttons on the status bar.

3. **Click** Web Layout button **in the Document Views group on the View tab**

   The view changes to Web Layout view, as shown in Figure A-13. This view shows how the document will look if you save it as a Web page.

   > **QUICK TIP**
   > You can also use the Zoom button in the Zoom group of the View tab to enlarge or reduce a document's appearance.

4. **Click the** Zoom in button ⊕ **on the status bar** eight times **until the zoom percentage reads** 180%

   **Zooming in**, or choosing a higher percentage, makes a document appear bigger on screen, but less of it fits on the screen at once; **zooming out**, or choosing a lower percentage, lets you see more of the document but at a reduced size.

5. **Drag the** Zoom slider ▽ **on the status bar to the** center mark

   The Zoom slider lets you zoom in and out without opening a dialog box or clicking buttons.

6. **Click the** Print Layout button **on the View tab**

   You return to Print Layout view, the default view in Microsoft Word.

7. **Click the** Office button ⊛, **point to** Print, **then click** Print Preview

   The Print Preview presents the most accurate view of how your document will look when printed, displaying the entire page on screen at once. Compare your screen to Figure A-14. The Ribbon in Print Preview contains a single tab, also known as a **program** tab, with commands specific to Print Preview. The commands on this tab facilitate viewing and changing overall settings such as margins and page size.

   > **QUICK TIP**
   > You can open the Print dialog box from any view by clicking the Office button, then clicking Print.

8. **Click the** Print button **on the Ribbon**

   The Print dialog box opens, as shown in Figure A-15. You can use this dialog box to change which pages to print, the number of printed copies, and even the number of pages you print on each page. If you have multiple printers from which to choose, you can change from one installed printer by clicking the Name list arrow, then clicking the name of the installed printer you want to use.

9. **Click** OK, **then click the** Close Print Preview button **on the Ribbon**

   A copy of the document prints, and Print Preview closes.

**FIGURE A-13:** Web Layout view

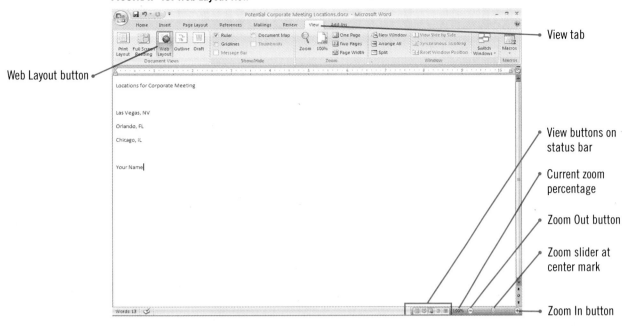

Web Layout button

View tab

View buttons on status bar

Current zoom percentage

Zoom Out button

Zoom slider at center mark

Zoom In button

**FIGURE A-14:** Print Preview screen

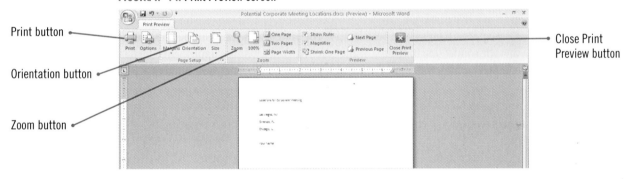

Print button

Orientation button

Zoom button

Close Print Preview button

**FIGURE A-15:** Print dialog box

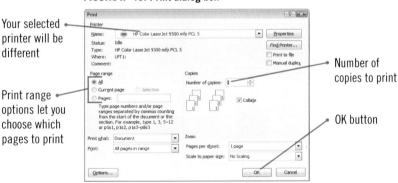

Your selected printer will be different

Print range options let you choose which pages to print

Number of copies to print

OK button

## Using the Print Screen feature to create a screen capture

At some point you may want to create a screen capture. A **screen capture** is a snapshot of your screen, as if you took a picture of it with a camera. You might want to take a screen capture if an error message occurs and you want Technical Support to see exactly what's on the screen. Or perhaps your instructor wants to see what your screen looks like when you create a particular document. To create a screen capture, press [PrtScn]. (Keyboards differ, but you may find the [PrtScn] button on the Insert key in or near your keyboard's function keys. You may have to press the [F Lock] key to enable the Function keys.) Pressing this key places a digital image of your screen in the Windows temporary storage area known as the **Clipboard**. Open the document where you want the screen capture to appear, click the Home tab on the Ribbon (if necessary), then click Paste on the Home tab. The screen capture is pasted into the document.

# Getting Help and Closing a File

You can get comprehensive help at any time by pressing [F1] in an Office program. You can also get help in the form of a ScreenTip by pointing to almost any icon in the program window. When you're finished working in an Office document, you have a few choices regarding ending your work session. You can close a file or exit a program by using the Office button or by clicking a button on the title bar. Closing a file leaves a program running, while exiting a program closes all the open files in that program as well as the program itself. In all cases, Office reminds you if you try to close a file or exit a program and your document contains unsaved changes. ░░░░░ Explore the Help system in Microsoft Office, and then close your documents and exit any open programs.

1. **Point to the Zoom button on the View tab of the Ribbon**
   A ScreenTip appears that describes how the Zoom button works.

If you are not connected to the Internet, the Help window displays only the help content available on your computer.

2. **Press [F1]**
   The Word Help window opens, as shown in Figure A-16, displaying the home page for help in Word. Each entry is a hyperlink you can click to open a list of related topics. This window also includes a toolbar of useful Help commands and a Search field. The connection status at the bottom of the Help window indicates that the connection to Office Online is active. Office Online supplements the help content available on your computer with a wide variety of up-to-date topics, templates, and training.

3. **Click the Getting help link in the Table of Contents pane**
   The icon next to Getting help changes and its list of subtopics expands.

You can also open the Help window by clicking the Microsoft Office Help button 🔘 to the right of the tabs on the Ribbon.

4. **Click the Work with the Help window link in the topics list in the left pane**
   The topic opens in the right pane, as shown in Figure A-17.

5. **Click the Hide Table of Contents button 📖 on the Help toolbar**
   The left pane closes, as shown in Figure A-18.

You can print the current topic by clicking the Print button 🖨 on the Help toolbar to open the Print dialog box.

6. **Click the Show Table of Contents button 📄 on the Help toolbar, scroll to the bottom of the left pane, click the Accessibility link in the Table of Contents pane, click the Use the keyboard to work with Ribbon programs link, read the information in the right pane, then click the Help window Close button**

7. **Click the Office button 🔵, then click Close; if a dialog box opens asking whether you want to save your changes, click Yes**
   The Potential Corporate Meeting Locations document closes, leaving the Word program open.

8. **Click 🔵, then click Exit Word**
   Microsoft Office Word closes, and the Excel program window is active.

9. **Click 🔵, click Exit Excel, click the PowerPoint button on the taskbar if necessary, click 🔵, then click Exit PowerPoint**
   Microsoft Office Excel and Microsoft Office PowerPoint both close.

**FIGURE A-16: Word Help window**

Help toolbar

Search field

Hide Table of
Contents
button

The colors
of your links
may differ

Connection status

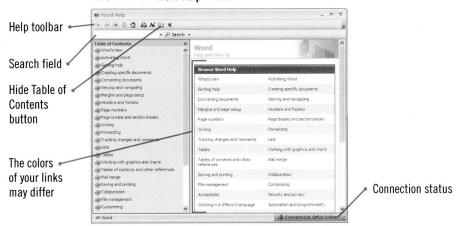

**FIGURE A-17: Work with the Help window**

Print button

Icon indicates
expanded topic

Work with
the Help
window link

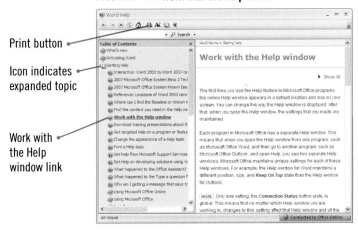

**FIGURE A-18: Help window with Table of Contents closed**

Show Table of
Contents button

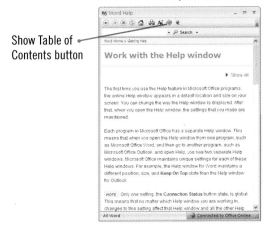

## Recovering a document

Sometimes while you are using Office, you may experience a power failure or your computer may "freeze," making it impossible to continue working. If this type of interruption occurs, each Office program has a built-in recovery feature that allows you to open and save files that were open at the time of the interruption. When you restart the program(s) after an interruption, the Document Recovery task pane opens on the left side of your screen displaying both original and recovered versions of the files that were open. If you're not sure which file to open (original or recovered), it's usually better to open the recovered file because it will contain the latest information. You can, however, open and review all versions of the file that were recovered and save the best one. Each file listed in the Document Recovery task pane displays a list arrow with options that allow you to open the file, save it as is, delete it, or show repairs made to it during recovery.

# Practice

If you have a SAM user profile, you may have access to hands-on instruction, practice, and assessment of the skills covered in this unit. Log in to your SAM account (http://sam2007.course.com/) to launch any assigned training activities or exams that relate to the skills covered in this unit.

## ▼ CONCEPTS REVIEW

**Label the elements of the program window shown in Figure A-19.**

FIGURE A-19

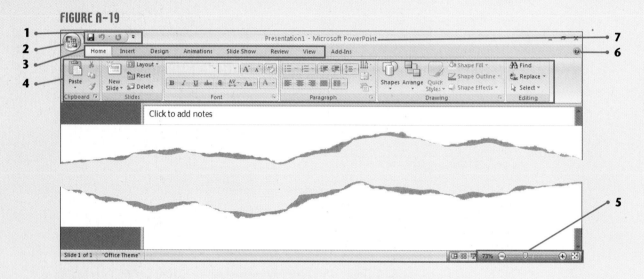

**Match each project with the program for which it is best suited.**

8. Microsoft Office PowerPoint
9. Microsoft Office Excel
10. Microsoft Office Word
11. Microsoft Office Access

a. Corporate expansion budget with expense projections
b. Business résumé for a job application
c. Auto parts store inventory
d. Presentation for Board of Directors meeting

## ▼ INDEPENDENT CHALLENGE 1

You just accepted an administrative position with a local car dealership that's recently invested in computers and is now considering purchasing Microsoft Office. You are asked to propose ways Office might help the dealership. You produce your proposal in Microsoft Word.

a. Start Word, then save the document as **Microsoft Office Proposal** in the drive and folder where you store your Data Files.

b. Type **Microsoft Office Word**, press [Enter] twice, type **Microsoft Office Excel**, press [Enter] twice, type **Microsoft Office PowerPoint**, press [Enter] twice, type **Microsoft Office Access**, press [Enter] twice, then type your name.

c. Click the line beneath each program name, type at least two tasks suited to that program, then press [Enter].

d. Save your work, then print one copy of this document.

### Advanced Challenge Exercise

- Press the [PrtScn] button to create a screen capture, then press [Ctrl][V].
- Save and print the document.

e. Exit Word.

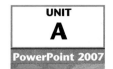

# Creating a Presentation in PowerPoint 2007

Microsoft Office PowerPoint 2007 is a powerful computer software program that enables you to create visually dynamic presentations. With PowerPoint, you can create individual slides and display them as a slide show on your computer, a video projector, or over the Internet. Ellen Latsky is the European tour developer for Quest Specialty Travel (QST), an adventure tour company committed to providing travel experiences that immerse travelers into world cultures. One of Ellen's responsibilities is to present new tour ideas for the upcoming travel season at the annual sales meeting held at the company's corporate offices. As a newly hired summer intern, Ellen has asked you to get acquainted with PowerPoint and then start work on the new tour ideas presentation.

**OBJECTIVES**

Define presentation software

Plan an effective presentation

Examine the PowerPoint window

Enter slide text

Add a new slide

Apply a design theme

Compare presentation views

Print a PowerPoint presentation

# Defining Presentation Software

**Presentation software** is a computer program you use to organize and present information to others. Whether you are explaining a new product or moderating a meeting, presentation software can help you effectively communicate your ideas. You can use PowerPoint to create presentations, as well as speaker notes for the presenter and handouts for the audience. Table A-1 explains how your information can be presented using PowerPoint. 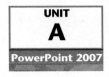 Ellen wants you to start work on the presentation that she will use to present the new European tour series. Because you are only somewhat familiar with PowerPoint, you get to work exploring its capabilities. Figure A-1 shows how a presentation looks printed as handouts. Figure A-2 shows how the same presentation might look printed as notes pages for a speaker.

**DETAILS**

### You can easily complete the following tasks using PowerPoint:

- **Enter and edit text easily**

  Text editing and formatting commands in PowerPoint are organized by the task you are performing at the time, so you can enter, edit, and format text information simply and efficiently to produce the best results in the least amount of time.

- **Change the appearance of information**

  PowerPoint has many effects that can transform the way text, graphics, and slides appear. By exploring some of these capabilities, you discover how easy it is to change the appearance of your presentation.

- **Organize and arrange information**

  Once you start using PowerPoint, you won't have to spend much time making sure your information is correct and in the right order. With PowerPoint, you can quickly and easily rearrange and modify text, graphics, and slides in your presentation.

- **Incorporate information from other sources**

  Often, when you create presentations, you use information from a variety of sources. With PowerPoint, you can import text, photographs, numerical data, and facts from files created in such programs as Microsoft Word, Corel WordPerfect, Adobe Photoshop, Microsoft Excel, and Microsoft Access. You can also import graphic images from a variety of sources such as the Internet, other computers, a digital camera, or other graphics programs.

- **Present information in a variety of ways**

  With PowerPoint, you can present information using a variety of methods. For example, you can print handout pages or an outline of your presentation for audience members. You can display your presentation as an electronic slide show using your computer, or if you are presenting to a large group, you can use a video projector and a large screen. If you want to reach an even wider audience, you can publish the presentation to the Internet so people anywhere in the world can use a browser to view your presentation.

- **Collaborate on a presentation with others**

  PowerPoint makes it easy to collaborate with colleagues and coworkers to create a presentation using the Internet. You can use your e-mail program to send a presentation as an attachment to a colleague for feedback. If you have a large number of people that need to collaborate on a presentation, you can set up a shared workspace on the Internet so everyone in your group has access to the presentation.

**FIGURE A-1:** PowerPoint Handout

**FIGURE A-2:** PowerPoint Notes page

**TABLE A-1:** Presenting information using PowerPoint

| method | description |
| --- | --- |
| On-screen presentations | Run a slide show from your computer or through a video projector to a large screen |
| Notes | Print a page with the image of a slide and notes about each slide for yourself or your audience |
| Audience handouts | Print handouts with one, two, three, four, six, or nine slides on a page |
| Online meetings | View or work on a presentation with your colleagues in real time |
| Outline pages | Print a text outline of your presentation to highlight the main points |
| Overheads | Print PowerPoint slides directly to transparencies using a standard printer |

# Planning an Effective Presentation

Before you create a presentation, you need to have a basic idea of the information you want to communicate. PowerPoint is a powerful and flexible program that gives you the ability to start a presentation simply by entering the text of your message. If you have a design or theme you want to use, you can start the presentation by working on the design. In most cases you'll probably enter the text of your presentation into PowerPoint first and then tailor the design to the message and audience. When preparing your presentation, you need to keep in mind not only to whom you are giving it, but also where you are giving it. It is important to know what equipment you will need, such as a sound system, computer, or projector. 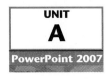 Use the planning guidelines below to help plan an effective presentation. Figure A-3 illustrates a storyboard for a well thought-out presentation.

## DETAILS

### In planning a presentation, it is important to:

- **Determine and outline the message you want to communicate**

  The more time you take developing the message and outline of your presentation, the better your presentation will be. A presentation with a clear message that reads like a story and is illustrated with visual aids will have the greatest impact on your audience. Start the presentation by describing the tour development goals, defining focus group data, and stating the tour strategy objectives. See Figure A-3.

- **Verify the audience and the delivery location**

  Audience and delivery location should be major factors in the type of presentation you create. For example, a presentation you develop for a staff meeting that is held in a conference room would not necessarily need to be as elaborate or detailed as a presentation that you develop for a large audience held in an auditorium. Room lighting, natural light, screen position, and room layout all affect how the audience responds to your presentation. This presentation will be delivered in a small auditorium to QST's management and sales team.

- **Determine the type of output**

  Output choices for a presentation include black-and-white or color handouts, on-screen slide show, or an online meeting. Consider the time demands and computer equipment availability as you decide which output types to produce. Because you are speaking in a small auditorium to a large group and have access to a computer and projection equipment, you decide that an on-screen slide show is the best output choice for your presentation.

- **Determine the design**

  Visual appeal, graphics, and design work to communicate your message. You can choose one of the professionally designed themes that come with PowerPoint, modify one of these themes, or create one of your own. You decide to choose one of PowerPoint's design themes to convey the new tour information.

- **Decide what additional materials will be useful in the presentation**

  You need to prepare not only the slides themselves but also supplementary materials, including speaker notes and handouts for the audience. You use speaker notes to help remember key details, and you pass out handouts for the audience to use as a reference during the presentation.

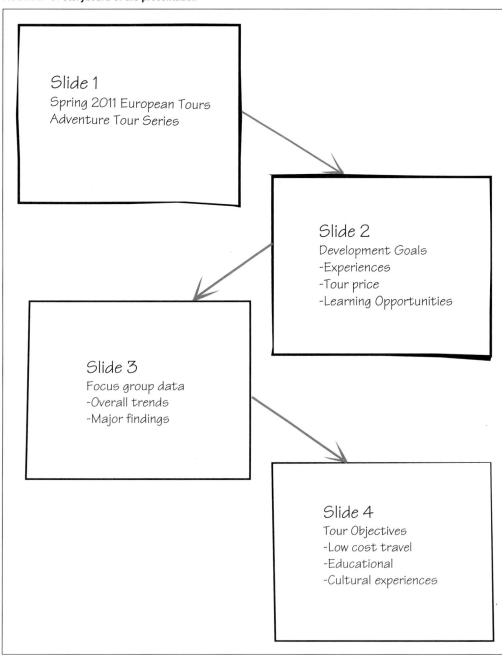

## Understanding copyright

Intellectual property is any idea or creation of the human mind. Copyright law is a type of intellectual property law that protects works of authorship, including books, Web pages, computer games, music, artwork, and photographs. Copyright protects the expression of an idea, but not the underlying facts or concepts. In other words, the general subject matter is not protected, but how you express it is, such as when several people photograph the same sunset. Copyright attaches to any original work of authorship *as soon* as it is created, you *do not* have to register it with the Copyright Office or display the copyright symbol, ©.

Fair use is an exception to copyright and permits the public to use copyrighted material for certain purposes without obtaining prior consent from the owner. Determining whether fair use applies to a work depends on its purpose, the nature of the work, how much of the work you want to copy, and the effect on the work's value. Unauthorized use of protected work (such as downloading a photo or a song from the Web) is known as copyright infringement, and can lead to legal action.

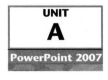

# Examining the PowerPoint Window

When you first start PowerPoint, a blank slide appears in the PowerPoint window. PowerPoint has different **views** that allow you to see your presentation in different forms. By default, the PowerPoint window opens in **Normal view**, which is the primary view that you use to write, edit, and design your presentation. Normal view is divided into three areas called **panes**: the pane on the left contains the Outline and Slides tabs, the large pane is the Slide pane, and the small pane below the Slide pane is the Notes pane. You move around in each pane using the scroll bars. The PowerPoint window and the specific parts of Normal view are described below.

## STEPS

1.  **Click the Start button ● on the taskbar, point to All Programs, click Microsoft Office, then click Microsoft Office PowerPoint 2007**
    PowerPoint starts and the PowerPoint window opens, as shown in Figure A-4.

**Using Figure A-4 as a guide, examine the elements of the PowerPoint window, then find and compare the elements described below:**

*   The **Ribbon**—a wide (toolbar-like) band that runs across the entire PowerPoint window—is a new feature that organizes all of PowerPoint's primary commands. Each set of primary commands is identified by a **tab**; for example, the Home tab is selected by default as shown in Figure A-4. Commands are further arranged into **groups** on the Ribbon based on their function. So, for example, text formatting commands such as Bold, Underline, and Italic are located on the Home tab, in the Font group.

*   The **Outline tab** displays the text of your presentation in the form of an outline, without showing graphics or other visual objects. Using this tab, it is easy to move text on or among slides by dragging text to reorder the information.

*   The **Slides tab** displays the slides of your presentation as small images, called **thumbnails**. You can quickly navigate through the slides in your presentation by clicking the thumbnails on this tab. You can also add, delete, or rearrange slides using this tab.

*   The **Slide pane** displays the current slide in your presentation.

*   The **Notes pane** is used to type text that references a slide's content. You can print these notes and refer to them when you make a presentation or print them as handouts and give them to your audience. The Notes pane is not visible to the audience when you show a slide presentation in Slide Show view.

*   The **Quick Access toolbar** provides immediate access to common commands that you use all the time, such as Save, Undo, and Redo. The Quick Access toolbar is always visible no matter which Ribbon tab you select. This toolbar is fully customizable. Click the Customize Quick Access Toolbar button to add or remove commands.

*   The **View Shortcuts** on the status bar allow you to switch quickly between PowerPoint views.

*   The **status bar**, located at the bottom of the PowerPoint window, shows messages about what you are doing and seeing in PowerPoint, including which slide you are viewing, and the design theme applied to the presentation. In addition, the status bar displays the Zoom slider controls, the **Fit slide to current window button** ▣, and information on other functionality such as signatures and permissions.

*   The **Zoom slider**, located in the lower-right corner of the status bar, allows you to zoom the slide in and out quickly.

**FIGURE A-4:** PowerPoint window in Normal view

Office button

Quick Access toolbar

Tabs

Slides tab

Outline tab

Notes pane

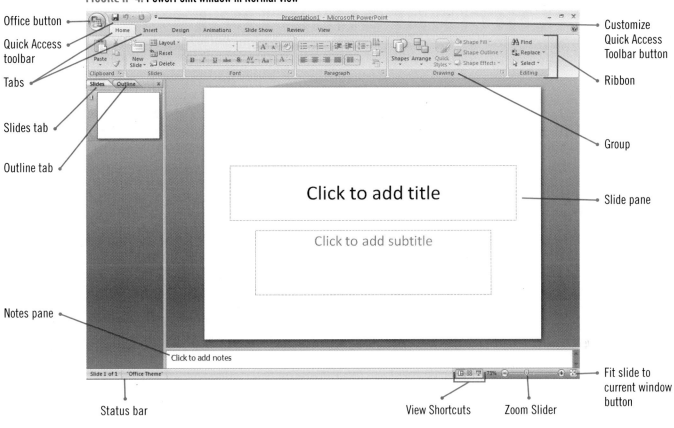

Customize Quick Access Toolbar button

Ribbon

Group

Slide pane

Fit slide to current window button

Status bar

View Shortcuts

Zoom Slider

## Viewing your presentation in grayscale or black and white

Viewing your presentation in grayscale (using shades of gray) or pure black and white is very useful when you are printing a presentation on a black-and-white printer and you want to make sure your presentation prints correctly. To see how your color presentation looks in grayscale or black and white, click the View tab, then click either the Grayscale or Pure Black and White button. Depending on which button you select, the Grayscale or the Black and White tab appears and the Ribbon displays different settings that you can customize. If you don't like the way an individual object looks in black and white or grayscale, you can change its color. Right-click the object, point to Black and White Setting or Grayscale Setting (depending on which view you are in), and choose from the options on the submenu.

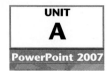
# Entering Slide Text

Each time you launch PowerPoint, a new presentation with a blank title slide appears in Normal view. The title slide has two **text placeholders**—boxes with dotted borders—where you enter text. The top text placeholder on the title slide is the **title placeholder**, labeled "Click to add title." The bottom text placeholder on the title slide is the **subtitle text placeholder**, labeled "Click to add subtitle." To enter text in a placeholder, click the placeholder and then type your text. After you enter text in a placeholder, the placeholder becomes a text object. An **object** is any item on a slide that can be modified. Objects are the building blocks that make up a presentation slide. Begin working on your presentation by entering text on the title slide.

## STEPS

1. **Move the pointer over the title placeholder labeled "Click to add title" in the Slide pane**
   The pointer changes to I when you move the pointer over the placeholder. In PowerPoint, the pointer often changes shape, depending on the task you are trying to accomplish.

2. **Click the title placeholder in the Slide pane**
   The **insertion point**, a blinking vertical line, indicates where your text appears when you type in the placeholder. A **selection box** with a dashed line border and sizing handles appears around the placeholder, indicating that it is selected and ready to accept text. See Figure A-5.

**TROUBLE**

If you press a wrong key, press [Backspace] to erase the character.

3. **Type Spring 2011 European Tour Proposal**
   PowerPoint wraps and then center-aligns the title text within the title placeholder, which is now a text object. Notice that the text also appears on the slide thumbnail on the Slides tab.

4. **Click the subtitle text placeholder in the Slide pane**
   The subtitle text placeholder is ready to accept text.

5. **Type Adventure Tour Series, then press [Enter]**
   The insertion point moves to the next line in the text object.

6. **Type Your Name, press [Enter], type Tour Developer-Europe, press [Enter] then type Quest Specialty Travel**
   Notice that the AutoFit Options button ⊟ appears near the text object. The AutoFit Options button on your screen indicates that PowerPoint has automatically decreased the size of all the text in the text object so that it fits inside the text object.

7. **Click the Autofit Options button ⊟, then click Stop Fitting Text to This Placeholder on the shortcut menu**
   The text in the text object changes back to its original size and no longer fits in the text object.

8. **Position I to the right of Series, drag left to select the entire line of text, press [Backspace], then click outside the text object in a blank area of the slide**
   The Adventure Tour Series line of text is deleted and the Autofit Options button closes, as shown in Figure A-6. Clicking a blank area of the slide deselects all selected objects on the slide.

9. **Click the Save button 🖫 on the Quick Access toolbar to open the Save As dialog box, then save the presentation as QuestA in the drive and folder where you store your Data Files**

**FIGURE A-5:** Title text placeholder ready to accept text

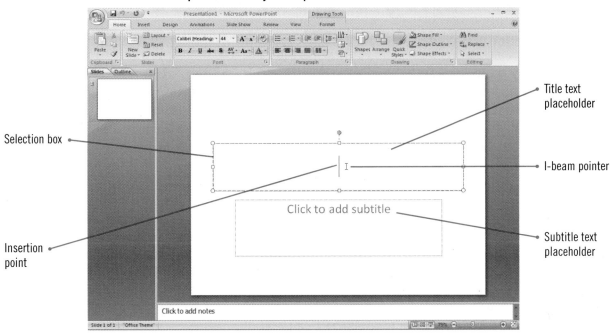

Title text placeholder

I-beam pointer

Subtitle text placeholder

Selection box

Insertion point

**FIGURE A-6:** Text on title slide

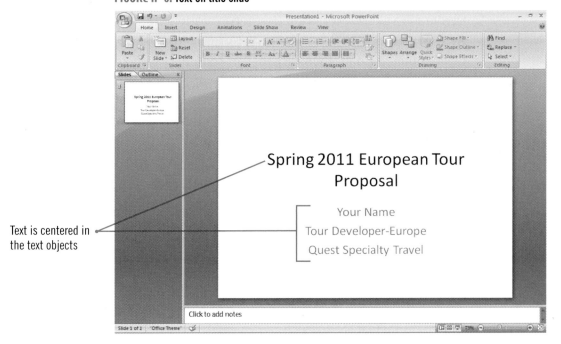

Text is centered in the text objects

Spring 2011 European Tour Proposal

Your Name
Tour Developer-Europe
Quest Specialty Travel

## Saving fonts with your presentation

When you create a presentation, it uses the fonts that are installed on your computer. If you need to open the presentation on another computer, the fonts might look different if that computer has a different set of fonts. To preserve the look of your presentation on any computer, you can save, or embed, the fonts in your presentation. Click the Office button, then click the PowerPoint Options button. The PowerPoint Options dialog box opens. Click Save in the left pane, then click the Embed fonts in the file check box. Click the Embed all characters option button, then click OK to close the dialog box. Click Save on the Quick Access toolbar. Now the presentation looks the same on any computer that opens it. Using this option, however, significantly increases the size of your presentation, so only use it when necessary. You can freely embed any TrueType font that comes with Windows. You can embed other TrueType fonts only if they have no license restrictions.

# Adding a New Slide

Ordinarily when you add a new slide to a presentation, you have a pretty good idea of what you want the slide to look like. For example, you may want to add a slide that has a title over bulleted text and a picture. To help you add a slide like this quickly and easily, PowerPoint provides nine standard slide layouts. A **slide layout** contains text and object placeholders that are arranged in a specific way on the slide. You have already worked with the Title Slide layout in the previous lesson. In the event that a standard slide layout does not meet your needs, you can modify an existing slide layout or create a brand new, custom slide layout.  To continue developing the presentation, you create a slide that defines the QST development goals for the new tour series.

**QUICK TIP**
If you know which slide layout you want to use on the new slide, you can click the New Slide list arrow to open the slide layout gallery and then select a specific slide layout.

1. **Click the New Slide button in the Slides group on the Home tab on the Ribbon**

   A new blank slide (now the current slide) appears as the second slide in your presentation as shown in Figure A-7. The new slide in the Slide pane contains a title placeholder and a content placeholder. A **content placeholder** can be used to insert text or objects such as clip art, tables, or charts. Table A-2 describes the content placeholder icons. Notice that the status bar indicates Slide 2 of 2 and that the Slides tab now contains two slide thumbnails. You can easily change the current slide's layout using the Layout button in the Slides group.

2. **Click the Layout button in the Slides group**

   The Layout gallery opens. Each layout is identified by a descriptive name.

3. **Point to the Two Content slide layout, then click the Two Content slide layout**

   A slide layout with a title placeholder and two content placeholders replaces the Title and Content layout for the current slide.

4. **Type Tour Development Goals, then click the left content placeholder**

   The text you type appears in the title placeholder and the insertion point appears at the top of the left content placeholder.

5. **Type Focus on significant experiences, then press [Enter]**

   A new first-level bullet automatically appears when you press [Enter].

6. **Press [Tab]**

   The new first-level bullet indents and becomes a second-level bullet.

**QUICK TIP**
You can also press [Shift][Tab] to decrease the indent level.

7. **Type Preserve QST values, press [Enter], then click the Decrease List Level button** 📑 **in the Paragraph group**

   The Decrease List Level button changes the second-level bullet into a first-level bullet.

8. **Type Price tours reasonably, press [Enter], type Create learning opportunities, press [Enter], then click the Increase List Level button** 📑 **in the Paragraph group**

9. **Type Offer local guides, press [Enter], type Provide experts, then click the Save button** 💾 **on the Quick Access toolbar**

   The Increase List Level button creates a second-level bullet from a first-level bullet. The Save button saves all of the changes to the file. Compare your screen with Figure A-8.

**FIGURE A-7:** New blank slide in Normal view

New Slide button

New slide thumbnail added to Slides tab

Total number of slides

Current slide number

Title text placeholder

Content placeholder

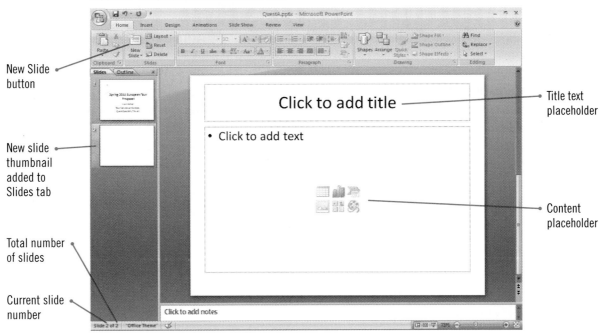

**FIGURE A-8:** New slide with Two Content slide layout

Decrease List Level button

Increase List Level button

First-level bullet

Second-level bullet

Two content placeholders based on the slide layout

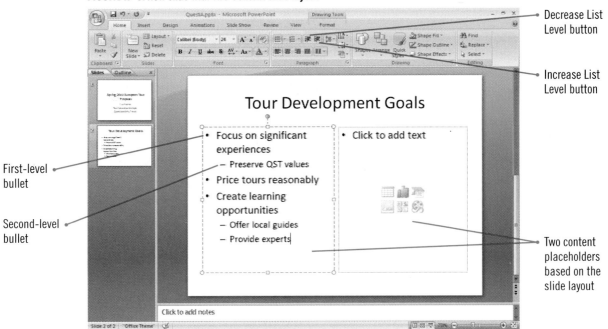

**TABLE A-2:** Content placeholder icons

| click this icon | to insert a |
| --- | --- |
|  | Table |
|  | Graph chart |
|  | Piece of clip art |
|  | Picture from a file |
|  | SmartArt graphic |
|  | Movie or video clip |

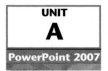

# Applying a Design Theme

PowerPoint provides a number of design themes to help you quickly create a professional and contemporary looking presentation. A design **theme** incorporates sets of colors for fill, line, and shadow, called **theme colors**; fonts for titles and other text, called **theme fonts**; and effects for lines and fills, called **theme effects** to create a cohesive look. In most cases, you would apply one theme to an entire presentation; you can, however, apply multiple themes to the same presentation, or even a different theme on each presentation slide. You can use a design theme as is, or you can alter individual elements of the theme as needed. Unless you need to use a specific design theme, such as a company theme or product design theme, it is faster and easier to use one of the themes supplied with PowerPoint. If you design a custom theme, you can save it to use in the future. ⬛⬛⬛ You decide to change the default design theme in the presentation to a new one.

## STEPS

1. **Click the Slide 1 thumbnail on the Slides tab**

    Slide 1, the title slide, appears in the Slide pane.

2. **Click the Design tab on the Ribbon, then point to the Civic theme in the Themes group as shown in Figure A-9**

    The Design tab appears and a live preview of the Civic theme is displayed on the slide. A **live preview** allows you to see how your changes affect the slides before actually making the change. The live preview lasts about one minute and then your slide reverts back to its original state. The first (far left) theme thumbnail identifies the current theme applied to the presentation, in this case, the default design theme called the Office Theme. Depending on your monitor resolution and screen size, you can see between five and seven design themes visible in the Themes group. However, there are a total of 20 standard built-in themes available to use.

3. **Slowly move your pointer ⬚ over the other design themes, then click the Themes group down scroll arrow once**

    A live preview of the theme appears on the slide each time you pass your pointer over the theme thumbnails, and a ScreenTip identifies the theme names.

4. **Move ⬚ over the design themes, then click the Metro theme**

    The Metro design theme is applied to all the slides in the presentation. Notice the new slide background color, graphic elements, fonts, and text color. You decide that this theme isn't right for this presentation.

<table>
<tr><td>

**QUICK TIP**

One way to apply multiple themes to the same presentation is to click the Slide Sorter button in the status bar, select a slide or a group of slides, then click the theme.

</td></tr>
</table>

5. **Click the More button ▾ in the Themes group**

    The Themes gallery window opens. At the top of the gallery window in the This Presentation section are the current theme(s) applied to the presentation. Notice that just the Metro theme is listed here because when you changed the theme in the last step, you replaced the default theme with the Metro theme. The Built-In section identifies all of the standard themes that come with PowerPoint.

6. **Right-click the Solstice theme in the Themes group, then click Apply to Selected Slides**

    The Solstice theme is applied only to Slide 1. You like the Solstice theme better and decide to apply it to both slides.

7. **Right-click the Solstice theme in the Themes group, then click Apply to All Slides**

    The Solstice theme is applied to both slides. Preview the other slide in the presentation to see how it looks.

8. **Click the Next Slide button ⬇ at the bottom of the vertical scroll bar**

    Compare your screen to Figure A-10.

9. **Click the Previous Slide button ⬆ at the bottom of the vertical scroll bar, then save your changes**

FIGURE A-9: Slide showing a different design theme

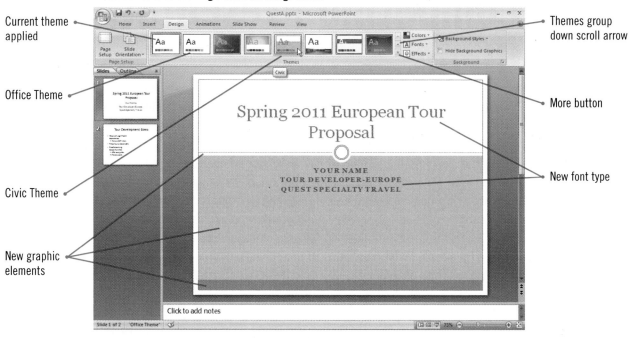

Current theme applied

Office Theme

Civic Theme

New graphic elements

Themes group down scroll arrow

More button

New font type

FIGURE A-10: Presentation with Solstice theme applied

Solstice theme

Solstice theme applied

Previous Slide button

Next Slide button

## Customizing themes

You are not limited to using the standard themes PowerPoint provides; you can also modify a theme to create your own custom theme. For example, you might want to incorporate your company's colors on the slide background of the presentation or be able to type using fonts your company uses for brand recognition. To modify an existing theme, you can change the color theme, font theme, or the effects theme and then save it for future use by clicking the

Themes group More button, then clicking Save Current Theme. You also have the ability to create a new font theme or a new color theme from scratch by clicking the Theme Fonts button or the Theme Colors button and then clicking Create New Theme Fonts or Create New Theme Colors. You work in the Create New Theme Fonts or Create New Theme Colors dialog box to define the custom theme fonts or colors.

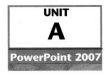

# Comparing Presentation Views

PowerPoint has four basic views: Normal view, Slide Sorter view, Notes Page view, and Slide Show view. Each PowerPoint view displays your presentation in a different way and is used for different purposes. Normal view is the primary editing view where you add text, graphics, and other elements to the slides. Slide Sorter view is primarily used to rearrange slides, however, you can also add slide effects and design themes in this view. You use Notes Page view to type notes you want to remember about each slide. Slide Show view displays your presentation filling the computer screen and is the view used to give a presentation. To move easily among three of the PowerPoint views, use the View Shortcuts buttons located in the Status bar next to the Zoom slider. All PowerPoint views can be accessed using the View tab on the Ribbon. Table A-3 provides a brief description of the PowerPoint views. ███ Examine each of the PowerPoint views, starting with Normal view.

## STEPS

1.  **Click the Outline tab, then click the small slide icon ▭ next to Slide 2 in the Outline tab**
    The text for Slide 2 is selected in the Outline tab and Slide 2 appears in the Slide pane as shown in Figure A-11. Notice that the status bar identifies the number of the slide you are viewing, the total number of slides in the presentation, and the name of the applied design theme.

2.  **Click the Previous Slide button ▲ at the bottom of the vertical scroll bar**
    Slide 1 appears in the Slide pane. The scroll box in the vertical scroll bar moves back up the scroll bar.

3.  **Click the Slides tab**
    Thumbnails of the slides in your presentation appear again on the Slides tab. Since the Slides tab is narrower than the Outline tab, the Slide pane enlarges.

    > **QUICK TIP**
    > You can also switch between views using the commands in the Presentation Views group on the View tab.

4.  **Click the Slide Sorter button ▦ on the status bar**
    A thumbnail of each slide in the presentation appears as shown in Figure A-12. You can examine the flow of your slides and drag any slide or group of slides to rearrange the order of the slides in the presentation.

5.  **Double-click Slide 1 in Slide Sorter view**
    Slide 1 appears in Normal view.

6.  **Click the Slide Show button ▣ on the status bar**
    The first slide fills the entire screen. In this view, you can practice running through your slides as they would appear in the slide show.

    > **QUICK TIP**
    > You can also press [Enter] or [Spacebar] to advance the slide show.

7.  **Click the left mouse button to advance through the slides one at a time until you see a black slide, then click once more to return to Normal view**
    The black slide at the end of the slide show indicates that the slide show is finished. At the end of a slide show you automatically return to the slide and PowerPoint view you were in before you ran the slide show, in this case Slide 1 in Normal view.

8.  **Click the View tab on the Ribbon, then click the Notes Page button in the Presentation Views group**
    Notes Page view appears, showing a reduced image of the current slide above a large text placeholder. You can enter text in this placeholder and then print the notes page for your own use.

9.  **Click the Normal button in the Presentation Views group**

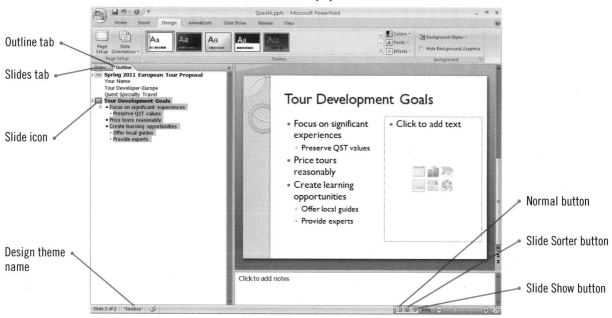

**FIGURE A-11:** Normal view with the outline tab displayed

Outline tab

Slides tab

Slide icon

Design theme name

Normal button

Slide Sorter button

Slide Show button

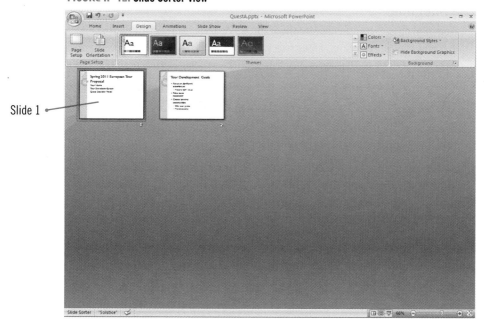

**FIGURE A-12:** Slide Sorter view

Slide 1

**TABLE A-3:** PowerPoint views

| view name | button | button name | description |
|---|---|---|---|
| Normal | ⊞ | Normal | Displays the Outline and Slides tabs, the Slide pane, and the Notes pane at the same time; use this view to work on your presentation's content, layout, and notes concurrently |
| Slide Sorter | ▦ | Slide Sorter | Displays thumbnails of all slides in the order in which they appear in your presentation; use this view to rearrange and add special effects to your slides |
| Slide Show | 🖵 | Slide Show | Displays your presentation as an electronic slide show |
| Notes Page | (no View Shortcut button) | | Displays a reduced image of the current slide above a large text box where you can enter or view notes |

# Printing a PowerPoint Presentation

You print your presentation when you want to review your work or when you have completed it and want a hard copy. Reviewing your presentation at different stages of development gives you a better perspective of the overall flow and feel of the presentation. You can also preview your presentation to see exactly how each slide looks before you print the presentation. When you are finished working on your presentation, even if it is not yet complete, you can close the presentation file and exit PowerPoint. █████ You are done working on the tour presentation for now. You save and preview the presentation, then you print the slides and notes pages of the presentation so you can review them later. Before leaving for the day, you close the file and exit PowerPoint.

## STEPS

1. **Click the Office button 🔘, point to Print, then click Print Preview**
   The Print Preview window opens as shown in Figure A-13. Notice the Print Preview tab appears on the Ribbon, which now displays associated commands for the Print Preview window.

2. **Click the Next Page button in the Preview group, then click the Print button in the Print group**
   You view Slide 2 before opening the Print dialog box. In the Print dialog box, you can specify what you want to print (slides, handouts, notes pages, or outline), the slide range, the number of copies to print, as well as other print options. The default options for the available printer are selected in the dialog box.

3. **Click the Slides option button in the Print range section of the dialog box to select it, type 2 to print only the second slide, then click OK**
   The second slide prints. To save paper when you are reviewing your slides, you can print in handout format, which lets you print up to nine slides per page.

4. **Click the Close Print Preview button in the Preview group, click the Office button 🔘, then click Print**
   The Print dialog box opens again. The options you choose in the Print dialog box remain there until you close the presentation.

5. **Click the All option button in the Print range section, click the Print what list arrow, click Handouts, click the Slides per page list arrow in the Handouts section, then click 3**

6. **Click the Color/grayscale list arrow, click Pure Black and White as shown in Figure A-14, then click OK**
   The presentation prints as handouts showing slide thumbnails next to blank lines. Using the Handouts with three slides per page printing option is a great way to print your presentation when you want to provide a way for audience members to take notes. Printing in pure black and white prints without any gray tones and can save printer toner.

7. **Click the Office button 🔘, then click Close**
   If you have made changes to your presentation, a Microsoft PowerPoint alert box opens asking you if you want to save changes you have made to your presentation file.

8. **Click Yes, if necessary, to close the alert box**
   Your presentation closes.

9. **Click the Office button 🔘, then click the Exit PowerPoint button**
   The PowerPoint program closes, and you return to the Windows desktop.

**FIGURE A-13:** Print Preview window

Print Preview tab

Print button

The color of the slide changes to reflect the grayscale printer that is attached to the computer

**FIGURE A-14:** Print dialog box with Handouts selected

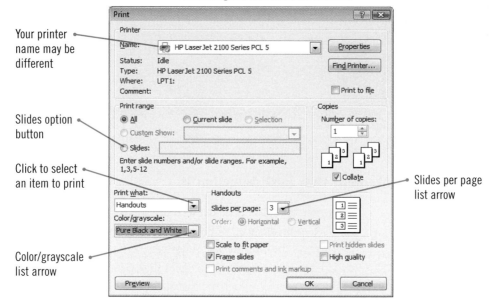

Your printer name may be different

Slides option button

Click to select an item to print

Color/grayscale list arrow

Slides per page list arrow

## Animating in PowerPoint

Providing emphasis to the information in your presentation can help your audience retain that information. Animating text and other objects is one dramatic way to provide emphasis. Animations make a presentation engaging and enjoyable to watch. You can animate text, shapes, diagrams, charts, and other objects, which provides you a wide variety of options to create a dynamic presentation. You can also add interesting effects to the way slides are presented or transition on the screen. Types of animation effects include flying in or out, fading, and changing color.

# Practice

**SAM**

If you have a SAM user profile, you may have access to hands-on instruction, practice, and assessment of the skills covered in this unit. Log in to your SAM account (http://sam2007.course.com/) to launch any assigned training activities or exams that relate to the skills covered in this unit.

## ▼ CONCEPTS REVIEW

**Label each element of the PowerPoint window shown in Figure A-15.**

FIGURE A-15

**Match each term with the statement that best describes it.**

| | |
|---|---|
| 10. **Ribbon** | **a.** A view that displays slides as thumbnails |
| 11. **Normal view** | **b.** Used to organize all of PowerPoint's commands |
| 12. **Slide Sorter view** | **c.** Displays the Outline and Slides tabs, as well as the Slide and Notes panes |
| 13. **Zoom slider** | **d.** Used to type text that references slide content |
| 14. **Notes pane** | **e.** Allows you to change the size of the slide in the window |

**Select the best answer from the list of choices.**

**15. When you type text in a placeholder, it becomes:**
- **a.** A label
- **b.** A text object
- **c.** A text processing object
- **d.** A selection box

**16. The buttons you use to switch between the PowerPoint views in the status bar are called:**
- **a.** Toolbar buttons
- **b.** View buttons
- **c.** PowerPoint buttons
- **d.** View Shortcuts

**17. All of the following are PowerPoint views, except:**
- **a.** Notes Page view
- **b.** Outline Page view
- **c.** Normal view
- **d.** Slide Sorter view

**18. What does the slide layout do in a presentation?**
- **a.** A slide layout defines how all the elements on a slide are arranged.
- **b.** A slide layout automatically applies all the objects you can use on a slide.
- **c.** The slide layout puts all your slides in order.
- **d.** The slide layout enables you to apply a template to the presentation.

**19. The view that fills the entire screen with each slide in the presentation is called:**
- **a.** Presentation view
- **b.** Slide Sorter view
- **c.** Slide Show view
- **d.** Slide view

**20. According to the unit, which of the following is not a guideline for planning a presentation?**
- **a.** Determine how much time you need to give the presentation.
- **b.** Determine the purpose of the presentation.
- **c.** Determine what you want to produce when the presentation is finished.
- **d.** Determine which type of output you need to best convey your message.

**21. Other than the Slide pane, where else can you enter slide text?**
- **a.** Slides tab
- **b.** Outline tab
- **c.** Tab Preview
- **d.** Notes Page view

## ▼ SKILLS REVIEW

**1. Start PowerPoint and examine the PowerPoint window.**
- **a.** Start PowerPoint, if necessary.
- **b.** Identify as many elements of the PowerPoint window as you can without referring to the unit material.
- **c.** Be able to describe the purpose or function of each element.
- **d.** For any elements you cannot identify, refer to the unit.

**2. Enter slide text.**
- **a.** In the Slide pane in Normal view, enter the text **Historic Middle Fork Land & Camps Protection Proposal** in the title placeholder. Refer to Figure A-16 as you complete the slide.
- **b.** In the subtitle text placeholder, enter **Historic Lands Preservation Society**

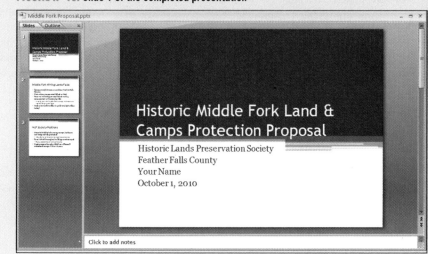

**FIGURE A-16: Slide 1 of the completed presentation**

    **c.** On the next line of the placeholder, enter **Feather Falls County**.

    **d.** On the next line of the placeholder, enter **Your Name**.

    **e.** On the next line of the placeholder, enter **October 1, 2010**. Let PowerPoint AutoFit the text in the text object.

    **f.** Deselect the text object.

    **g.** Save the presentation using the filename **Middle Fork Proposal** to the drive and folder where you store your Data Files.

**3. Add new slides.**

    **a.** Create a new slide.

    **b.** Using Figure A-17, enter text on the slide.

    **c.** Create another new slide.

    **d.** Using Figure A-18, enter text on the slide.

    **e.** Save your changes.

**4. Apply a design theme.**

    **a.** Click the Design tab.

    **b.** Click the Themes group More button, then point to all of the themes.

    **c.** Locate the Verve theme, then apply it to all the slides.

    **d.** Move to Slide 1.

    **e.** Locate the Urban theme, then apply it to Slide 1.

    **f.** Apply the Urban theme to all of the slides in the presentation.

    **g.** Use the Next Slide button to move to Slide 3, then save your changes.

**5. Compare presentation views.**

    **a.** Click the View tab.

    **b.** Click the Slide Sorter button in the Presentation Views group.

    **c.** Click the Notes Page button in the Presentation Views group, then click the Previous Slide button twice.

    **d.** Click the Normal button in the Presentation Views group, then click the Slide Show button.

    **e.** Click until a black screen appears, then click to end the presentation.

    **f.** Save your changes.

**6. Print and close a presentation, and exit PowerPoint.**

    **a.** Print Slide 1 as slides in grayscale. (*Hint*: Click the Current slide option button in the Print dialog box.)

    **b.** Print all the slides as handouts, 3 slides per page, in pure black and white.

    **c.** Print the presentation outline.

    **d.** Close the file, saving your changes.

    **e.** Exit PowerPoint.

**FIGURE A-17**

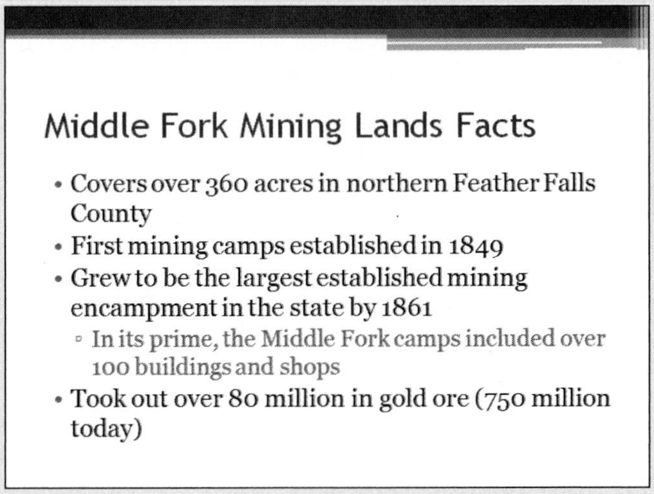

## Middle Fork Mining Lands Facts

- Covers over 360 acres in northern Feather Falls County
- First mining camps established in 1849
- Grew to be the largest established mining encampment in the state by 1861
  - In its prime, the Middle Fork camps included over 100 buildings and shops
- Took out over 80 million in gold ore (750 million today)

**FIGURE A-18**

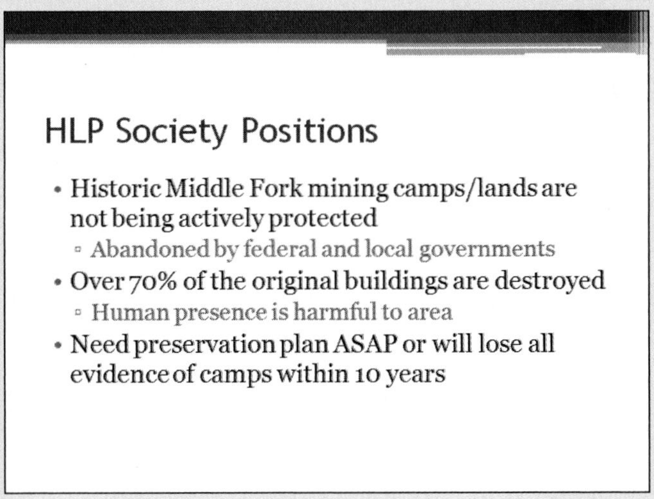

## HLP Society Positions

- Historic Middle Fork mining camps/lands are not being actively protected
  - Abandoned by federal and local governments
- Over 70% of the original buildings are destroyed
  - Human presence is harmful to area
- Need preservation plan ASAP or will lose all evidence of camps within 10 years

# ▼ INDEPENDENT CHALLENGE 1

You work for Resource Industries, a business that that offers environmental hazard clean up and project management. In an effort to expand the business, your boss has asked you to create a sales presentation that describes the services Resource Industries offers.

a. Start PowerPoint.

b. In the title placeholder on Slide 1, type **Resource Industries**

c. In the sub-title placeholder, type **Professional & Client Services**, press **[Enter]**, type **Your Name**, press **[Enter]**, then type **Today's Date**

d. Apply the Equity design theme to the slide.

e. Save your presentation with the filename **Resource Industries** to the drive and folder where you store your Data Files.

f. Use Figures A-19 and A-20 to add two more slides to your presentation. (*Hint*: Slide 2 uses the Comparison layout.)

g. Use the commands on the View tab to switch between all of PowerPoint's views.

h. Preview the presentation using the Print Preview command, print the presentation using the Slides option, save and close the file, then exit PowerPoint.

**FIGURE A-19**

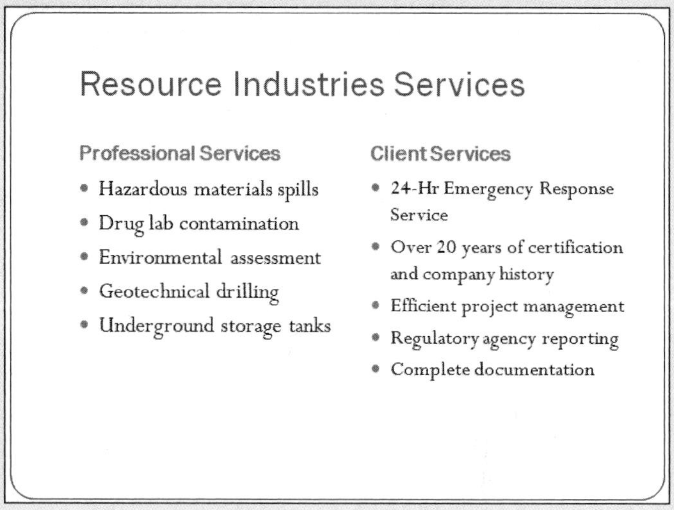

### Resource Industries Services

**Professional Services**
- Hazardous materials spills
- Drug lab contamination
- Environmental assessment
- Geotechnical drilling
- Underground storage tanks

**Client Services**
- 24-Hr Emergency Response Service
- Over 20 years of certification and company history
- Efficient project management
- Regulatory agency reporting
- Complete documentation

**FIGURE A-20**

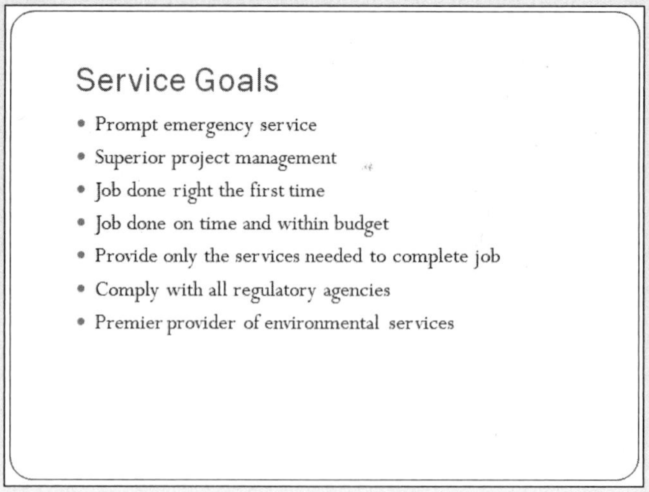

### Service Goals
- Prompt emergency service
- Superior project management
- Job done right the first time
- Job done on time and within budget
- Provide only the services needed to complete job
- Comply with all regulatory agencies
- Premier provider of environmental services

# ▼ INDEPENDENT CHALLENGE 2

You have recently been promoted to national sales manager at Windman Power Industries, which manufactures personal watercraft, including items such as paddle boats, canoes, kayaks, sail boats, and rafts. Part of your job is to present company sales figures at a yearly sales meeting. Use the following information as the basis for units sold nationally in your presentation: 797 canoes, 1302 kayaks, 421 paddle boats, 4219 sail boats, 230 rafts. Assume that Windman Power has five sales regions throughout the country: West, East, South, Midwest, and Northeast. Also, assume overall sales rose 22% during the last year and gross sales reached $230 million. The presentation should have at least five slides.

a. Spend some time planning the slides of your presentation. What is the best way to show the information provided? What other information could you add that might be useful for this presentation?

b. Start PowerPoint.

c. Give the presentation an appropriate title on the title slide and enter today's date and your name in the subtitle place-holder.

d. Add slides and enter appropriate slide text.

# ▼ INDEPENDENT CHALLENGE 2 (CONTINUED)

**e.** On the last slide of the presentation, include the
following information:

Windman Power Industries

PO Box 777

West Chester, IN 39022

**f.** Apply a design theme. A typical slide might look like
the one shown in Figure A-21.

### Advanced Challenge Exercise

■ Open the Notes Page view.

■ Add notes to three slides.

■ Print the Notes Page view for the presentation.

**g.** Switch views. Run through the slide show at
least once.

**h.** Save your presentation with the filename **Windman** where you store your Data Files.

**i.** Close the presentation and exit PowerPoint.

FIGURE A-21

## An Overall View

**Sales Figures**
- This year's results!
  - $230 million gross sales
- Comparison to last year
  - $65 million increase in overall sales
- Region by region
  - West-up by 12%
  - East-down by 5%
  - Northeast-up by 6%
  - South-up by 11%
  - Midwest-up by 7%

**National Sales**
- Product Sales
  - Canoes- 797 units
  - Kayaks- 1302 units
  - Paddle boats- 421 units
  - Sail boats- 4219 units
  - Rafts- 230 units

# ▼ INDEPENDENT CHALLENGE 3

You work for ThaiMade Trade Co., an emerging company that exports goods from Thailand. The company wants to expand its business globally. The Internet marketing director has asked you to plan and create a PowerPoint presentation that he will use to convey an expanded Internet service that will target Western countries. This new Internet service will allow customers to purchase all kinds of Thai made goods. Sample items for sale include silver and turquoise jewelry, hand crafts, folk art, terra cotta kitchenware, wooden decorative items, and bamboo furniture. Your presentation should contain product information and pricing. Use the Internet, if possible, to research information that will help you formulate your ideas. The presentation should have at least five slides.

**a.** Spend some time planning the slides of your presentation. What information would a consumer need to have to purchase items on this Web site?

**b.** Start PowerPoint.

**c.** Give the presentation an appropriate title on the title slide and enter today's date and your name in the subtitle placeholder.

**d.** Add slides and enter appropriate slide text.

**e.** On the last slide of the presentation, type the following information:

ThaiMade Trade Co.

Satrani Condominium Room 214

36/980 Moo 5 Sethup Sub District, Muang district,

Chiangmai 50208 Thailand

Tel/Fax: +90-49-39850 Hotline: (03)249347

FIGURE A-22

## Fine Jewelry Product List

| Silver Jewelry | Turquoise Jewelry |
|---|---|
| ☐ Bracelets | ☐ Bracelets |
| ☐ Necklaces | ☐ Necklaces |
| ☐ Rings | ☐ Rings |
| ☐ Earrings | ☐ Earrings |
| ☐ Watches | |
| ☐ Pendants | |

**f.** Apply a design theme. A typical slide might look like the one shown in Figure A-22.

**g.** Switch views. Run through the slide show at least once.

**h.** Save your presentation with the filename **ThaiMade** where you store your Data Files.

**i.** Close the presentation and exit PowerPoint.

# ▼ REAL LIFE INDEPENDENT CHALLENGE

Every year your college holds a large fund raising event to support a local charity. This year the Student Advisory Committee has chosen to help the East Hills Cerebral Palsy Center. To help them decide what kind of an event to hold this year, the Advisory Committee has appealed to the student body for fund raising ideas. Your idea is to host a regional Bar-B-Q cook off competition that includes local and professional cooking teams. Your idea was chosen as one of the finalist ideas and you need to present your proposal in a meeting of the Advisory Committee.

a. Spend some time planning the slides of your presentation. Assume the following: there are four competition categories (beef brisket, pork shoulder, pork ribs, and chicken); the competition is a two day event; event advertising will be city- and region-wide; local music groups will also be invited; there will be a kids section with games; the event will be held on the college football field. Use the Internet, if possible, to research information that will help you formulate your ideas.

b. Start PowerPoint.

c. Give the presentation an appropriate title on the title slide and enter your name and today's date in the subtitle placeholder.

d. Add slides and enter appropriate slide text. A typical slide might look like the one shown in Figure A-23.

e. View the presentation.

f. Save your presentation with the filename **Bar-B-Q Cookoff** where you store your Data Files.

g. Close the presentation and exit PowerPoint.

FIGURE A-23

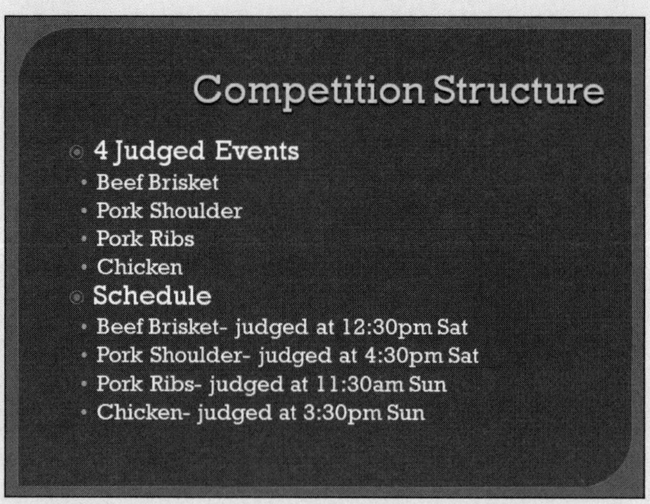

## Competition Structure

- **4 Judged Events**
  - Beef Brisket
  - Pork Shoulder
  - Pork Ribs
  - Chicken
- **Schedule**
  - Beef Brisket- judged at 12:30pm Sat
  - Pork Shoulder- judged at 4:30pm Sat
  - Pork Ribs- judged at 11:30am Sun
  - Chicken- judged at 3:30pm Sun

# ▼ VISUAL WORKSHOP

Create the presentation shown in Figures A-24 and A-25. Make sure you include your name on the title slide. Save the presentation as **PackJet Project Tests** where you store your Data Files. Print the slides.

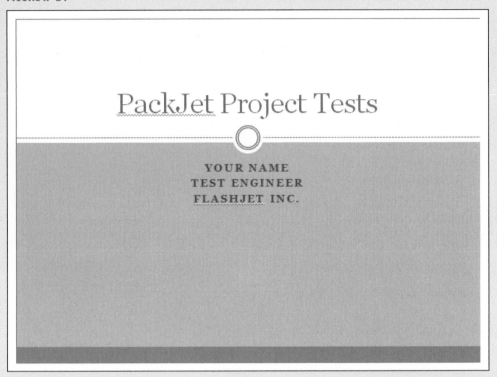

PackJet Project Tests

YOUR NAME
TEST ENGINEER
FLASHJET INC.

Component Tests

- Interface module board
- Security codes
- Flash system codes
  - Temporary access
  - Print reader
- Rocket pack system

# Modifying a Presentation

**Files You Will Need:**

PPT B-1.pptx
PPT B-2.pptx
PPT B-3.pptx
PPT B-4.pptx
PPT B-5.pptx

In the previous unit you learned how to enter slide text, add a new slide, and apply a design theme. Now, you are ready to take the next step in creating professional-looking presentations by learning to format text and work with drawn objects. In this unit, you'll enter text in the Outline tab, format text, draw and modify objects, add slide footer information, and check the spelling in the presentation. You continue working on the European tour proposal presentation for Ellen Latsky.

**OBJECTIVES**

Enter text in the Outline tab

Format text

Convert text to SmartArt

Insert and modify shapes

Edit and duplicate shapes

Align and group objects

Add slide headers and footers

Check spelling in a presentation

# Entering Text in the Outline Tab

You can enter presentation text by typing directly on the slide in the Slide pane, or, if you'd rather focus on the presentation text without worrying about the layout, you can enter text in the Outline tab. The outline is organized so that the headings, or slide titles, appear at the top of the outline. Beneath the title, each subpoint, or each line of bulleted text, appears as one or more indented lines under the title. Each indent in the outline creates another level of bulleted text on the slide. ⬛⬛⬛⬛ You switch to the Outline tab to enter text for two more slides in the European tour proposal presentation. Begin by entering more text using the Outline tab.

1. **Start PowerPoint, open the presentation PPT B-1.pptx from the drive and folder where you store your Data Files, save it as QuestB, click the View tab on the Ribbon, then click the Arrange All button in the Window group**

   The Slide pane, Notes pane, and Slide and Outline tabs are now in their own window with the presentation title at the top.

2. **Click the Slide 2 thumbnail in the Slides tab, then click the Outline tab**

   The Outline tab enlarges to display the text that is on the slides. The slide icon and the text for Slide 2 are highlighted, indicating that it's selected. Notice the number 1 that appears to the left of the first-level bullet for Slide 2, indicating that there are multiple content placeholders on the slide.

3. **Click the Home tab on the Ribbon, click the New Slide button list arrow in the Slides group, then click Title and Content**

   A new slide, Slide 3, with the Title and Content layout appears as the current slide below Slide 2. A blinking insertion point appears next to the new slide in the Outline tab. See Figure B-1. Text that you enter next to a slide icon becomes the title for that slide.

4. **Type Focus Group Data Analyzed, press [Enter], then press [Tab]**

   When you first press [Enter] you create a new slide, but because you want to enter bulleted text on Slide 3 you press [Tab] so that the text you type is entered as bullet text on Slide 3.

5. **Type Trends, press [Enter], type Major Findings, press [Enter], type Conclusions, then press [Enter]**

   The last time you press [Enter], you create a bullet that has no text at the end of this slide.

6. **Press [Shift][Tab]**

   The last bullet that was created on Slide 3 becomes a new slide.

7. **Type Tour Strategy Objectives, press [Ctrl][Enter], then type the rest of the information on Slide 4 as shown in Figure B-2**

   Pressing [Ctrl][Enter] while the cursor is in the title text object moves the cursor into the content placeholder. Make sure you misspell the word "Utilze" as shown on the slide.

8. **Position the pointer on the Slide 4 icon in the Outline tab**

   The pointer changes to ✛. Slide 4 is out of order.

9. **Drag the Slide 4 icon up until a horizontal indicator line appears above the Slide 3 icon, then release the mouse button**

   The fourth slide moves up and switches places with the third slide.

10. **Click the Slides tab, then save your work**

    The Outline tab closes and the Slides tab is now visible in the window.

**FIGURE B-1:** Outline tab open showing new slide

Outline tab

New slide

Text you type here becomes the slide title

Drag the pane divider line to change the width of the Outline tab

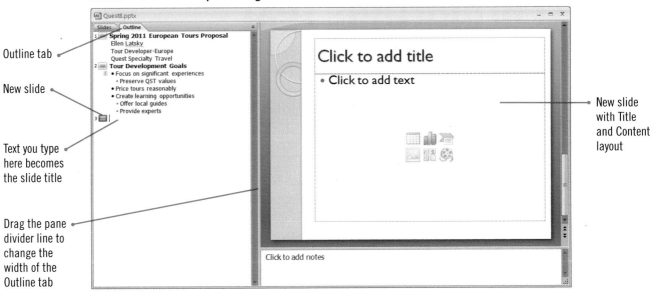

New slide with Title and Content layout

**FIGURE B-2:** Slide 4 with new information

Make sure you misspell this word

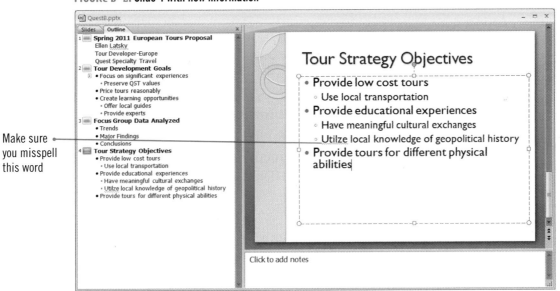

### Setting permissions

In PowerPoint, you can set specific access permissions for people who review or edit your work, so you have better control over your content. For example, you may want to give a user permission to edit or change your presentation but not allow them to print it. You can also restrict a user by permitting them to view the presentation, without the ability to edit or print the presentation, or you can give the user full access or control of the presentation. To use this feature, you first have to install the Windows Rights Management Services software using the Add or Remove Programs feature in the Control Panel, which installs the Restrict Permissions feature on the Office button. Then, to set user access permissions, click the Office button, point to Prepare, point to Restrict Permission, then click the appropriate option.

# Formatting Text

Once you have entered and edited the text in your presentation, you can modify the way the text looks to emphasize your message. Important text should be highlighted in some way to distinguish it from other text or objects on the slide. For example, if you have two text objects on the same slide, you could draw attention to one text object by changing its color, font, or size. In order to enhance the European tour proposal presentation, you format text on Slide 4.

## STEPS

**QUICK TIP**

Open the PowerPoint Options dialog box to set the option to show or hide the Mini toolbar.

1. **Click the Slide 4 thumbnail in the Slides tab, then double-click Trends in the text object**

   The word Trends is selected and a small semitransparent Mini toolbar appears above the text. The **Mini toolbar** contains basic text formatting commands, such as bold and italic, and appears when you select text using the mouse. This toolbar makes it quick and easy to format text, especially when the Home tab is not open.

2. **Move the pointer over the Mini toolbar, click the Font Color button list arrow A ⁻, then click the Dark Red color box under Standard Colors**

   The text changes color to dark red as shown in Figure B-3. As soon as you move the pointer over the Mini toolbar, the toolbar becomes clearly visible. When you click the Font Color button list arrow, the Font Color gallery appears showing the Theme Colors and Standard Colors. Notice that the Font Color button on the Mini toolbar and the Font Color button on the Home tab change color to reflect the new color choice.

**QUICK TIP**

You can also select the entire text object by clicking its border when the text object is already selected.

3. **Click outside the text object in a blank area of the slide, press and hold [Shift], click the text object, then release [Shift]**

   A selection box with small circles and squares called **sizing handles** appears around the text object. The entire text object is selected, and changes you make now affect all of the text in the text object. If you click a text object without pressing [Shift], a dotted selection box appears, indicating that the object is active and ready to accept text, but the text object itself is not selected. When the whole text object is selected, you can change its size, shape, or other attributes. Changing the color of the text helps emphasize it.

4. **Click the Font Color button A ⁻ in the Font group**

   All of the text in the text object changes to the dark red color.

5. **Click the Font list arrow in the Font group**

   A list of available fonts opens with Gill Sans MT, the current font used in the text object, selected at the top of the list with the Theme Fonts.

6. **Click Arial Narrow**

   The Arial Narrow font replaces the original font in the text object. Notice that as you move the pointer over the font names in the font list the text on the slide displays a live preview of the different font choices.

7. **Click the Text Shadow button S in the Font group, click the Change Case button Aa ⁻ in the Font group, then click UPPERCASE**

   All of the text now displays a gray shadow and is uppercase.

8. **Click the Bullets button list arrow ≣ ⁻ in the Paragraph group, click None, then click the Center button ≣ in the Paragraph group**

   The bullets no longer appear next to the text and the text moves to the center of the text box. Compare your screen to Figure B-4.

9. **Click a blank area of the slide outside the text object to deselect it, then save your work**

**FIGURE B-3:** Selected word with Mini toolbar open

Font list arrow

Mini toolbar

Changed text color

Font Color button list arrow

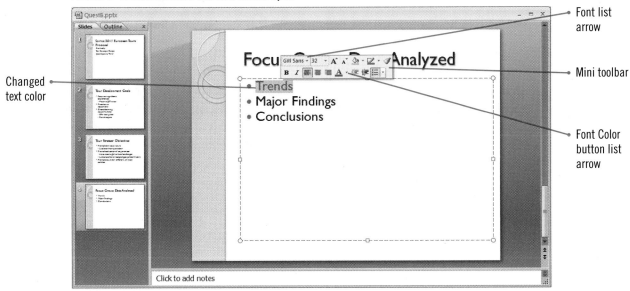

**FIGURE B-4:** Formatted text

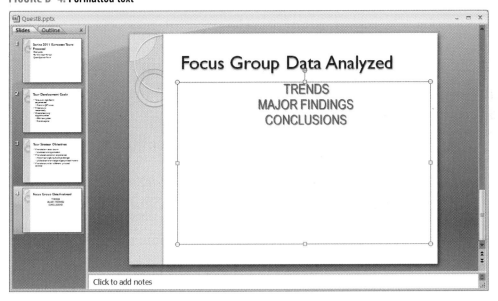

## Replacing text and fonts

As you review your presentation, you may decide to replace certain text or fonts throughout the entire presentation using the Replace command. Text can be a word, phrase, or sentence. To replace specific text, click the Home tab on the Ribbon, then click the Replace button in the Editing group. In the Replace dialog box, enter the text you want to replace then enter the text you want to use as its replacement. You can also use the Replace command to replace one font for another. Simply click the Replace button list arrow in the Editing group, then click Replace Fonts to open the Replace Font dialog box.

# Converting Text to SmartArt

Sometimes when you are working with text it just doesn't capture your attention, no matter how you dress it up with color or other formatting attributes. The introduction of the SmartArt graphic in PowerPoint 2007 increases your ability to create dynamic-looking text. A **SmartArt** graphic is a professional-quality diagram that visually illustrates text. There are seven basic categories, or types, of SmartArt graphics that illustrate text differently. For example, you can show steps in a process or timeline, show proportional relationships, or show how parts relate to a whole. You can create a SmartArt graphic from scratch or create one by converting existing text you have entered on a slide with a few simple clicks of the mouse. At QST, Ellen wants the text to appear visually dynamic so you convert the text on Slide 4 to a SmartArt graphic.

**STEPS**

1. **On Slide 4, click anywhere in the text object, then click the Convert to SmartArt Graphic button in the Paragraph group**

   A gallery of SmartArt graphic layouts opens. As with many features in PowerPoint, you can preview how your text will look prior to applying the SmartArt graphic layout by using PowerPoint's Live Preview feature. You can review each SmartArt graphic layout and see how it changes the appearance of text.

2. **Move the pointer over the SmartArt graphic layouts in the gallery**

   Notice how the text becomes part of the graphic and the color and font changes each time you move the pointer over a different graphic layout. SmartArt graphic names appear as ScreenTips.

3. **Click the Basic Timeline layout in the SmartArt graphics gallery**

   A SmartArt graphic appears on the slide in place of the text object and a new SmartArt Tools Design tab opens on the Ribbon as shown in Figure B-5. A SmartArt graphic consists of two parts: the SmartArt graphic itself and a text pane where you type and edit text.

   > **QUICK TIP**
   > The text objects in the SmartArt graphic can be moved and edited like any other text object in PowerPoint.

4. **If necessary, click the Text Pane button in the Create Graphic group to open the text pane, then click each bullet point in the text pane**

   Notice that each time you select a bullet point in the text pane, a selection box appears around the text objects in the SmartArt graphic.

5. **Click the Text Pane button, click the More button in the Layouts group, then click the Alternating Flow layout**

   The text pane closes and the SmartArt graphic changes to the new graphic layout. You can radically change how the SmartArt graphic looks by applying a SmartArt Style. A **SmartArt Style** is a pre-set combination of simple and 3-D formatting options that follows the presentation theme.

   > **QUICK TIP**
   > Click the Reset Graphic button in the Reset group to revert the SmartArt graphic to its original state.

6. **Move the pointer slowly over the styles in the SmartArt Styles group, then click the More button in the SmartArt Styles group**

   A live preview of each style is displayed on the SmartArt graphic. The SmartArt styles are organized into sections; the top group offers suggestions for the best match for the document.

7. **Move the pointer over the styles in the 3-D section of the gallery, then click Powder**

   Notice how the new Powder style adds a bevel to the text boxes and makes them semi-transparent. Now move the SmartArt graphic more toward the center of the slide.

8. **Press [left-arrow key] twice, click a blank area of the slide outside the SmartArt graphic object to deselect it, then save your work**

   Compare your screen to Figure B-6.

**FIGURE B-5:** Text converted to a SmartArt graphic

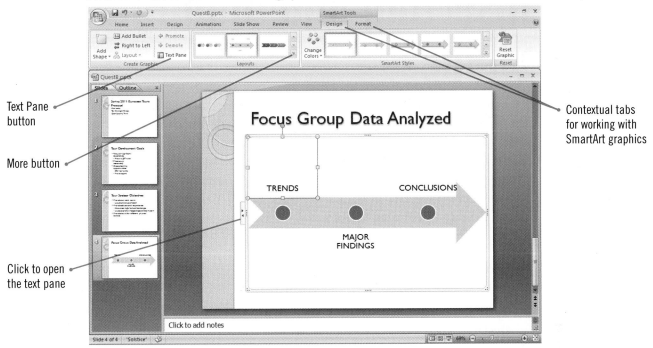

Text Pane button

More button

Click to open the text pane

Contextual tabs for working with SmartArt graphics

**FIGURE B-6:** Final SmartArt graphic

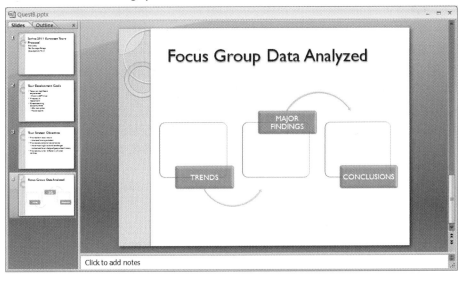

## Choosing SmartArt graphics

When choosing a SmartArt graphic to use on your slide, remember that you want the SmartArt graphic to communicate the message of the text effectively; not every SmartArt graphic layout achieves that goal. So, you must consider the type of text you want to illustrate. For example, does the text show steps in a process, does it show a continual process, or does it show non-sequential information? The answer to this question will dictate the type of SmartArt graphic layout you should choose. Also, the amount of text you want to illustrate will have an effect on the SmartArt graphic layout you choose. Most of the time key points will be the text you use in a SmartArt graphic. Finally, some SmartArt graphic layouts are limited by the number of shapes that they can accommodate. So, if you have four points you want to illustrate and you choose a graphic layout with only two shapes, you will not communicate your message correctly. Experiment with the SmartArt graphic layouts until you find the right one, and have fun in the process!

# Inserting and Modifying Shapes

In PowerPoint you can insert many different types of shapes including lines, geometric figures, arrows, stars, callouts, and banners to enhance your presentation. You can create single shapes or combine several shapes together to make a more complex figure. You can modify many aspects of a shape including its fill color, line color, and line style, as well as add other effects like shadow, and 3-D effects. Instead of changing individual attributes, you can apply a Quick Style to a shape. A **Quick Style** is a set of formatting options, including line style, fill color, and effects. You decide to draw some shapes on Slide 3 of your presentation to complete the slide.

**STEPS**

1. **Click the Slide 3 thumbnail in the Slides tab**
   Slide 3 appears in the Slide pane.

2. **Press and hold [Shift], click the text object, then release [Shift]**
   The text object is selected.

3. **Position the pointer over the bottom-middle sizing handle, notice the pointer change to ↕, then drag the sizing handle up until the text object looks like Figure B-7**
   The text object decreases in size. When you position the pointer over a sizing handle, it changes to ↕. The pointer points in different directions depending on which sizing handle it is positioned over. When you drag a sizing handle, the pointer changes to +, and a faint gray outline appears, representing the size of the text object.

**TROUBLE**

If you see the Shapes gallery on the Ribbon, you are working at a higher resolution than the figures in this book, skip to step 5.

4. **Click the Shapes button in the Drawing group**
   A gallery of shapes organized by type opens. Notice that there is a section at the top of the gallery where all of the recently used shapes are placed.

5. **Click the Chevron shape ⟫ in the Block Arrows section, position + in the blank area of the slide below the text object, press and hold [Shift], drag down and to the right to create the chevron shape, as shown in Figure B-8, release the mouse button, then release [Shift]**
   A chevron arrow shape appears on the slide, filled with the default color. Pressing [Shift] while you create the object maintains the object's proportions as you change its size. To change the shape style apply a Quick Style from the Shape Styles group.

**TROUBLE**

If your shape is not approximately the same size as the one shown in Figure B-8, press [Shift] and drag one of the corner sizing handles to resize the object.

6. **Click the Drawing Tools Format tab, click the More button ▼ in the Shape Styles group, move the pointer over the styles in the gallery to review them, then click Moderate Effect — Accent 3**
   A red Quick Style with coordinated gradient fill, line, and shadow color is applied to the shape.

7. **Click the Shape Effects button in the Shape Styles group, then move the pointer over the effects to review them**
   The shape changes every time you move the pointer over a different effect.

8. **Point to Bevel, click Divot, then save your work**

**FIGURE B-7: Resized text object**

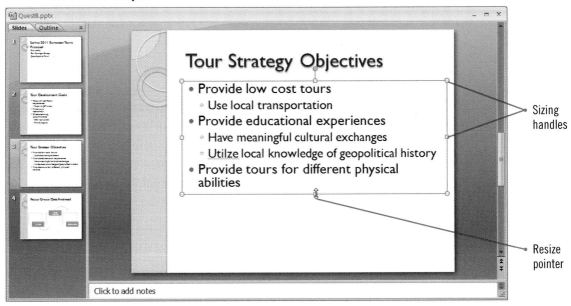

Sizing handles

Resize pointer

**FIGURE B-8: Chevron arrow shape**

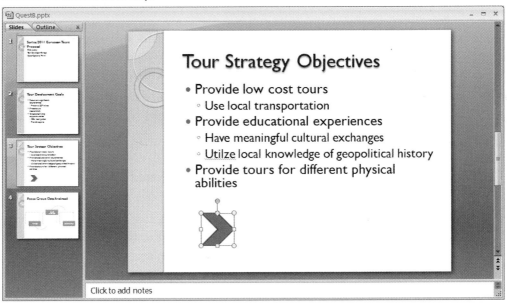

## Changing the size and position of shapes

Usually when you resize a shape you can simply drag one of the sizing handles around the outside of the shape, but sometimes you may need to resize a shape more precisely. When you select a shape, the Drawing Tools Format tab appears on the Ribbon, offering you many different formatting options including some sizing commands located in the Size group. The Width and Height commands in the Size group allow you to change the width and height of a shape. You also have the option to open the Size and Position dialog box, which allows you to change the size of a shape, as well as the rotation, scale, and position of a shape on the slide.

# Editing and Duplicating Shapes

Once you have created a shape you still have the ability to refine the aspects of the object. PowerPoint allows you to adjust various aspects of shapes to help change the look of them. For example, if you create a shape with an arrowhead but the head of the arrow does not look quite like you want it to look, you can change it. You can also add text to most PowerPoint shapes, and you can move or copy shapes. ███████ You want two identical arrows on Slide 3 to break up the look of the slide. You first change the shape of the arrow you've already created, and then you make a copy of it.

## STEPS

1.  **Click the arrow shape on Slide 3 to select it, if it is not already selected**
    In addition to sizing handles, two other handles appear on the selected object. You use the **adjustment handle**—a small yellow diamond—to change the appearance of an object. The adjustment handle appears next to the most prominent feature of the object, like the head of an arrow in this case. You use the **rotate handle**—a small green circle—to manually rotate the object.

2.  **Press and hold [Shift], drag the right-middle sizing handle on the arrow shape to the right approximately 1/2", release [Shift], then release the mouse button**

3.  **Position the pointer over the middle of the selected arrow shape so that it changes to ⭢, then drag the arrow shape so that the arrow aligns with the left edge of the text in the text object as shown in Figure B-9**
    A semitransparent copy of the shape appears as you move the arrow shape to help you position it. PowerPoint uses a hidden grid to align objects; it forces objects to "snap" to the grid lines. Make any needed adjustments to the arrow shape position so it looks similar to Figure B-9.

    > **TROUBLE**
    > If you are having trouble making precise adjustments, press and hold [Alt] to turn off the snap to grid feature, then drag the adjustment handle.

4.  **Position the pointer over the adjustment handle of the arrow shape so that it changes to ▷, then drag the adjustment handle to the right so it is halfway between the sizing handles**
    The arrow shape appearance changes.

5.  **Position ⭢ over the arrow shape then press and hold [Ctrl]**
    The pointer changes to ⭢, indicating that PowerPoint makes a copy of the arrow shape when you drag the mouse.

6.  **Holding [Ctrl], drag the arrow shape to the right until the arrow shape copy is in a blank area of the slide, release the mouse button, then release [Ctrl]**
    An identical copy of the arrow shape appears on the slide.

    > **TROUBLE**
    > If the text does not fit on one line, drag the right-middle sizing handle slightly to the right until the text moves onto one line.

7.  **Type Higher**
    The text appears in the selected arrow shape. The text is now part of the shape, so if you move or rotate the object, the text moves with it. Compare your screen with Figure B-10.

8.  **Click the other arrow shape, type Aim, then click in a blank area of the slide**
    Clicking a blank area of the slide deselects all objects that are selected.

9.  **Save your work**

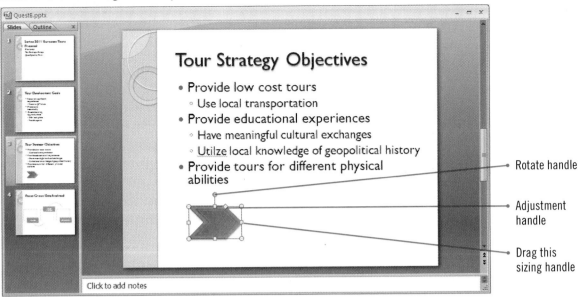

FIGURE B-10: Slide showing duplicated shape

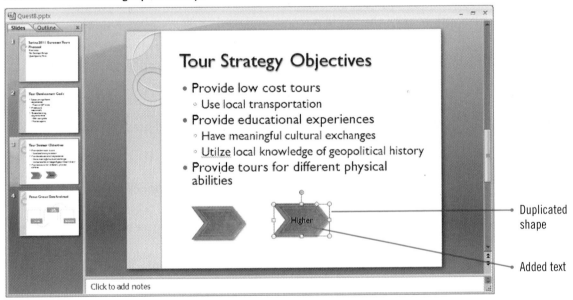

## Understanding PowerPoint objects

Every object on a slide, whether it is a text object, a shape, a chart, a picture, or any other object, is stacked on the slide in the order it was created. So, for example, if you add three shapes to a slide, the first shape you create is on the bottom of the stack and the last shape you create is on the top of the stack. Each object, including Title and Content objects, can be moved up or down in the stack depending on how you want the objects to look on the slide. To move an object to the front of the stack, select the object, then click the Bring to Front button in the Arrange group on the Drawing Tools Format tab. To move an object to the back of the stack, click the Send to Back button in the Arrange group on the Drawing Tools Format tab. You can also open the Selection and Visibility pane by clicking the Selection Pane button in the Arrange group to view and rearrange all of the objects on the slide.

# Aligning and Grouping Objects

After you are finished creating and modifying your objects, you can position them accurately on the slide to achieve the look you want. Using the Align commands in the Arrange group, you can align objects relative to each other by snapping them to a grid of evenly spaced vertical and horizontal lines. The Group command groups objects into one object, which secures their relative position to each other and makes it easy to edit and move them. The Distribute commands found with the Align commands evenly space objects horizontally or vertically relative to each other or the slide.  You are ready to position and group the arrow shapes on Slide 3 to make the slide look consistent and planned.

## STEPS

1. **Right-click a blank area of the slide, then click Grid and Guides on the shortcut menu**
   The Grid and Guides dialog box opens.

2. **Click the Display drawing guides on screen check box, then click OK**
   The PowerPoint guides appear as dotted lines on the slide and intersect at the center of the slide. They help you position the arrow shape.

3. **Position ⌖ over the vertical guide in a blank area of the slide, press and hold the mouse button until the pointer changes to a measurement guide, then drag the guide to the right until the guide position box reads 1.00**

4. **Position ✛ over the Higher arrow shape (not over the text in the shape), then drag the arrow shape so that the left edge of the selection box touches the vertical guide as shown in Figure B-11**
   The arrow shape attaches or "snaps" to the vertical guide.

5. **With the Higher arrow shape selected, press and hold [Shift], click the Aim arrow shape, then release [Shift]**
   The two objects are now selected.

6. **Click the Drawing Tools Format tab on the Ribbon, click the Align button in the Arrange group, then click Align Bottom**
   The objects are now aligned horizontally along their bottom edges. Notice that the Higher arrow shape moves to align with the Aim arrow shape.

7. **Click the Group button in the Arrange group, then click Group**
   The objects group to form one object without losing their individual attributes. Notice that the sizing handles and rotate handle now appear on the outer edge of the grouped object, not around each individual object.

8. **Click the Align button, click Distribute Horizontally, then click a blank area of the slide**
   The objects are now distributed equally between the edges of the slide. Compare your screen with Figure B-12.

9. **Right-click a blank area of the slide, click Grid and Guides on the shortcut menu, click the Display drawing guides on screen check box, click OK, then save your work**
   The guides are no longer displayed on the slide.

**FIGURE B-11:** Repositioned shape

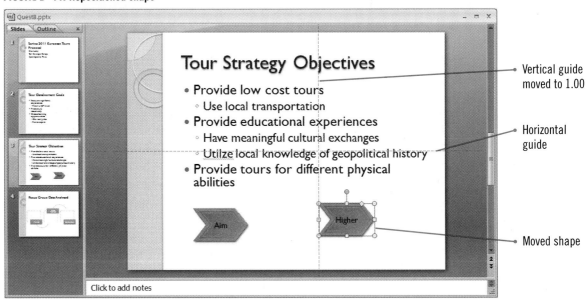

Vertical guide moved to 1.00

Horizontal guide

Moved shape

**FIGURE B-12:** Aligned and grouped shapes

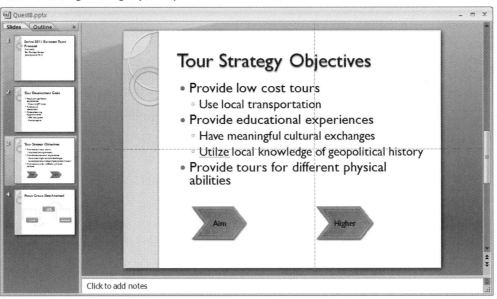

## Distributing objects

There are two ways to distribute objects in PowerPoint: relative to each other and relative to the slide edge. If you choose to distribute objects relative to each other, PowerPoint evenly divides the empty space between all of the selected objects. When distributing objects in relation to the slide, PowerPoint evenly splits the empty space from slide edge to slide edge between the selected objects. To distribute objects relative to each other, click the Align button in the Arrange group on the Format tab, then click Align Selected Objects. To distribute objects relative to the slide, click the Align button in the Arrange group on the Format tab, then click Align to Slide.

# Adding Slide Headers and Footers

Header and footer text, such as your company or product name, the slide number, and the date, can give your slides a polished look and make it easier for your audience to follow your presentation. On slides, you can add text to the footer; however, notes or handouts can include both header and footer text. Footer information that you apply to the slides of your presentation is visible in the PowerPoint views and when you print the slides. Notes and handouts header and footer text is visible when you print notes pages, handouts, and the outline. ▰▰▰▰▰ You add footer text to the slides of the European tour proposal presentation to make it easier for the audience to follow.

## STEPS

**QUICK TIP**

The placement of the footer text objects on the slide is dependent upon the presentation theme.

1. **Click the Insert tab on the Ribbon, then click the Header & Footer button in the Text group**

   The Header and Footer dialog box opens, as shown in Figure B-13. The Header and Footer dialog box has two tabs: a Slide tab and a Notes and Handouts tab. The Slide tab is selected. There are three types of footer text, Date and time, Slide number, and Footer. The rectangles at the bottom of the Preview box identify the default position and status of the three types of footer text placeholders on the slides.

2. **Click the Date and time check box to select it**

   The date and time sub-options are now available and the far-left rectangle at the bottom of the Preview box has a dark border around it, signifying where the date and time information will appear on the slide. The Update automatically date and time option button is selected by default. This option updates the date and time every time you open or print the file.

**QUICK TIP**

If you want a specific date—such as the original date that the presentation was created—to appear every time you view or print the presentation, click the Fixed date option button, then type the date in the Fixed text box.

3. **Click the Update automatically list arrow, then click the fourth option in the list**

   The date format changes to display the month spelled out, the date number, and the four-digit year.

4. **Click the Slide number check box, click the Footer check box, then type Your Name**

   The Preview box now shows that all three footer placeholders are selected.

5. **Click the Don't show on title slide check box**

   Selecting this check box prevents the footer information you entered in the Header and Footer dialog box from appearing on the title slide.

6. **Click Apply to All**

   The dialog box closes and the footer information is applied to all of the slides in your presentation except the title slide. Compare your screen to Figure B-14.

7. **Click the Slide 1 thumbnail in the Slides tab, then click the Header & Footer button in the Text group**

   The Header and Footer dialog box opens again. You want to show your company tag line in the footer on the title slide.

8. **Click the Don't show on title slide check box to deselect it, click the Footer check box, then select the text in the Footer text box**

**TROUBLE**

If you click Apply to All in Step 9, click the Undo button on the Quick Access toolbar and repeat Steps 7, 8, and 9.

9. **Type "Explore with us...learn from the world", click Apply, then save your work**

   Only the text in the Footer text box appears on the title slide. Clicking Apply applies the footer information to just the current slide.

**FIGURE B-13:** Header and Footer dialog box

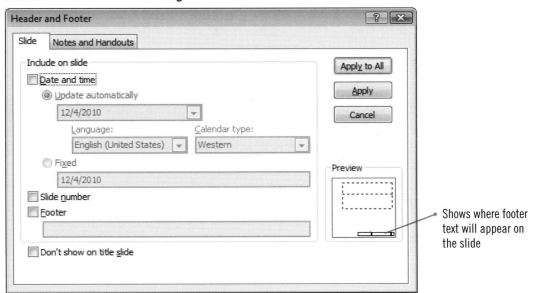

Shows where footer text will appear on the slide

**FIGURE B-14:** Slide showing footer information

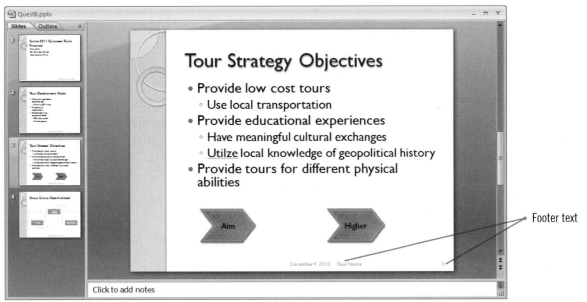

Footer text

### Entering and printing notes

You can add notes to your slides when there are certain facts you want to remember during a presentation or when there is information you want to hand out to your audience. Notes do not appear on the slides when you run a slide show. Use the Notes pane in Normal view or Notes Page view to enter notes for your slides. To enter text notes on a slide, click in the Notes pane, then type. If you want to insert graphics as notes, you must use Notes Page view. To open Notes Page view, click the View tab on the Ribbon, then click the Notes Page button in the Presentation Views group. You can print your notes by clicking the Print what list arrow and then clicking Notes Pages in the Print dialog box. The notes page can be a good handout to give your audience to use during the presentation and then after as a reminder. If you don't enter any notes in the Notes pane, and print the notes pages, the slides print as thumbnails with blank lines to the right of the thumbnails to handwrite notes.

# Checking Spelling in a Presentation

As your work on the presentation file nears completion, you need to review and proofread your slides thoroughly for errors. You can use the spellchecking feature in PowerPoint to check for and correct spelling errors. This feature compares the spelling of all the words in your presentation against the words contained in PowerPoint's electronic dictionary. You still must proofread your presentation for punctuation, grammar, and word-usage errors because the spellchecker recognizes only misspelled and unknown words, not misused words. For example, the spellchecker would not identify the word "lost" as an error, even if you had intended to type the word "cost." 〰〰〰 Ellen wants to present a professional presentation, one without spelling errors. You're finished working with the European tour proposal presentation for now; this is a good time to check the spelling.

## STEPS

1. **Click the Review tab on the Ribbon, then click the Spelling button in the Proofing group**
   PowerPoint begins to check the spelling in your presentation. When PowerPoint finds a misspelled word or a word it doesn't recognize, the Spelling dialog box opens, as shown in Figure B-15. In this case, PowerPoint does not recognize the name "Latsky" on Slide 1. It suggests that you replace it with the word "Lastly." You want the word to remain as you typed it.

2. **Click Ignore All**
   Clicking Ignore All tells the spellchecker not to stop at and question any more occurrences of this word in this presentation. The next word the spellchecker identifies as an error is the word "Utilze" in the text object on Slide 3. In the Suggestions list box, the spellchecker suggests "Utilize."

3. **Verify that Utilize is selected in the Suggestions list box, then click Change**
   If PowerPoint finds any other words it does not recognize, either change or ignore them. When the spellchecker finishes checking your presentation, the Spelling dialog box closes, and an alert box opens with a message that the spelling check is complete.

4. **Click OK**
   The alert box closes. You are satisfied with the presentation so far and you decide to print it. Compare your screen to Figure B-16.

5. **Click the Office button, then click the Print button**
   The Print dialog box opens.

6. **Make sure Slides is selected in the Print what list box, then click the Frame slides check box**
   The slides of your presentation print with a frame around each page.

7. **Click OK in the Print dialog box, then save your presentation**

8. **Click the Office button, then click Exit PowerPoint**

FIGURE B-15: Spelling dialog box

Selected word from Suggestions list

Suggestions list

Unrecognized word

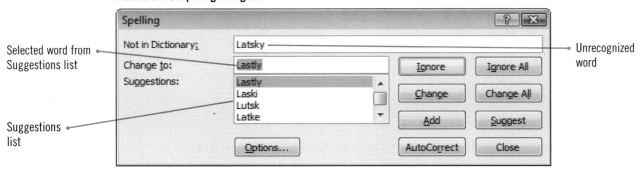

FIGURE B-16: Slide showing fixed spelling error

Fixed spelling error

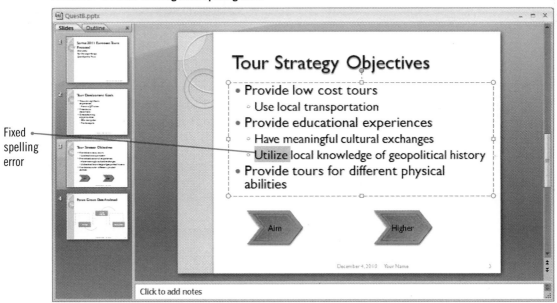

## Checking spelling as you type

PowerPoint checks your spelling as you type. If you type a word that is not in the electronic dictionary, a wavy red line appears under it. To correct an error, right-click the misspelled word, then review the suggestions, which appear in the shortcut menu. You can select a suggestion, add the word you typed to your custom dictionary, or ignore it. To turn off automatic spellchecking, click the Office button, then click the PowerPoint Options button to open the PowerPoint Options dialog box. Click the Proofing button, then click the Check spelling as you type check box to deselect it. To temporarily hide the wavy red lines, click the Hide spelling errors check box to select it.

# Practice

If you have a SAM user profile, you may have access to hands-on instruction, practice, and assessment of the skills covered in this unit. Log in to your SAM account (http://sam2007.course.com/) to launch any assigned training activities or exams that relate to the skills covered in this unit.

## ▼ CONCEPTS REVIEW

**Label each element of the PowerPoint window shown in Figure B-17.**

FIGURE B-17

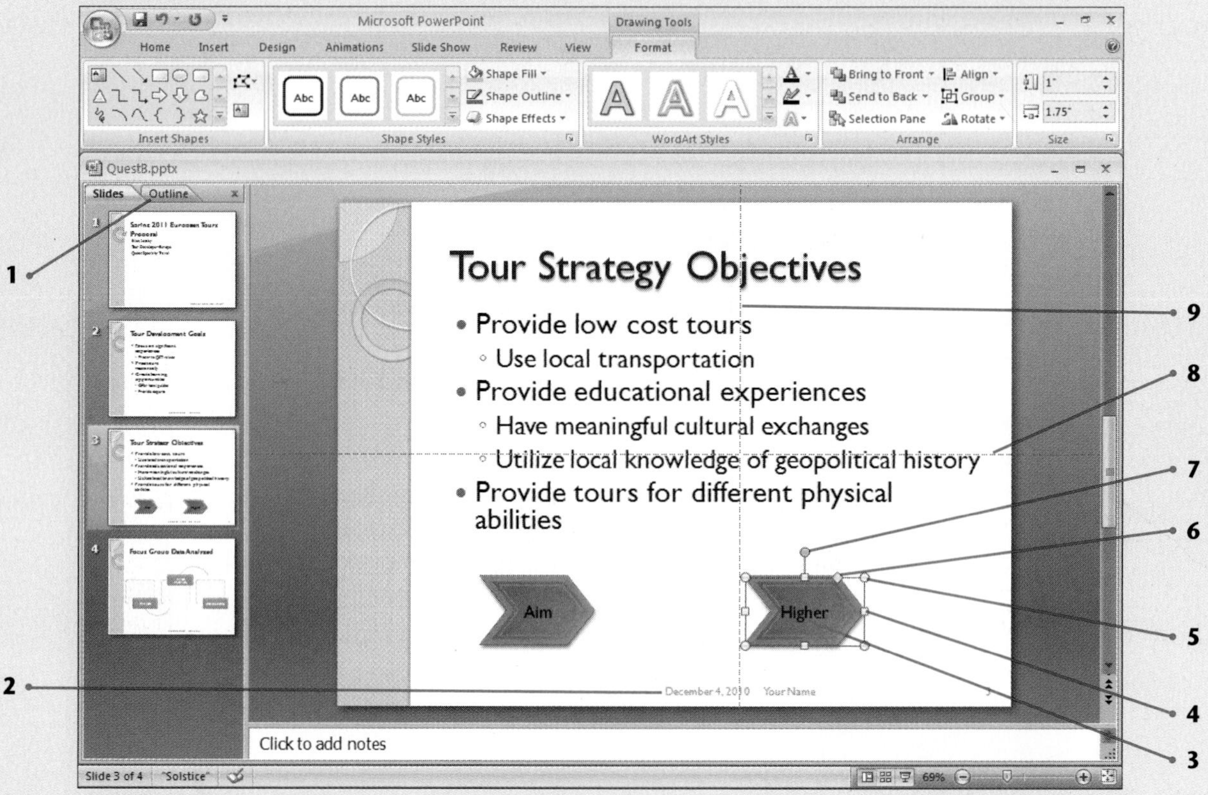


**Match each term with the statement that best describes it.**

**10. Mini toolbar**
**11. SmartArt graphic**
**12. Adjustment handle**
**13. Quick Style**
**14. Rotate handle**
**15. Sizing handle**

**a.** A circle or square that appears around a selected object
**b.** A pre-set combination of formatting options that you apply to an object
**c.** A formatting toolbar
**d.** Changes the appearance of an object
**e.** Allows you to manually rotate an object
**f.** A diagram that visually illustrates text

**Select the best answer from the list of choices.**

**16. Which of the following statements about the Mini toolbar is incorrect?**

   **a.** It is semitransparent until you move the pointer over it.

   **b.** It is used to change the layout of a slide.

   **c.** It is used to format text.

   **d.** It appears when you select text.

**17. Which statement about the PowerPoint spellchecker is true?**

   **a.** PowerPoint only identifies spelling errors when you run the spellchecker.

   **b.** The spellchecker catches grammar problems.

   **c.** The spellchecker identifies misspelled and unknown words.

   **d.** Most misused words are caught by the spellchecker.

**18. A professional-quality diagram that visually illustrates text best describes which of the following?**

   **a.** A SmartArt graphic         **c.** A slide layout

   **b.** A shape                 **d.** A content object

**19. What does the adjustment handle do to a shape?**

   **a.** Changes the shape to another     **c.** Changes the size of a shape

   **b.** Changes the rotation of a shape   **d.** Changes the appearance of a shape

**20. How do you make a shape smaller?**

   **a.** Drag the adjustment handle.      **c.** Drag the rotate handle.

   **b.** Drag the sizing handle.          **d.** Drag the shape edge.

**21. What would you use to place a shape in a specific position on a slide?**

   **a.** PowerPoint guides          **c.** PowerPoint distribution angles

   **b.** PowerPoint placeholders      **d.** PowerPoint anchor points

**22. What is *not* true about grouped objects?**

   **a.** Grouped objects have one rotate handle.

   **b.** Sizing handles appear around the grouped object.

   **c.** Grouped objects lose some of their individual characteristics.

   **d.** Grouped objects act as one object.

# ▼ SKILLS REVIEW

**1. Enter text in the Outline tab.**

   **a.** Open the presentation PPT B-2.pptx from the drive and folder where you store your Data Files, then save it as **TechJet**. The completed presentation is shown in Figure B-18.

   **b.** Create a new slide after Slide 3 with the Title and Content layout.

   **c.** Open the Outline tab, then type **Network Integration**.

   **d.** Press [Enter], press [Tab], type **Protocols and Conversions**, press [Enter], press [Tab], then type **Server codes and routing protocols**.

   **e.** Press [Enter], type **File transfer**, press [Enter], type **Data conversion**, press [Enter], then type **Platform functionality ratings**.

   **f.** Move Slide 4 to the Slide 3 position.

**FIGURE B-18**

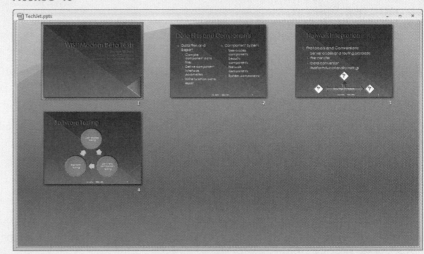

   **g.** Switch back to the Slides tab.

   **h.** Save your changes.

**2. Format text.**

   **a.** Go to Slide 1.

   **b.** Select the name Joseph M. Sera, then move the pointer over the Mini toolbar.

   **c.** Click the Font Color list arrow, then click Orange under Standard Colors.

   **d.** Using [Shift] select the text object, then change all of the text to the color Orange.

   **e.** Click the Font Size list arrow, then click 24.

   **f.** Click the Bold button.

   **g.** Save your changes.

**3. Convert text to SmartArt.**

   **a.** Click the text object on Slide 4.

   **b.** Apply the Basic Cycle SmartArt graphic layout to the text object.

   **c.** Click the More button in the SmartArt Styles group, then apply the Inset style to the graphic.

   **d.** Reposition the diagram to the center of the slide, if necessary.

   **e.** Click outside the SmartArt graphic in an empty part of the slide.

   **f.** Save your changes.

**4. Insert and modify shapes.**

   **a.** Go to Slide 3.

   **b.** Using [Shift] select the text object, then drag the bottom-middle sizing handle up to decrease the size of the text object.

   **c.** Click the Insert tab on the Ribbon, then insert the Left-Right-Up Arrow shape from the Shapes gallery similar to the one in Figure B-19.

   **d.** Type **Routing protocols**, then click Moderate Effect – Accent 3 in the Shape Styles group.

   **e.** Click the Shape Effects button in the Shape Styles group, point to Shadow, then click Offset Bottom.

   **f.** Click the Shape Fill button in the Shape Styles group, point to Gradient, then click Linear Up.

   **g.** Click a blank area of the slide, then save your changes.

**FIGURE B-19**

**5. Edit and duplicate shapes.**

   **a.** Insert a Diamond shape from the Shapes gallery to the left of the arrow shape.

   **b.** Click the More button in the Shape Styles group, click Colored Outline – Accent 4, then type **File 1**.

   **c.** Drag to select the text File 1, click the Home tab, click the Font Size button in the Font group, then click 14.

   **d.** Using [Ctrl] make two copies of the diamond shape, then change the text in one shape to **File 2** and the text in the other shape to **File 3**.

   **e.** Move the File 2 diamond shape to the top of the arrow shape and the File 3 diamond shape to the right of the arrow shape, as shown in Figure B-19.

   **f.** Click a blank area of the slide, then save your changes.

**6. Align and group objects.**

   **a.** Hold down [Shift], click the File 1 diamond shape, click the File 3 diamond shape, then release [Shift].

   **b.** Click the Drawing Tools Format tab if necessary, click Align, click Align Middle.

   **c.** Hold down [Shift], click the arrow shape, click the File 2 diamond shape, click the Group button in the Arrange group, then click Group.

   **d.** Click the Align button in the Arrange group, then click Distribute Horizontally.

   **e.** Save your work.

# ▼ SKILLS REVIEW (CONTINUED)

**7. Add slide headers and footers.**

   **a.** Open the Header and Footer dialog box.

   **b.** In the Slide tab, type today's date into the Fixed text box.

   **c.** Add the slide number to the footer.

   **d.** Type your name in the Footer text box.

   **e.** Apply the footer to all of the slides except the title slide.

   **f.** Open the Header and Footer dialog box again, then click the Notes and Handouts tab.

   **g.** Enter today's date in the Fixed text box.

   **h.** Type the name of your class in the Header text box, then click the Page number check box.

   **i.** Type your name in the Footer text box.

   **j.** Apply the header and footer information to all the notes and handouts.

   **k.** Save your changes.

**8. Check spelling in a presentation.**

   **a.** Perform a spelling check on the document and change any misspelled words. Ignore any words that are correctly spelled but that the spellchecker doesn't recognize. There is at least one misspelled word in the presentation.

   **b.** Save your changes, then close the file and exit PowerPoint.

# ▼ INDEPENDENT CHALLENGE 1

You are the Director of the Westminster Theater Arts Center in Kansas City, Missouri, and one of your many duties is to raise funds to cover operation costs. One of the primary ways you do this is by speaking to businesses, community clubs, and other organizations throughout the Kansas City region. Every year you speak to many organizations, where you give a short presentation detailing what the theater center plans to do for the coming season. You need to continue working on the presentation you started already.

   **a.** Start PowerPoint, open the presentation PPT B-3.pptx from the drive and folder where you store your Data Files, and save it as **WTAC 2011**.

   **b.** Use the Outline tab to enter the following as bulleted text on the Commitment to Excellence slide:
     **Study**
     **Diligence**
     **Testing**
     **Excellence**

   **c.** Apply the Verve design theme to the presentation.

   **d.** Change the font color of each play name on Slide 3 to Yellow.

   **e.** Change the bulleted text on Slide 5 to the Basic Cycle SmartArt graphic layout, then apply the Polished SmartArt Style.

## Advanced Challenge Exercise

   ■ Open the Notes Page view.

   ■ To at least two slides, add notes that relate to the slide content that you think would be important when giving this presentation.

   ■ Save the presentation as **WTAC 2011 ACE** to the drive and folder where you store your Data Files, then print the Notes Page view for the presentation.

   **f.** Check the spelling in the presentation then view the presentation in Slide Show view.

   **g.** Add your name as a footer on the notes and handouts, print handouts (three slides per page), and then print the presentation outline.

   **h.** Save your changes, close your presentation, then exit PowerPoint.

# ▼ INDEPENDENT CHALLENGE 2

You are a manager for Schweizerhaus, Ltd., a Swiss mortgage loan company headquartered in Bern, Switzerland. You have been asked by your boss to develop a presentation outlining important details and aspects of the mortgage process for clients and investors. The focus of the presentation is the use of mortgage brokers to secure loans for clients.

**a.** Start PowerPoint, open the presentation PPT B-4.pptx from the drive and folder where you store your Data Files, and save it as **Loan Broker**.

**b.** Apply the Technic design theme to the presentation.

**c.** On Slide 4 select the three shapes, Banks, Mortgage Bankers, and Private Investors, then using the Align command distribute them vertically and align them to their left edges.

**d.** On Slide 4 select the three shapes, Borrower, Mortgage Broker, and Mortgage Bankers, then using the Align command distribute them horizontally and align them to their bottom edges.

**e.** Select all of the shapes, then apply Moderate Effect – Accent 2 from the Shape Styles group.

**f.** Using the Arrow shape from the Shapes gallery, draw a 3pt arrow between all of the shapes as shown in Figure B-20. (*Hint*: Draw one arrow shape, change the line weight to 3 pt using the Shape Outline button, then duplicate the shape.)

**g.** Create a sixth slide to end the presentation with the following information:
**Schweizerhaus, Ltd.**
**Zieglerstrasse 765, Bern**
**TEL: 3937095, FAX: 9375719**

**h.** Check the spelling in the presentation, view the presentation in Slide Show view, then view the slides in Slide Sorter view.

**i.** Add your name as a footer on the notes and handouts, print the presentation as handouts (two slides per page), then print the presentation outline.

**j.** Save your changes, close your presentation, then exit PowerPoint.

**FIGURE B-20**

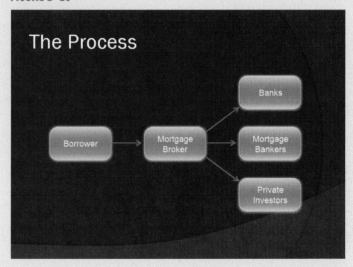

# ▼ INDEPENDENT CHALLENGE 3

You are an independent distributor of natural foods in Bellingham, Washington. Your business, NorthWest Natural Foods, has grown progressively since its inception five years ago, but sales and profits have leveled off over the last nine months. In an effort to stimulate growth, you decide to acquire All Natural Inc., a major natural food dealer in California, which would allow your company to begin expanding into surrounding states. Use PowerPoint to develop a presentation that you can use to gain a financial backer for the acquisition. Create your own information for the presentation.

**a.** Start PowerPoint, create a new presentation, then apply the Concourse design theme to the presentation.

**b.** Enter **A Plan for Growth** as the main title on the title slide, and **NorthWest Natural Foods** as the subtitle.

**c.** Save the presentation as **NW Natural** to the drive and folder where you store your Data Files.

**d.** Add five more slides with the following titles: Slide 2-Background; Slide 3-Current Situation; Slide 4-Acquisition Goals; Slide 5-Our Management Team; Slide 6-Funding Required.

**e.** Enter text into the text placeholders of the slides. Use both the Slide pane and the Outline tab to enter text.

**f.** Convert text on one slide to a SmartArt graphic, then apply the SmartArt graphic style Subtle Effect.

# ▼ INDEPENDENT CHALLENGE 3 (CONTINUED)

**Advanced Challenge Exercise**

- Click the Replace button arrow in the Editing group on the Home tab, then click Replace Fonts.
- Replace the Eras Medium ITC font with the Arial font.
- Save the presentation as **NW Natural ACE** to the drive and folder where you store your Data Files.

 

**g.** Check the spelling in the presentation, view the presentation as a slide show, then view the slides in Slide Sorter view.

**h.** Add your name as a footer on the slides, save your changes, then print the slides.

**i.** Close your presentation, then exit PowerPoint.

# ▼ REAL LIFE INDEPENDENT CHALLENGE

Your computer professor at Central State University has been asked by the department head to convert his Applied Technology course into an accelerated course that both students and professional working people can take. Your professor has asked you to help him create a presentation for the class that he can post on the Internet and use as a promotional tool at local businesses. Most of the raw information is already on the slides, you primarily need to jazz it up by adding a theme, and some text formatting.

**a.** Start PowerPoint, open the presentation PPT B-5.pptx from drive and folder where you store your data files, and save it as **Applied Tech**.

**b.** Add a new slide after the Course Facts slide with the same layout, type **Course Details** in the title text placeholder, then enter the following as bulleted text in the Outline tab:
**Unix/Information Systems**
**Networking**
**Applied Methods**
**Technology Solutions**
**Software Design**
**Applications**

**c.** Apply the Origin theme to the presentation.

**d.** Select the title text object on Slide 1 (*Hint*: Press [Shift] to select the whole object), then change the text color to Dark Red.

**e.** Change the font of the title text object to Bernard MT Condensed.

**f.** Change the text on Slide 4 to a SmartArt graphic. The text on this slide is a list so make sure the diagram type you choose is appropriate for the text.

**g.** Change the style of the SmartArt diagram using one of the SmartArt Styles, then view the presentation in Slide Show view.

**h.** Add the slide number and your name as a footer on the notes and handouts, print handouts (four slides per page), and then print the presentation outline.

**i.** Save your changes, close your presentation, then exit PowerPoint.

Create the presentation shown in Figures B-21 and B-22. Add today's date as the date on the title slide. Save the presentation as **Trade Analysis** to the drive and folder where you store your Data Files. Review your slides in Slide Show view, then add your name as a footer to the notes and handouts. Print the slides of your presentation, then print the outline. Save your changes, close the presentation, then exit PowerPoint.

FIGURE B-21

FIGURE B-22

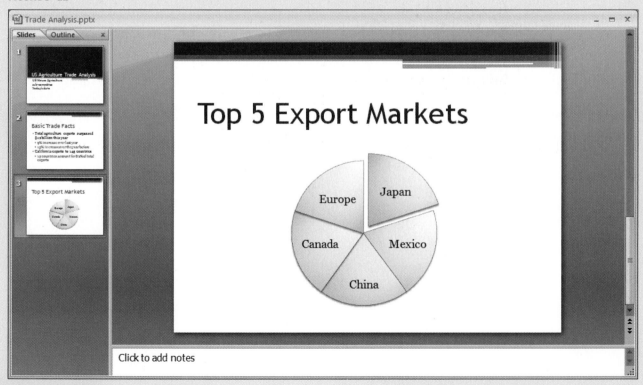

# Inserting Objects into a Presentation

**Files You Will Need:**

PPT C-1.pptx
PPT C-2.docx
PPT C-3.jpg
PPT C-4.pptx
PPT C-5.docx
PPT C-6.jpg
PPT C-7.pptx
PPT C-8.pptx
PPT C-9.docx
PPT C-10.pptx
PPT C-11.docx
PPT C-12.jpg
PPT C-13.jpg
PPT C-14.jpg

A good presenter will make use of visual elements, such as charts, graphics, and photographs, in conjunction with text to help communicate the presentation message. Visual elements keep the presentation interesting and help the audience focus on what the presenter is saying. In this unit, you continue working on the presentation for your boss Ellen Latsky by inserting visual elements, including clip art, a picture, and a chart, into the presentation. You format these objects using PowerPoint's powerful object editing features.

**OBJECTIVES**

Insert text from Microsoft Word

Insert clip art

Insert and style a picture

Insert a text box

Insert a chart

Enter and edit chart data

Insert a table

Insert and format WordArt

# Inserting Text from Microsoft Word

PowerPoint makes it easy to insert text from other sources into a presentation. Documents saved in Microsoft Word format (.docx), Rich Text Format (.rtf), plain text format (.txt), and HTML format (.htm) can be inserted into a presentation. If you have an existing Word document or outline, you can import it into PowerPoint to create a new presentation or use it to insert additional slides in an existing presentation. When you import a Microsoft Word or a Rich Text Format document into a presentation, PowerPoint creates an outline structure based on the styles in the document. For example, a Heading 1 style in the Word document becomes a slide title in PowerPoint and a Heading 2 style becomes the first level of text in a bulleted list. If you insert a plain text format document into a presentation, PowerPoint creates an outline based on the tabs at the beginning of the document's paragraphs. Paragraphs without tabs become slide titles; paragraphs with one tab indent become first-level text in bulleted lists; paragraphs with two tabs become second-level text in bulleted lists; and so on. Ron Dawson, QST's Vice President of Marketing, sent you a Microsoft Word document with data from a focus group study QST held last spring. You use this information in the presentation.

## STEPS

1. **Start PowerPoint, open the presentation** PPT C-1.pptx **from the drive and folder where you store your Data Files, save it as** QuestC, **click the** View tab **on the Ribbon, then click the** Arrange All button **in the Window group**

2. **Click the** Outline tab, **then click the** Slide 4 icon **in the Outline tab**

   Slide 4 appears in the Slide pane. Each time you click a slide icon in the Outline tab, the slide title and text are highlighted indicating the slide is selected. Before you insert information into a presentation, you must first designate where you want the information to be placed. In this case, the Word document will be inserted after Slide 4, the selected slide.

3. **Click the** Home tab **on the Ribbon, click the** New Slide button list arrow **in the Slides group, then click** Slides from Outline

   The Insert Outline dialog box opens.

4. **Select the Word document file** PPT C-2.docx **from the drive and folder where you store your Data Files, then click** Insert

   Four new slides (5, 6, 7, and 8) are added to the presentation. See Figure C-1.

5. **Read the text for the new Slide 5 in the Slide pane, then review the text on slides 6, 7, and 8 in the Outline tab**

   After reviewing the text on the new slides, you realize that the information on Slide 8 is not necessary for the presentation.

6. **Click the** Slides tab, **then right-click the** Slide 8 thumbnail

   A shortcut menu opens displaying a number of common commands. Right-clicking most objects in PowerPoint opens a shortcut menu.

7. **Click** Delete Slide **on the shortcut menu**

   Slide 8 is deleted from the presentation. The last slide in the presentation displaying a picture placeholder now appears in the Slide pane. You also notice that Slide 6 should come before Slide 5.

8. **Click** Slide 6 **in the Slides tab, then drag it above Slide 5**

   Slide 6 and Slide 5 change places. Compare your screen to Figure C-2.

9. **Click the** Save button 📄 **on the Quick Access Toolbar**

**FIGURE C-1:** Outline tab showing imported text

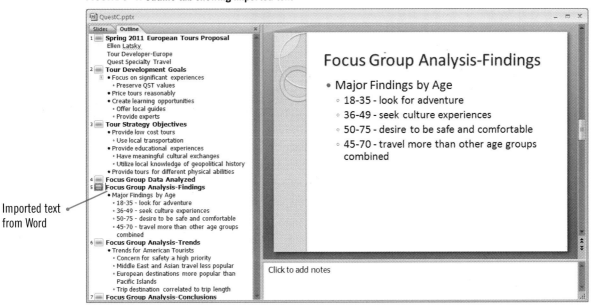

Imported text from Word

**FIGURE C-2:** Presentation after moving a slide

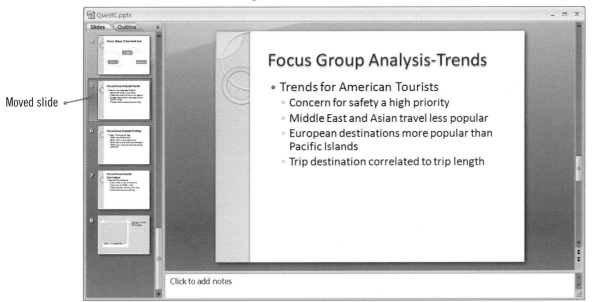

Moved slide

## Inserting slides from other presentations

To insert slides from another presentation into the current presentation, click the New Slide button list arrow in the Slides group, then click Reuse Slides. The Reuse Slides task pane opens on the right side of the window. Click the Open a PowerPoint File link, locate the presentation you want to use, then click Open. Click the slide(s) to place them in the presentation. The new slides automatically take on the theme of the current presentation. You can also copy slides from one presentation to another. Open both presentations, change the view of each presentation to Slide Sorter view or use the Arrange All command to see both presentations, select the desired slides, then copy and paste them (or use drag and drop) into the desired presentation.

# Inserting Clip Art

PowerPoint has access to many professionally designed graphics, called **clip art**, which you can place in your presentation. In Microsoft Office, clip art and other media files, including photographs, movies, and sounds, are stored in a file index system called the Microsoft Clip Organizer and are identified by descriptive keywords. The Clip Organizer sorts the clip art into groups, including My Collections, Office Collections, and Web Collections. The Office Collections group holds all the media files that come with Microsoft Office. You can customize the Clip Organizer by adding clips to a collection, moving clips from one collection to another, or creating a new collection. As with drawn objects, you can modify clip art images by changing their shape, size, fill, or shading. Clip art is available from many sources outside the Clip Organizer, including the Microsoft Office Online Web site and commercially available collections that you can purchase. ▰▰▰▰ To enhance the QST presentation, you add a clip from the Clip Organizer to one of the slides and then adjust its size and placement.

## STEPS

1. **Click the up scroll arrow in the Slides tab until Slide 2 appears, click the Slide 2 thumbnail, then click the Clip Art icon ▦ in the Content placeholder**

   The Clip Art task pane opens. At the top of the task pane in the Search for text box, you enter a keyword to search for clips that meet that description. You can search for a clip in a specific collection or in all collections. You can also search for a clip that is a specific media type, such as clip art, photographs, movies, or sounds. At the bottom of the task pane, you can click a hyperlink to organize clips, locate other pieces of clip art at the Office Online Web site, or read tips on how to find clip art.

2. **Select any text in the Search for text box, type travel, click the Results should be list arrow, then click the Photographs check box, the Movies check box, and the Sounds check box to remove the check marks**

   Since you are only interested in finding clip art, deselecting the Photographs, Movies, and Sounds check boxes significantly reduces the amount of media PowerPoint needs to search through to produce your results. PowerPoint searches for clips identified by the keyword "travel."

**QUICK TIP**

If an alert dialog box appears asking if you want to add additional images from Microsoft Office Online, click Yes

3. **Click the Go button, then click the clip art thumbnail shown in Figure C-3**

   The clip art object appears in the content placeholder and the Picture Tools Format tab appears on the Ribbon. If you don't see the clip shown in Figure C-3, select another one. Although you can change a clip's size by dragging a corner sizing handle, you can also **scale** it to change its size by a specific percentage.

4. **Click the Size and Position dialog box launcher in the Size group, in the Scale section make sure the Lock aspect ratio check box has a check mark, in the Scale section click the Height up arrow until the Height and Width percentages display 110%, then click Close**

   The clip proportionally increases in size.

5. **Click the Picture Border button in the Picture Styles group, then click the Aqua, Accent 1 color box in the top row**

   A light blue border appears around the object.

**QUICK TIP**

You can use the Reset Picture button in the Adjust group to reset the object formatting.

6. **Click the Picture Border button, point to Weight, then click the 3 pt solid line style**

   The clip now has a 3-point solid border. It appears to be framed.

7. **Drag the clip art object straight down even with the bottom line of text**

   You don't like the new placement of the clip.

8. **Click the Undo button ↺ on the Quick Access toolbar, click a blank area of the slide, then save your changes**

9. **Click the Results should be list arrow in the Clip Art task pane, click the All media types check box, click Go, then click the task pane Close button**

   Now the next time you search for a clip, PowerPoint will search through all media types. Compare the slide on your screen to the slide shown in Figure C-4.

**FIGURE C-3:** Screen showing Clip Art task pane

Select this clip

Clip Art icon

Click to locate clips on the Office Online Web site

**FIGURE C-4:** Slide with formatted clip art object

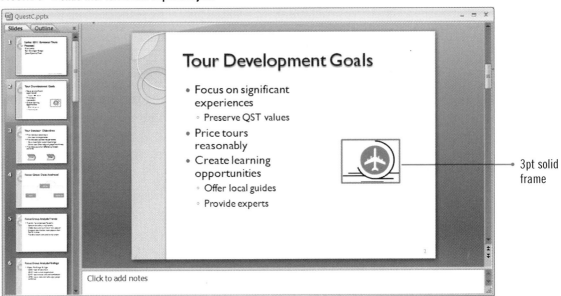

3pt solid frame

### Finding more clips online

If you can't find exactly what you want in the Clip Organizer, you can easily download and use clips from the Clip Art and Media Web page in the Microsoft Office Online Web site. To get clips from the Clip Art Web page, click the Clip art on Office Online hyperlink at the bottom of the Clip Art task pane. If your computer is connected to the Internet, this will launch your Web browser and automatically connect you to the Microsoft Office Online Web site. You can search the site by keyword or browse by media type category. Each clip you download is automatically inserted into the Clip Organizer Web Collections folder and appears in the Clip Art task pane.

# Inserting and Styling a Picture

In PowerPoint, a **picture** is defined as a digital photograph, a piece of line art or clip art, or other artwork that is created in another program and inserted into a PowerPoint presentation. PowerPoint gives you the ability to insert 17 different types of pictures including JPEG File Interchange Format and BMP Windows Bitmap. As with all objects in PowerPoint, you can format and style inserted pictures to help them fit the theme of your presentation. You can also hide a portion of the picture you don't want visible by **cropping** it. The cropped portion of a picture, unlike other objects such as clip art, is automatically deleted when the presentation is saved unless you change the setting in the Compression Settings dialog box. █████ QST has a library of pictures from tours available to use in presentations. In this lesson, you insert a picture that has previously been saved to a file, and then you crop it and style it.

## STEPS

**QUICK TIP**
You can also insert a picture by clicking the Picture button in the Illustrations group on the Insert tab.

1. **Click the down scroll arrow in the Slides tab until Slide 8 appears, click the Slide 8 thumbnail, then click the Insert Picture from File icon 🖼 in the content placeholder on the slide**

   The Insert Picture dialog box opens displaying the pictures available in the Pictures folder. The Pictures folder is the default folder.

2. **Select the picture file PPT C-3.jpg from the drive and folder where you store your Data Files, then click Insert**

   The picture appears in the Picture placeholder on the slide and the Picture Tools Format tab opens on the Ribbon. The picture would look better if you cropped some of the beach off the bottom.

3. **Click the Crop button in the Size group, then place the pointer over the bottom-middle sizing handle of the picture**

   The pointer changes to **T**. When the Crop button is active, the sizing handles appear as straight black lines.

4. **Press and hold [Alt], drag the bottom edge of the picture up until the lower-left corner of the picture is at the water line as shown in Figure C-5, then click the Crop button**

   Pressing [Alt] while dragging or drawing an object in PowerPoint overrides the automatic snap-to-grid setting. PowerPoint has a number of picture formatting options, and you decide to experiment with some of them.

5. **Click the Picture Styles More button ▾, then click Bevel Rectangle (3rd row)**

   The picture changes shape. Notice that this particular style includes an adjustment handle so that you can adjust the shape of the picture.

6. **Click the Recolor button in the Adjust group, click Sepia in the Color Modes section, then click the Slide Show button 🖵 in the status bar**

   The slide fills your screen. After evaluating the slide you conclude that the shape and color changes you've made to the picture don't improve the look of the slide.

7. **Press [Esc], click the Undo button list arrow on the Quick Access toolbar, then click Format Picture**

   All of the formatting changes you made to the picture are removed. The cropped portion of the picture does not change and remains hidden.

8. **Click the Picture Styles More button, click Drop Shadow Rectangle (1st row), click a blank area on the slide, then save your changes**

   Compare your screen to Figure C-6.

**FIGURE C-5:** Using the cropping pointer to crop a picture

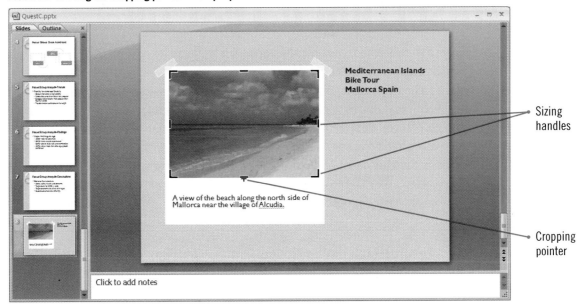

Sizing handles

Cropping pointer

**FIGURE C-6:** Cropped and styled picture

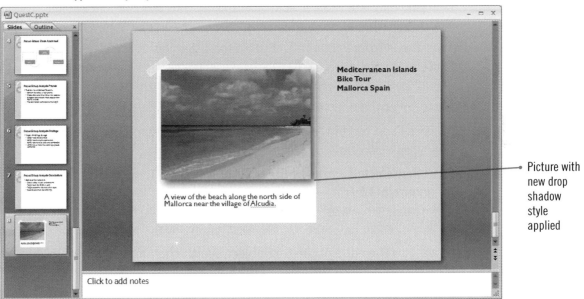

Picture with new drop shadow style applied

## Picture compression

By default, all inserted pictures in PowerPoint 2007 are automatically compressed every time you save your presentation. If you want to prohibit the automatic compression of pictures or be able to choose individual pictures to compress, select a picture, then click the Picture Tools Format tab. Click the Compress Pictures button in the Adjust group, then click Options in the Compress Pictures dialog box. The Compression Settings dialog box opens. Notice that PowerPoint compresses pictures every time the presentation is saved and deletes cropped portions of pictures to save space. To compress individual pictures, make sure the top option in the Compression Settings dialog box is deselected, select a picture, click the Compress Pictures button, then click OK. To stop PowerPoint from automatically deleting cropped portions of pictures, deselect the check box next to the Delete cropped areas of pictures option in the Compression Settings dialog box.

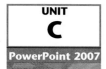
# Inserting a Text Box

As you've already learned, you enter text on a slide using a title or content placeholder that is arranged on the slide based on a particular slide layout. Every so often you need additional text on a slide where the traditional placeholder does not place text effectively for your message. You can create an individual text object by clicking the Text Box button in the Text group on the Insert tab on the Ribbon. There are two types of text objects that you can create: a text label, used for a small phrase where text doesn't automatically wrap to the next line inside the box; and a word processing box, used for a sentence or paragraph where the text wraps inside the boundaries of the box. Either type of text box can be formatted and edited just like any other text object. ▰▰▰ You decide to add a text object to Slide 8 to finish the information about the bike tour. You create a word processing box on the slide, enter text, edit text, and then format the text.

## STEPS

1. **Click the Insert tab on the Ribbon, click the Text Box button in the Text group, then move the pointer to the blank area of the slide to the right of the picture**
   The pointer changes to ↓.

2. **Drag down and toward the right side of the slide about an inch and a half to create a word processing box**
   When you begin dragging, an outline of the text object appears, indicating how large a text object you are drawing. After you release the mouse button, an insertion point appears inside the text object, in this case a word processing box, which indicates that you can enter text. The font and font style appear in the Font group on the Ribbon.

3. **Type Travel from Palma to La Puebla for 135 miles over 6 days**
   Notice that the text object increases in size as your text wraps inside the text object. Your screen should look similar to Figure C-7. After entering the text you realize there is a mistake.

4. **Drag I over the phrase for 135 miles to select it**

5. **Position ⇗ on top of the selected phrase and press and hold the mouse button**
   The pointer changes to ⇗.

6. **Drag the selected words to the right of the word Travel in the text object, then release the mouse button**
   A light blue insertion line appears as you drag, indicating where PowerPoint places the text when you release the mouse button. The phrase "for 135 miles" moves after the word "Travel".

7. **Move ⇗ to the edge of the text object, which changes to ⁺⇗, click the text object border, then click the Italic button I in the Font group**
   All of the text in the text object is italicized.

8. **Drag the right-middle sizing handle of the text object to the right until the text is on two lines, position ⁺⇗ over the text object edge, then drag it next to the picture caption**
   Your screen should look similar to Figure C-8.

9. **Click a blank area of the slide outside the text object, then save your changes**

FIGURE C-7: **New text object**

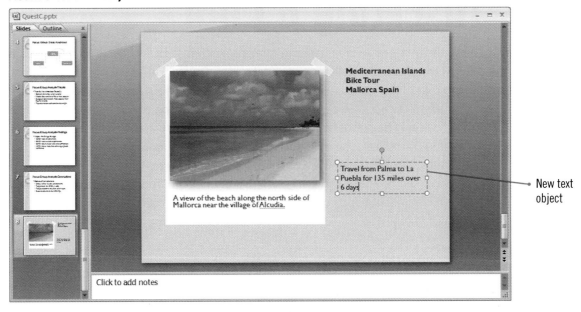

New text object

FIGURE C-8: **Formatted text object**

Formatted text

## Sending a presentation using e-mail

You can send a copy of a presentation over the Internet to a reviewer for them to edit and add comments. You can use Microsoft Outlook, or any other compatible e-mail program, to send your presentation. Although your e-mail program allows you to attach files, you can send a presentation using Outlook from within PowerPoint. Click the Office button, point to Send, then click Email. Outlook opens and automatically creates an e-mail with the presentation attached to it. The recipient of the presentation can use PowerPoint 2007 or an earlier version of PowerPoint to edit the presentation or add comments. To open a PowerPoint 2007 file in an earlier version of PowerPoint, you must save the presentation as a PowerPoint 97-2003 presentation or install the Compatibility Pack for the Office 2007 Office system files from Microsoft's Web site. Once the presentation is back in your hands, you can view, edit, or delete the reviewer's comments.

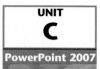

# Inserting a Chart

Often, the best way to communicate numerical information is with a visual aid such as a chart. If you have Microsoft Excel installed on your computer, PowerPoint uses Excel to create charts. If you don't have Excel installed, a charting program called **Microsoft Graph** opens that you can use to create charts for your slides. A **chart** is the graphical representation of numerical data. Every chart has a corresponding **worksheet** that contains the numerical data displayed by the chart. When you insert a chart object into PowerPoint, you are actually embedding it. An **embedded** object is one that is a part of your presentation (just like any other object you insert into PowerPoint) except that an embedded object's data source can be opened, in this case Excel, for editing purposes. Changes you make to an embedded object in PowerPoint using PowerPoint's features do not affect the data source for the data. ⬛⬛⬛ You insert a chart on a new slide that graphically shows results from an online survey Ellen Latsky conducted.

## STEPS

**QUICK TIP**
You can also add a chart to a slide by clicking the Insert Chart button in the Illustrations group on the Insert tab.

1. **Verify that Slide 8 is selected, click the New Slide button list arrow in the Slides group, then click Title and Content**

    A new slide is added to your presentation with the Title and Content slide layout.

2. **Click the Insert Chart icon 📊 in the Content placeholder**

    The Insert Chart dialog box opens as shown in Figure C-9. Each chart type includes a number of 2-D and 3-D styles. The Column chart type, for example, includes 19 different styles and the Line chart type includes 7 different styles. The Clustered Column chart is the default chart style. For a brief explanation of how each of these chart types graphs data, refer to Table C-1.

**QUICK TIP**
Microsoft Graph opens if Excel is not installed on your computer.

3. **Click OK**

    Excel opens in a split window sharing the computer screen with the PowerPoint window as shown in Figure C-10. The PowerPoint window displays the clustered column chart and the Excel window displays sample data in a worksheet. The Chart Tools Design tab on the Ribbon contains commands you use in PowerPoint to work with the chart. The worksheet consists of rows and columns. The intersection of a row and a column is called a **cell**. Cells are referred to by their row and column location; for example, the cell at the intersection of column A and row 1 is called cell A1. Cells in the first or left column contain **axis labels** that identify the data in a row for example, "Category 1" is an axis label. Cells in the first or top row are **legend** names and provide further information about the data. Cells below and to the right of the axis labels and legend names contain the data values that are represented in the chart. Each column and row of data in the worksheet is called a **data series**. Each data series has corresponding **data series markers** in the chart, which are graphical representations such as bars, columns, or pie wedges. The gray boxes with the numbers along the left side of the worksheet are called **row headings**, and the gray boxes with the letters along the top of the worksheet are called **column headings**.

**TROUBLE**
If the Excel window covers the slide in PowerPoint, click View on the PowerPoint Ribbon, click Window, then click Arrange All

4. **Move the pointer over the worksheet in the Excel window**

    The pointer changes to ➕. Cell A6 is the **active cell**, which means that it is selected. The active cell has a thick black border around it.

5. **Click cell C4**

    Cell C4 is now the active cell.

6. **Click the Excel Window Close button ✕ on the title bar**

    The Excel window closes and the PowerPoint window fills the screen. A new chart object appears on the slide displaying the data from the Excel worksheet.

7. **Click in a blank area of the slide to deselect the chart object**

    The Chart Tools Design Ribbon is no longer active.

8. **Click the slide Title placeholder, type On-line Survey Results, then save your changes**

**FIGURE C-9:** Insert Chart dialog box

Default chart

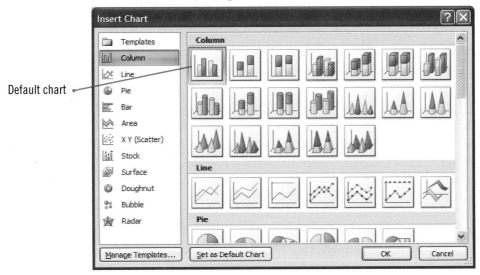

**FIGURE C-10:** The PowerPoint and Excel split windows

Chart Tools
Design tab
on the
Ribbon

Inserted
chart in
PowerPoint

Excel window

Column heading

Data for the
inserted chart

Row heading

Data series
marker

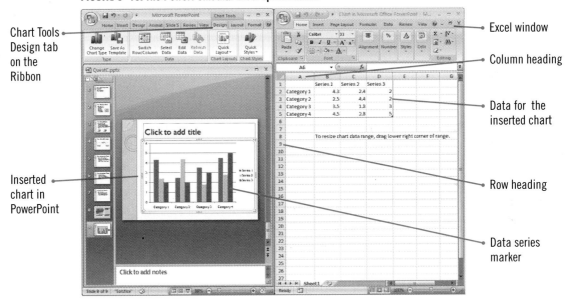

**TABLE C-1:** Chart types

| chart type | icon looks like | use to |
|---|---|---|
| Column | | Track values over time or across categories |
| Line | | Track values over time |
| Pie | | Compare individual values to the whole |
| Bar | | Compare values in categories or over time |
| Area | | Show contribution of each data series to the total over time |
| XY (Scatter) | | Compare pairs of values |
| Stock | | Show stock market information or scientific data |
| Surface | | Show value trends across two dimensions |
| Doughnut | | Compare individual values to the whole with multiple series |
| Bubble | | Indicate relative size of data points |
| Radar | | Show changes in values in relation to a center point |

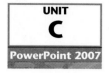

# Entering and Editing Chart Data

After you insert a chart into your presentation, you need to replace the sample data with the correct information. If you have data in an Excel worksheet or another source, you can import it into Excel; otherwise you can type your own information into the worksheet. As you enter data and make other changes in the Excel worksheet, the chart in PowerPoint automatically reflects the new changes. You enter and format the survey data collected by Ellen.

1. **Click the chart on Slide 9, click the Chart Tools Design tab on the Ribbon, then click the Edit Data button in the Data group**

   The chart is selected in PowerPoint and the worksheet opens in a separate Excel window. The data in the worksheet needs to be replaced with the correct information.

   > **QUICK TIP**
   > You can double-click the column divider lines between the column headings to automatically resize the column width to accommodate the widest entry.

2. **Click the Series 1 cell, type Safety, press [Tab], type Price, press [Tab], then type Experience**

   The Legend labels are entered. Pressing [Tab] in Excel moves the active cell from left to right one cell at a time in a row. Pressing [Enter] in the worksheet moves the active cell down one cell at a time in a column.

3. **Click the Category 1 cell, type 2 Years Past, press [Enter], type Last Year, press [Enter], then type This Year**

   The axis labels are entered and the chart in the PowerPoint window reflects all the changes.

   > **QUICK TIP**
   > Click the chart in the PowerPoint window, then move your pointer over each bar in the chart to see the data source values.

4. **Enter the remainder of the data shown in Figure C-11 to complete the worksheet, then press [Enter]**

   The sample information in Row 5 of the worksheet is not needed.

5. **Right-click the Row 5 row heading, then click Delete**

   Clicking a row heading selects the entire row. The chart currently shows the rows grouped by year, and the legend represents the columns in the datasheet. It would be more effective if the row data appeared in the legend so you could compare yearly results.

6. **Click the Switch Row/Column button in the Data group in the PowerPoint window**

   You have finished entering data in the Excel worksheet.

7. **Click the Excel window Close button** ☒

   Notice that the height of each column in the chart, as well as the values along the vertical axis, adjust to reflect the numbers you typed. The vertical axis is also called the **Value axis**. The horizontal axis is called the **Category axis**. The column labels are now on the Category axis of the chart, and the row labels are listed in the legend.

8. **Click a blank area on the slide, then save the presentation**

   Compare your chart to Figure C-12.

FIGURE C-11: Worksheet showing chart data

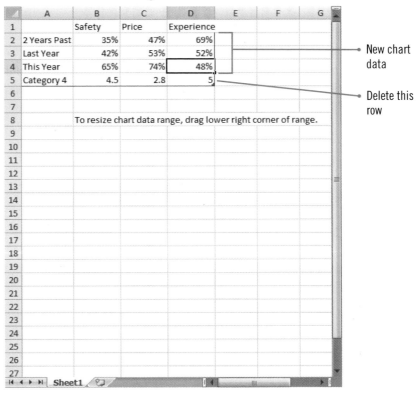

New chart data

Delete this row

FIGURE C-12: Formatted chart

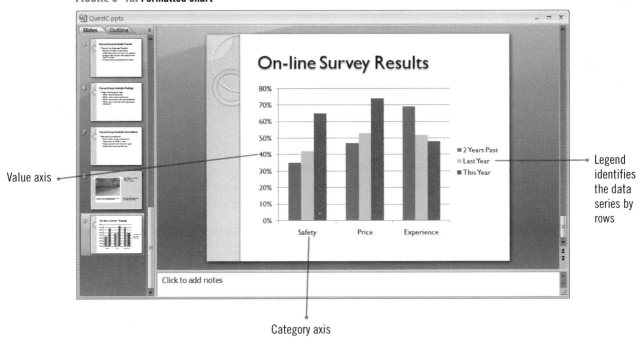

Value axis

Legend identifies the data series by rows

Category axis

## Series in rows vs. series in columns

If you have difficulty visualizing what the Switch Row/Column command does, think about what is represented in the legend. **Series in Rows** means that the information in the datasheet rows will be on the Value or vertical axis and is the information shown in the legend.

The column labels will be on the Category or horizontal axis. **Series in Columns** means that the information in the columns becomes the information shown on the Value axis and in the legend; the row labels will be on the horizontal or Category axis.

# Inserting a Table

As you create your presentation, you may have some information that would look best organized in rows and columns. For example, if you wanted to compare the basic details of three different cruise tours side by side, a table is ideal for this type of information. Once you have created a table, two new tabs, the Table Tools Design tab and the Table Tools Layout tab, appear on the Ribbon. You can use the Design tab to apply color styles, change cell borders and add cell effects. Using the Layout tab, you can add rows and columns to your table, adjust the size of cells, and align text in the cells. You decide that a table best illustrates the new adventure tour series being proposed by Ellen.

## STEPS

1. **Verify that Slide 9 is selected, click the New Slide button list arrow in the Slides group, click Title Only, click the Insert tab on the Ribbon, then click the Table button in the Tables group**

   The Insert Table gallery opens where you can drag the mouse to specify the number of columns and rows you need in the table.

2. **Move the pointer over the grid to select a 4x3 cell area so that 4x3 Table appears in the gallery title bar, then click the lower right corner of the 4x3 grid**

   A table with four columns and three rows appears on the slide, and the Table Tools Design tab opens on the Ribbon. The table has 12 cells. The insertion point is in the first cell of the table and is ready to accept text.

**QUICK TIP**
Pressing [Tab] when the insertion point is in the last cell of a table creates a new row.

3. **Type Self Guided, press [Tab], type Family, press [Tab], type Cruise, press [Tab], type Extreme, then press [Tab]**

   The text you typed appears in the top four cells of the table. Pressing [Tab] moves the insertion point to the next cell. Pressing [Enter] moves the insertion point to the next line in the cell. Pressing [Tab] in the last row, last column inserts a new row.

4. **Enter the rest of the table information shown in Figure C-13, then drag the right-middle sizing handle slightly to the right**

   The word Mediterranean now fits on one line. The table would look better if it were formatted differently.

5. **Click the Table Styles More button ⬇ in the Table Styles group, scroll to the bottom of the gallery, then click Dark Style 1 – Accent 6**

   The background and text color change to reflect the table style you applied.

**QUICK TIP**
You can change the height or width of any table cell by dragging its top or side borders.

6. **Click the upper-left cell, click the Table Tools Layout tab, click the Select button in the Table group, click Select Row, then click the Center button ▤ in the Alignment group**

   The text in the top row is centered horizontally in each cell.

7. **Click the Select button in the Table group, click Select Table, then click the Center Vertically button ▤ in the Alignment group**

   The text in the whole table is centered vertically within each cell. The table would look better if all the rows were the same height.

8. **Click the Distribute Rows button ▦ in the Cell Size group, click the Table Tools Design tab, then click the Effects button ◩▾ in the Table Styles group**

   The Table Effects gallery opens. Apply a 3-D effect to the cells so that they stand out.

9. **Point to Cell Bevel, click Cool Slant, drag the table to the center of the blank area of the slide, click the slide title placeholder, type Adventure Series, click a blank area of the slide, then save the presentation**

   The effect makes the cells of the table stand out. Compare your screen with Figure C-14.

FIGURE C-13: The inserted table with data

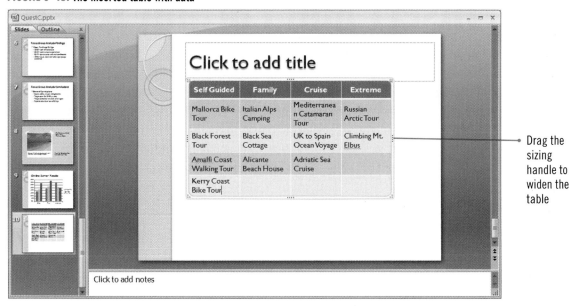

Drag the sizing handle to widen the table

FIGURE C-14: Formatted table

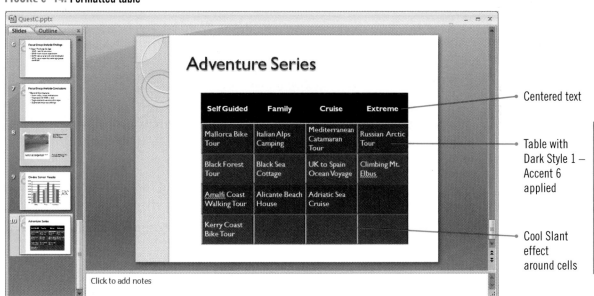

Centered text

Table with Dark Style 1 – Accent 6 applied

Cool Slant effect around cells

## Saving slides as graphics

You can save PowerPoint slides as graphics and later use them in other presentations, in graphics programs, and on Web pages. Display the slide you want to save, click the Office button, then click Save As. In the Save As dialog box, click the Save as type list arrow, select the desired graphics format (for example, Web Page (*.htm;*.html), JPEG File Interchange Format (*.jpg), TIFF Tag Image Format (*.tif), or Device Independent Bitmap (*.bmp)), then name the file. Click Save, then click the desired option when the alert box appears asking if you want to save all the slides or only the current slide.

# Insert and Format WordArt

As you work to create an interesting presentation, your goal should include making your slides visually appealing. Sometimes plain text can come across as dull and unexciting in a presentation. **WordArt** is a set of decorative text styles, or text effects, that you can apply to any text object to help direct the attention of your audience to a certain piece of information. You can use WordArt in two different ways: you can apply a WordArt text style to an existing text object that converts the text into WordArt, or you can create a new WordArt object. The WordArt text styles and effects include text shadows, reflections, glows, bevels, 3-D rotations, and transformations. ████ Use WordArt to convert the QST tours tag line on Slide 1 so it is easier to see.

## STEPS

1. **Click the Slide 1 thumbnail in the Slides tab, press [Shift], click the footer text object at the bottom of the slide, then drag the Zoom slider to the right until the Zoom percentage reaches 100%**

   Notice how the selected footer text object becomes the focal point as you zoom in. The footer text is hard to see and would look better with a WordArt style applied to it.

**QUICK TIP**
You can add a new WordArt object to a slide by clicking the Insert tab, then the WordArt button in the Text group.

2. **Click the Drawing Tools Format tab, click the WordArt Styles More button ⏷, move your mouse over the WordArt styles in the gallery, then click Gradient Fill – Accent 6, Inner Shadow**

   The WordArt gallery displays all of the WordArt styles, and the Live Preview lets you see how each style would look if applied to the text.

3. **Click the Text Effects button A▾ in the WordArt Styles group, point to Reflection, then click Tight Reflection, touching**

   The footer text object is now styled with a WordArt style and a reflection effect. You decide to increase the footer text font and give it a more prominent position on the slide.

4. **Click the Home tab on the Ribbon, click the Increase Font Size button A˄ in the Font group twice, then drag the left-middle sizing handle to the left until the text is on one line**

   Now the footer text object is easier to read.

5. **Position ⛾ over the edge of the text object, drag to position the text object to match Figure C-15**

**TROUBLE**
Your zoom percentage may be different depending on your screen size and resolution.

6. **Click a blank area of the slide, click the Fit slide to current window button ▥ in the status bar**

   The slide returns to its original zoom percentage of 66%.

7. **Click the Slide Show button ▤ on the status bar, view the presentation, press [Esc] at the end of the slide show, then click the Slide Sorter button ▦ on the status bar**

   Figure C-16 shows the final presentation.

8. **Add your name as a footer to the notes and handouts, save your changes, print the presentation as handouts (four per page), then exit PowerPoint**

FIGURE C-15: Footer text converted to WordArt

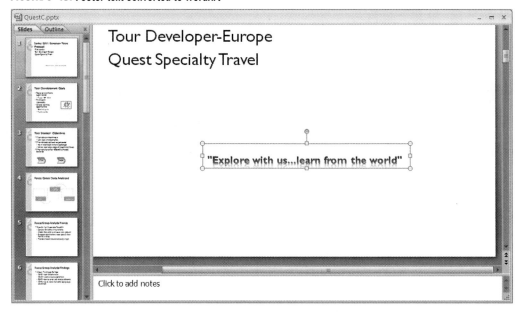

FIGURE C-16: Completed presentation in Slide Sorter view

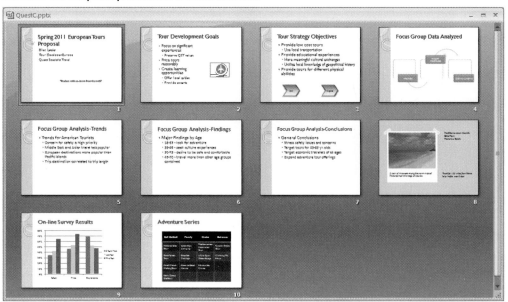

## Using content templates from the Web

When you create a presentation, you have the option of using one of the many design themes supplied with PowerPoint, or you can use a template from the Microsoft Office Online Web site. These templates are designed and formatted with sample text, background and text colors, pictures, charts, and other graphic elements. To access a template from the Microsoft Office Online Web site, you need to be connected to the Internet, then click the Microsoft Office button. Click New to open the New Presentation dialog box. Click one of the template categories in the Microsoft

Office Online template list in the left pane, then download and save the template in PowerPoint. Some of the template categories have subcategories that you need to select to display the individual templates. If you don't have access to the Internet or if you want to view more template choices, you can select one of the installed PowerPoint templates. In the New Presentation dialog box, click Installed Templates in the Template Categories list to select one of the installed templates.

# Practice

If you have a SAM user profile, you may have access to hands-on instruction, practice, and assessment of the skills covered in this unit. Log in to your SAM account (http://sam2007.course.com/) to launch any assigned training activities or exams that relate to the skills covered in this unit.

## ▼ CONCEPTS REVIEW

**Label each element of the PowerPoint window shown in Figure C-17.**

FIGURE C-17

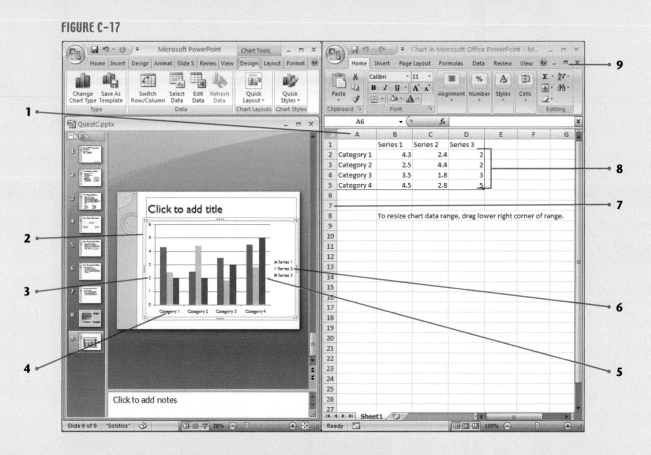

**Match each term with the statement that best describes it.**

10. Text label
11. Category axis
12. Value axis
13. Chart
14. WordArt

a. The graphical representation of numerical data
b. A set of decorative styles you can add to text
c. Another name for the vertical axis in a chart
d. A specific type of text object used to enter a small phrase
e. Another name for the horizontal axis in the chart

## Select the best answer from the list of choices.

**15.** Which of the following statements about inserting text from Microsoft Word is *not* true?

   **a.** Each line of inserted text is placed onto separate slides.

   **b.** An outline structure is created in PowerPoint based on the Word styles used in the text.

   **c.** PowerPoint can insert text that has tabs at the end of paragraphs.

   **d.** You can create a new presentation based on inserted Word text.

**16.** What is the file index system that stores clip art, photographs, and movies called?

   **a.** Microsoft Clip Organizer       **c.** Clip Art Index

   **b.** Office Media Collections       **d.** WordArt Gallery

**17.** Hiding a portion of a picture or piece of clip art best describes which of the following actions?

   **a.** Adjusting       **c.** Styling

   **b.** Hiding       **d.** Cropping

**18.** Where is the numerical data located for a chart?

   **a.** Table       **c.** Worksheet

   **b.** Legend       **d.** Chart

**19.** An object that has its own data source and becomes a part of your presentation after you insert it best describes which of the following?

   **a.** A Word outline       **c.** A WordArt object

   **b.** An embedded object       **d.** A table

**20.** According to the book, which of the following objects is ideal to compare data side by side?

   **a.** Table       **c.** Outline

   **b.** Chart       **d.** Grid

**21.** A set of decorative text styles you apply to text describes which of the following items?

   **a.** Text labels       **c.** WordArt

   **b.** Illustrations       **d.** Gallery

**22.** What is a column of data in a worksheet called?

   **a.** Column headings       **c.** Data series markers

   **b.** Data series       **d.** Axis labels

## ▼ SKILLS REVIEW

**1. Insert text from Microsoft Word.**

   **a.** Open the file **PPT C-4.pptx** from the drive and folder where you store your Data Files, then save it as **Blue Moon**. You will work to create the completed presentation as shown in Figure C-18.

   **b.** Click Slide 3 in the Slides tab, then use the Slides from Outline command to insert the file **PPT C-5.docx** from the drive and folder where you store your Data Files.

   **c.** In the Slides tab, drag Slide 5 above Slide 4.

   **d.** In the Slides tab, delete Slide 7, Expansion Potential.

**2. Insert clip art.**

   **a.** Select Slide 4, then change the slide layout to the Two Content slide layout.

**FIGURE C-18**

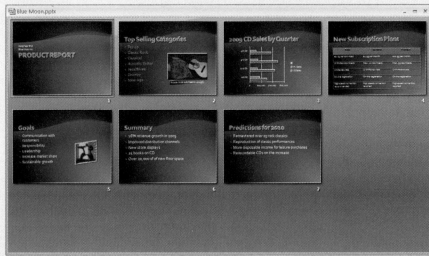

**b.** Click the clip art icon in the right content placeholder, search for clip art using the keyword **leadership**, then insert the first clip in the Clip Art task pane.

**c.** In the Size group on the Picture Tools Format Ribbon, use the Shape Width up arrow to change the width to 2.4".

**d.** Click the Picture Border button, change the color of the clip art border to Gold, Accent 4.

**e.** Click the Picture Border button, change the weight of the clip art border to 4½ pt.

**f.** Click the Picture Effects button, point to 3-D Rotation, then click Off Axis 1 Right.

**g.** Drag the clip art so the bottom lines up with the bottom of the text object, then save your changes.

**3. Insert and style a picture.**

**a.** Select Slide 2, then insert the picture **PPT C-6.jpg**.

**b.** Completely crop the light blue section off the top of the picture, then crop the right side of the picture about ¼".

**c.** Drag the picture up so it is in the center of the blank area of the slide.

**d.** Click the Recolor button, then change the picture color to Grayscale.

**e.** Save your changes.

**4. Insert a text box.**

**a.** On Slide 2, insert a text box below the picture.

**b.** Type **Private submissions for music up 19%**.

**c.** Delete the word for, then drag the word music after the word Private.

**d.** Select the text object, then click the Shape Styles More button in the Shape Styles group on the Drawing Tools Format tab.

**e.** Point to Other Theme Fills, then click Style 11.

**f.** Center the text object under the picture.

**5. Insert a chart.**

**a.** Go to Slide 3, 2009 CD Sales by Quarter, apply the Title and Content slide layout, then insert a Clustered Bar chart.

**b.** Close Excel.

**6. Enter and edit chart data.**

**a.** Show the chart data.

**b.** Enter the data shown in Table C-2 into the worksheet.

**c.** Delete the data in Column D, then close Excel.

**d.** Change the chart style to Style 16 in the Chart Styles group.

**e.** Save your changes.

**TABLE C-2**

|         | U.S. Sales | Int. Sales |
|---------|------------|------------|
| 1st Qtr | 290,957    | 163,902    |
| 2nd Qtr | 429,840    | 125,854    |
| 3rd Qtr | 485,063    | 135,927    |
| 4th Qtr | 365,113    | 103,750    |

**7. Insert a table.**

**a.** Add a new slide after Slide 3 with the Title and Content layout.

**b.** Add the slide title **New Subscription Plans**.

**c.** Insert a table with 3 columns and 6 rows.

**d.** Enter the information shown in Table C-3, then change the table style to Light Style 2 – Accent 1. (*Hint*: Use the Copy and Paste commands to enter duplicate information in the table.)

**e.** Center the text in the top row.

**TABLE C-3**

| Basic                             | Standard                       | Premium                        |
|-----------------------------------|--------------------------------|--------------------------------|
| $1.25 per download                | $4.99 per month                | $12.95 per month               |
| Unlimited downloads               | Max. 12 downloads              | Max. 35 downloads              |
| Limited access                    | Unlimited access               | Unlimited access               |
| Online registration              | Online registration            | Online registration            |
| High-speed connection recommended | High-speed connection required | High-speed connection required |

**f.** In the Table Tools Layout tab, distribute the table rows.

**g.** Save your changes.

**8. Insert and format WordArt.**

**a.** Go to Slide 2, then select the bulleted list text object.

**b.** Apply the WordArt style Fill – Accent 2, Warm Matte Bevel.

**c.** View the presentation in Slide Show view, then save your changes.

**d.** Add your name as a footer to the notes and handouts, print the slides as handouts (3 slides per page).

**e.** Save your work, close the file, and exit PowerPoint.

# ▼ INDEPENDENT CHALLENGE 1

You are a financial management consultant for Casey Investments, located in St. Louis, Missouri. One of your responsibilities is to create standardized presentations on different financial investments for use on the company Web site. As part of the presentation for this meeting, you insert some clip art, add a text box, and insert a chart.

**a.** Open the file PPT C-7.pptx from the drive and folder where you store your Data Files, then save it as **Casey**.

**b.** Add your name as the footer on all notes and handouts, then apply the Oriel Design Theme.

**c.** Insert a clustered column chart on Slide 6, then enter the data in Table C-4 into the worksheet.

**d.** Format the chart using Style 27.

**Advanced Challenge Exercise**

■ Click the Chart Tools Layout tab, click the Legend button, then click Show Legend at Top.

■ Click the Chart Tools Format tab, then click the Current Selection list arrow in the Current Selection group, then click Series "3 Year."

■ Click the Shape Fill button list arrow, then click the Orange color under Standard Colors.

**TABLE C-4**

| | 1 year | 3 year | 5 year | 7 year |
|---|---|---|---|---|
| Bonds | 4.2% | 5.2% | 7.9% | 6.5% |
| Stocks | 6.9% | 8.2% | 7.2% | 9.6% |
| Mutual Funds | 4.6% | 6.0% | 7.4% | 11.4% |

**e.** Insert clip art of a set of scales on Slide 2, then format as necessary. (*Hint*: Use the keyword scales to search for clips.)

**f.** On Slide 3, use the Align, and Distribute commands on the Drawing Tools Format tab in the Arrange group to align and distribute the objects so that the shapes are aligned on top and distributed horizontally.

**g.** Spell check the presentation, then save it.

**h.** View the slide show. Make changes if necessary.

**i.** The final presentation should look like Figure C-19.

**j.** Print the slides as handouts (6 slides per page), then close the presentation, and exit PowerPoint.

**FIGURE C-19**

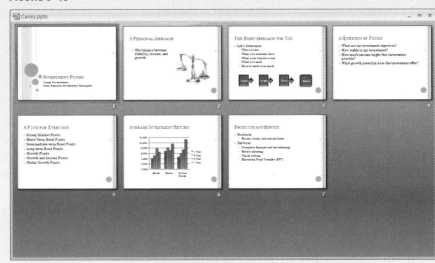

# ▼ INDEPENDENT CHALLENGE 2

You work for Alcom Home Systems, a company based out of Colorado Springs, Colorado that provides integrated data, security, and voice command systems for homes. You have been asked to enhance a marketing presentation on a new product that the company is going to promote at a large trade fair in Las Vegas. You work on completing a presentation for the show. You insert some clip art, add a text box, and insert a chart.

**a.** Start PowerPoint, open the file PPT C-8.pptx from the drive and folder where you store your Data Files, and save it as **Alcom**.

**b.** Add your name and today's date to Slide 1 in the Subtitle text box.

**c.** Organize the objects on Slide 2 using the Align, Distribute, and Group commands. Add and format additional shapes to enhance the presentation.

**d.** On Slide 3, style the picture, recolor the picture, and use a picture effect.

**e.** Apply the Median theme to the presentation.

**f.** Insert the Word document file **PPT C-9.docx** to create additional slides from an outline after Slide 2.

**g.** Create a new slide after Slide 4, title the slide **Growth of Integrated Systems**, then insert a chart.

**TABLE C-5**

|            | Last Yr. | Current Yr. | Next Yr. |
|------------|----------|-------------|----------|
| Traditional | 91       | 85          | 74       |
| Integrated  | 9        | 15          | 26       |

**FIGURE C-20**

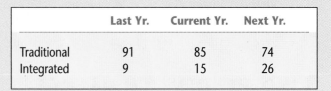

**h.** Enter the data in Table C-5, then format the chart using at least two formatting commands. Be able to name which formatting commands you applied to the chart.

**i.** Insert a text box on the Alcom Home Systems slide (Slide 7). Create your own company contact and address information. Format the text box.

**j.** Spell check, then view the final slide show (refer to Figure C-20). Make any necessary changes.

**k.** Save the presentation, print the slides as handouts, close the file, and exit PowerPoint.

# ▼ INDEPENDENT CHALLENGE 3

You work for LearnSource Ltd., a company that produces instructional software to help people learn foreign languages. Once a year, LearnSource holds a meeting with their biggest client, the Department of State, to brief the government on new products and to receive feedback on existing products. Your boss has started a presentation and has asked you to look it over and add other elements to make it look better.

**a.** Start PowerPoint, open the file PPT C-10.pptx from the drive and folder where you store your Data Files, and save it as **LearnSource**.

**b.** Add an appropriate design theme to the presentation.

**c.** Insert the Word outline PPT C-11.docx after the Product Revisions slide.

**d.** Format the text so that the most important information is the most prominent.

**e.** Insert an appropriate table on a slide of your choice. Use your own information. (*Hint*: You can convert a bulleted list to a table.)

**f.** Add at least two appropriate shapes that emphasize slide content. Format the objects using shape styles. If appropriate, use the Align, Distribute, and Group commands to organize your shapes.

# ▼ INDEPENDENT CHALLENGE 3 (CONTINUED)

## Advanced Challenge Exercise (*Internet connection required*)

- Open the Clip Art task pane, then click the Clip art on Office Online link to go to the Microsoft Office Online Web site.
- Insert an appropriate graphic.
- Format the graphic using Picture Tools Format tab.
- Be able to explain how you formatted the graphic object.

**g.** Spell check and view the final slide show (refer to Figure C-21). Make any necessary changes.

**h.** Add your name as footer text on the notes and handouts, save the presentation, then print the slides as handouts.

**i.** Save and close the file, and exit PowerPoint.

**FIGURE C-21**

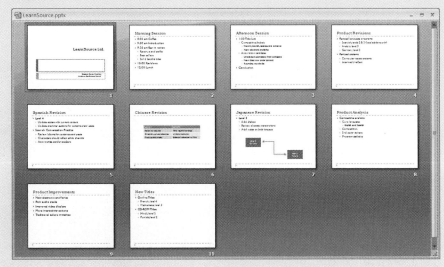

# ▼ REAL LIFE INDEPENDENT CHALLENGE

You are on the Foreign Exchange Commission at your college and one of your responsibilities is to present information on past foreign student exchanges to different organizations on and off campus. You need to create a pictorial presentation that highlights a trip to a different country. Create a presentation using your own pictures or photographs given to you with permission by a friend.

Note: Three photographs (PPT C-12.jpg, PPT C-13.jpg, and PPT C-14.jpg,) from Dijon, France are provided, if necessary to help you complete this Independent Challenge.

**a.** Start PowerPoint, create a new blank presentation, and save it as **Exchange** to the drive and folder where you store your Data Files.

**b.** Locate and insert the pictures you want to use. Place one picture on each slide using the Content with Caption slide layout.

**FIGURE C-22**

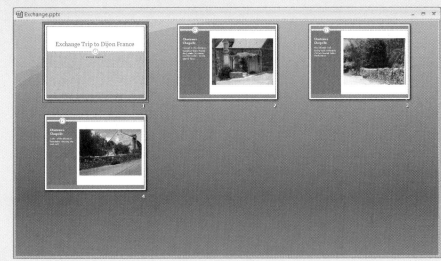

**c.** Add information about each picture in the text placeholder and enter a slide title. If you use the pictures provided, research Dijon, France using the Internet for relevant information to place on the slides. (*Internet connection required*)

**d.** Apply an appropriate design theme.

**e.** Apply an appropriate title and your name to the title slide. Spell check, then view the final slide show (refer to Figure C-22).

**f.** Add a slide number to the slides and your name as footer text to the notes and handouts, save the presentation, then print the slides and notes pages (if any).

**g.** Save your work, close the file, and exit PowerPoint.

Create a one-slide presentation that looks like Figure C-23. The slide layout shown in Figure C-23 is a specific layout designed for pictures. Insert the picture file PPT C-6.jpg to complete this presentation. Add your name as footer to the slide, save the presentation as **Guitar Lessons** to the drive and folder where you store your Data Files, then print the slide.

**FIGURE C-23**

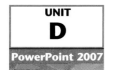

# Finishing a Presentation

Though not required, having a consistent professional-looking theme throughout your presentation is optimal if you want to peak and retain your audience's interest in the subject matter you are presenting. PowerPoint helps you achieve a consistent look by providing ways to customize your slides' layout and background. Once you are finished working with the text and other objects of your presentation, you are ready to apply slide show effects, which determine the way the slides and objects on the slides appear in Slide Show view. Ellen has reviewed the presentation and is pleased with the slides you created for the Quest Specialty Travel presentation. You are ready to finalize the layouts and add effects to make the presentation interesting to watch.

**OBJECTIVES**

Understand masters

Customize background style

Use slide show commands

Set slide show transitions and timings

Set slide animation effects

Inspect a presentation

Evaluate a presentation

Create a design template

# Understanding Masters

Each presentation in PowerPoint has a set of **masters**, which store information, including the position and size of text and content placeholders, text styles, background colors, effects, animations, and theme colors. There are three Master views: Slide Master view, Handout Master view, and Notes Master view. Changes made to the Slide Master are reflected on all the slides, changes made to the Notes Master are reflected in the Notes Page view, and changes made to the Handout Master are reflected when you print your presentation using one of the Handout print options. Design elements that you place on the Slide Master appear on every slide in the presentation. For example, you could insert a company logo in the upper-right corner of the slide master and that logo would then appear on every slide in your presentation. Each Slide Master has associated layouts. Changes made to a layout affect all slides that have that layout. ▃▃▃ You want to add the company logo to the presentation, so you open your presentation and examine the slide master.

**STEPS**

1. **Start PowerPoint, open the presentation** PPT D-1.pptx **from the drive and folder where you store your Data Files, save the presentation as** QuestD, **click the** View tab **on the Ribbon, then click the** Arrange All button **in the Window group**
   The title slide of the presentation appears.

2. **Click the** Slide Master button **in the Presentation Views group, then click the** Solstice Slide Master thumbnail (first thumbnail) **in the left pane**
   The Slide Master view appears with the slide master displayed in the Slide pane as shown in Figure D-1. This master slide is the theme master slide (the Solstice theme in this case). Each master text placeholder identifies the font size, style, color, and position of text placeholders on the slide in Normal view. For example, the Master title placeholder, labeled "Click to edit Master title style," is positioned at the top of the slide and uses a brown, shadowed, 44 pt, Gill Sans MT font. Any objects you place on the slide master will appear on all slides in the presentation. The slide layouts located below the master slide thumbnail in the left pane follow the information in the master slide and changes you make to this master slide, including font changes, are reflected in all of the slide layouts. Each slide layout in the presentation can be modified independently. Each theme comes with its own associated slide masters.

3. **Point to each** slide layout **in the left pane, then click the** Title Only Layout thumbnail
   As you point to each slide layout, a ScreenTip appears which identifies each slide layout by name and lists if any of the slides in the presentation are currently using the layout. Three slides are using the Title Only Layout, Slide 4, Slide 9, and Slide 10.

4. **Click the** Solstice Slide Master thumbnail, **click the** Insert tab **on the Ribbon, then click the** Picture button **in the Illustrations group**
   The Insert Picture dialog box opens.

5. **Select the picture file** PPT D-2.jpg **from the drive and folder where you store your Data Files, then click** Insert
   The QST graphic logo appears on the slide master and will appear on all slides in the presentation. The graphic is too large and needs to be repositioned on the slide so you reduce its size and move it to a better location on the slide.

6. **Click the** Shape Width down arrow **in the Size group until** 1.1" **appears, then drag the** graphic **to the upper left corner of the slide**
   Compare your screen to Figure D-2.

7. **Click the** Normal button ▣ **on the status bar, then save your changes**

**FIGURE D-1:** Slide Master view

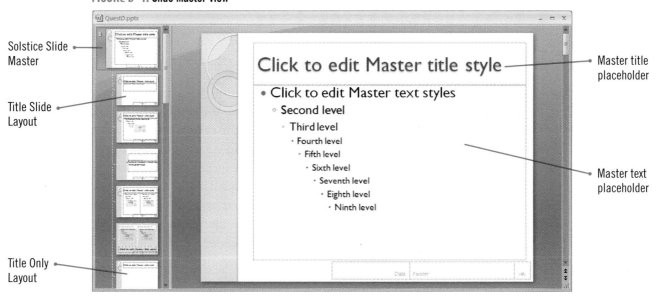

Solstice Slide Master

Title Slide Layout

Title Only Layout

Master title placeholder

Master text placeholder

**FIGURE D-2:** Graphic added to the slide master

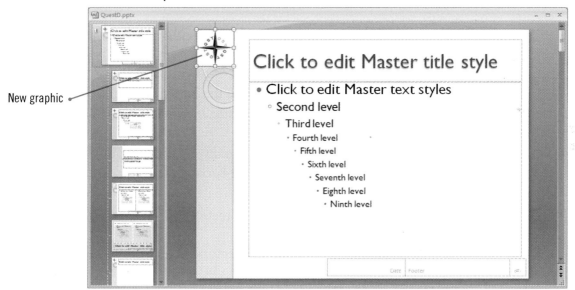

New graphic

## Create custom slide layouts

As you work with PowerPoint, you may find that you need to develop a customized slide layout. For example, you may need to create presentations for a client that has slides that display four pictures with a caption underneath each picture. To make everyone's job easier, you create a custom slide layout that includes only the placeholders needed for that particular slide layout. To create a custom slide layout, open Slide Master view, click the Insert Layout button in the Edit Master group. A new slide layout appears in the Slide pane. You can choose to add several different placeholders including Content, Text, Picture, Chart, Table, SmartArt, Media, and Clip Art. Click the Insert Placeholder button arrow in the Master Layout group, click the placeholder you want to add, drag ╅ to create the placeholder, then position the placeholder on the slide. In Slide Master view, you can add or delete placeholders in any of the slide layouts. You can rename a custom slide layout by clicking the Rename button in the Edit Master group and entering a descriptive name to better identify the layout.

# Customizing the Background Style

Every slide in a PowerPoint presentation has a **background**, the area behind the text and graphics. You modify the background to enhance the slides using images and color. A **background graphic** is an object placed on the slide master. You can quickly change the background appearance by applying a background style, which is a set of color variations derived from the theme colors. **Theme colors** are a set of twelve coordinated colors that determine the colors for all slide elements in your presentation including: slide background, text and lines, shadows, title text, fills, accents, and hyperlinks. Every theme, such as Civic and Solstice, has its own set of theme colors. See Table D-1 for a description of the theme colors. ▰▰▰▰▰ The QST presentation needs some design enhancements. You decide to modify the background of the slides in the presentation by applying a background style.

## STEPS

1. **Click the Design tab on the Ribbon, then click the Background Styles button in the Background group**

   A gallery of background styles opens. Review the different backgrounds using Live Preview.

**QUICK TIP**
To apply a new background style to only selected slides, select the slides on the Slides tab or in Slide Sorter view, right-click the background style in the Background Styles gallery, then click Apply to Selected Slides.

2. **Move the pointer over each style in the gallery, then click Style 6**

   Figure D-3 shows the new background on Slide 1 of the presentation. Even though you are working in Normal view, the new background style is applied to every slide in the presentation and to the master slide and master slide layouts. The new background style did not appear over the whole slide, which indicates there is a background graphic on the slide master that is preventing you from seeing the entire slide background.

3. **Click the Hide Background Graphics check box in the Background group**

   For the selected slide, all the background graphics are hidden from view and only the text objects on the slide remain visible.

4. **Click the Hide Background Graphics check box to display the background graphics, click the Background Styles button, then click Format Background**

   The Format Background dialog box opens.

**QUICK TIP**
You can also apply a gradient background style to a shape by right-clicking the shape, then clicking Format Shape in the shortcut menu.

5. **Click the Type list arrow, click Linear, click the Direction button, click Linear Down, click Apply to All, then click Close**

   The gradient fill of the background style now progresses from dark to light starting at the bottom of the slide and moving to the top. You need to fix the background color of the QST logo graphic so it does not obstruct the slide background graphics.

6. **Press [Shift], click the Normal button ▥ on the status bar, click the Solstice Slide Master thumbnail in the left pane, then click the QST graphic**

   The graphic is selected in the Slide Master view.

7. **Click the Picture Tools Format tab on the Ribbon, click the Recolor button in the Adjust group, click Set Transparent Color, then move the pointer over the slide**

   The pointer changes to the transparent pointer ⬚.

**TROUBLE**
If the white background does not become transparent, click the Undo button, then repeat the step.

8. **Position ⬚ over the white background of the QST logo graphic, then click**

   The white background of the QST graphic becomes transparent and the slide background appears behind the graphic.

9. **Click the Normal button ▥ on the status bar, then save your work**

   Compare your screen to Figure D-4.

**FIGURE D-3:** Slide with new background style applied

New background style is applied to all the slides

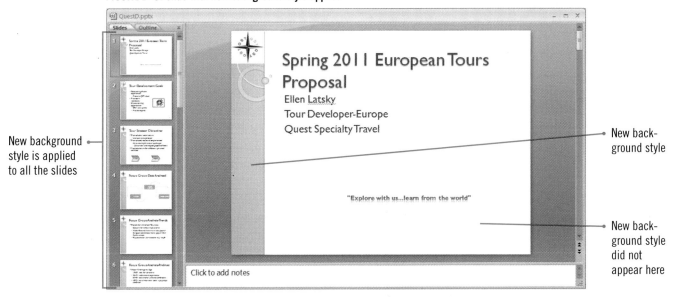

New background style

New background style did not appear here

**FIGURE D-4:** Finished slide

Graphic with transparent background

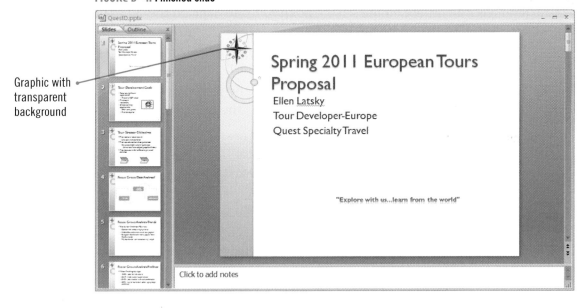

**TABLE D-1:** Theme colors

| scheme element | description |
| --- | --- |
| Background color | Color of the slide's background; fills the slide |
| Text and lines color | Used for any typed characters and drawn lines; contrasts with the background color |
| Shadows color | The shadow color for text and other objects; generally a darker shade of the background color |
| Title text color | Used for slide title; like the text and line colors and contrasts with the background color |
| Fills color | Used to fill shapes and other objects with color. Contrasts with both the background and the text and line colors |
| Accent colors | Colors used for other objects on slides, such as bullets |
| Accent and hyperlink colors | Colors used for accent objects and for hyperlinks you insert |
| Accent and followed hyperlink color | Color used for accent objects and for hyperlinks after they have been clicked |

# Using Slide Show Commands

With PowerPoint, you can show a presentation on any compatible computer using Slide Show view. As you've seen, Slide Show view fills your computer screen with the slides of the presentation, showing them one at a time. Once the presentation is in Slide Show view, you can use a number of slide show options to tailor the show to meet your needs. For example, you can draw, or **annotate**, on slides or jump to different slides in other parts of the presentation. ▓▓▓▓ Ellen wants you to learn how to run a slide show and use the slide show options so you can help her when she gives the presentation. You run the slide show of the presentation and practice using some of the custom slide show options.

## STEPS

1. **Click the View tab on the Ribbon, then click the Slide Show button in the Presentation Views group**

   The first slide of the presentation fills the screen.

2. **Press [Spacebar]**

   Slide 2 appears on the screen. Pressing [Spacebar] or clicking the left mouse button is the easiest way to move through a slide show. See Table D-2 for other Slide Show view key commands. You can also use the Slide Show shortcut menu for on-screen navigation during a slide show.

3. **Right-click anywhere on the screen, point to Go to Slide on the shortcut menu, then click 8 Mediterranean Islands Bike Tour**

   The slide show jumps to Slide 8. You can highlight or emphasize major points in your presentation by annotating the slide during a slide show using one of PowerPoint's annotation tools.

> **TROUBLE**
> The Slide Show toolbar buttons are semitransparent and will blend in with the background color on the slide.

4. **Move the pointer to the bottom left corner of the screen to display the Slide Show toolbar, click the Pen Options menu button ✏, then click Highlighter**

   The pointer changes to the highlighter pointer ▌.

5. **Drag ▌ to highlight the text below the picture**

   Compare your screen to Figure D-5. While the annotation tool is visible, mouse clicks do not advance the slide show; however, you can still move to the next slide by pressing [Spacebar] or [Enter].

> **QUICK TIP**
> You have the option of saving undeleted annotations you create while in Slide Show view when you end or quit the slide show.

6. **Click the Pen Options menu button ✏ on the Slide Show toolbar, click Erase All Ink on Slide, then press [Ctrl][A]**

   The annotations on Slide 8 are erased and the pointer returns to ▷ when you press [Ctrl][A].

7. **Click the Slide Show menu button ▤ on the Slide Show toolbar, point to Go to Slide, then click 10 Adventure Series on the menu**

   Slide 10 appears.

> **QUICK TIP**
> If you know the slide number of a slide you want to jump to during a slide show, type the number, then press [Enter].

8. **Press [Home], then press [Enter] to advance through the slide show, then when you see the black slide at the end of the slide show, press [Spacebar]**

   You are returned to Normal view. The black slide indicates the end of the slide show.

FIGURE D-5: Slide 8 in Slide Show view with highlight annotations

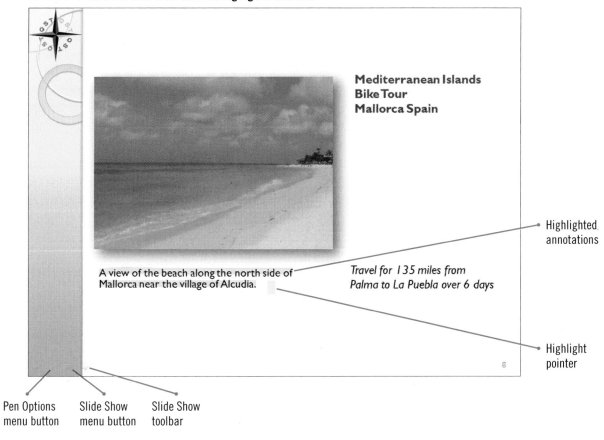

Mediterranean Islands
Bike Tour
Mallorca Spain

A view of the beach along the north side of
Mallorca near the village of Alcudia.

Travel for 135 miles from
Palma to La Puebla over 6 days

Highlighted annotations

Highlight pointer

Pen Options menu button

Slide Show menu button

Slide Show toolbar

TABLE D-2: Basic Slide Show keyboard controls

| control | description |
| --- | --- |
| [Enter], [Spacebar], [PgDn], [N], [down arrow key], or [right arrow key] | Advances to the next slide |
| [E] | Erases the annotation drawing |
| [Home], [End] | Moves to the first or last slide in the slide show |
| [H] | Displays a hidden slide |
| [up arrow key] or [PgUp] | Returns to the previous slide |
| [W] | Changes the screen to white; press again to return |
| [S] | Pauses the slide show; press again to continue |
| [B] | Changes the screen to black; press again to return |
| [Ctrl][M] | Shows or hides annotations on the slide |
| [Ctrl][A] | Changes pointer to |
| [Esc] | Stops the slide show |

# Setting Slide Show Transitions and Timings

In a slide show, you can specify how each slide advances in and out of view, and for how long each slide appears on the screen. **Slide transitions** are the special visual and audio effects you apply to a slide that determine how it moves in and out of view during the slide show. **Slide timing**, refers to the amount of time a slide is visible on the screen. Typically, you would set slide timings if you wanted the presentation to automatically progress through the slides during a slide show. Setting the correct slide timing, in this case, is important because it determines how long each slide is visible. Each slide can have a different slide timing. ⬛⬛⬛⬛ You decide to set slide transitions and 8 second slide timings for all the slides.

## STEPS

1. **Make sure Slide 1 is selected, click the Animations tab on the Ribbon, then point to each of the transition options in the Transition to This Slide group**

   A Live Preview of each transition is displayed on the slide. Transitions are organized by type into five groups.

**TROUBLE**

You'll need to wait a few seconds until the Live Preview of the transition finishes to see the transition ScreenTip.

2. **Click the More button in the Transition to This Slide group, then click Box In in the Wipes section (3rd row)**

   The new slide transition plays on the slide and a transition icon appears next to the slide thumbnail in the Slides tab as shown in Figure D-6. The slide transition would have more impact if it were slowed down.

3. **Click the Transition Speed list arrow in the Transition to This Slide group, then click Medium**

   The Box In slide transition plays again at the slower speed. You can apply this transition to all of the slides in the presentation.

**QUICK TIP**

Click the transition icon under any slide in Slide Sorter view to see its transition play.

4. **Click the Apply To All button in the Transition to This Slide group, then click the Slide Sorter button ⊞ on the status bar**

   All of the slides now have the Box In transition at the medium speed applied to them as identified by the transition icons located below each slide. The options under Advance Slide in the Transition to This Slide group determine how slides progress during a slide show—either by mouse click or automatically by slide timing.

5. **Click the Automatically After up arrow until 00.08 appears in the text box, then click the Apply To All button in the Transition to This Slide group**

   The timing between slides is 8 seconds as indicated by the time under each slide in Slide Sorter view. See Figure D-7. When you run the slide show, each slide will remain on the screen for 8 seconds. You can override a slide's timing and speed up the slide show by pressing [Spacebar], [Enter], or clicking the left mouse button during a slide show.

6. **Click Slide 8, click the Transition Sound list arrow in the Transition to This Slide group, then click Breeze**

   The Breeze sound will now play when Slide 8 appears during the slide show.

7. **Press [Home], click the Slide Show button ⬚ on the status bar, then watch the slide show advance automatically**

8. **When you see the black slide at the end of the slide show, press [Spacebar], then save your changes**

   The slide show ends and returns to Slide Sorter view with Slide 1 selected.

**FIGURE D-6:** Applied slide transition

Box In slide transition

More button

Transition icon

**FIGURE D-7:** Slide Sorter view showing applied transition and timing

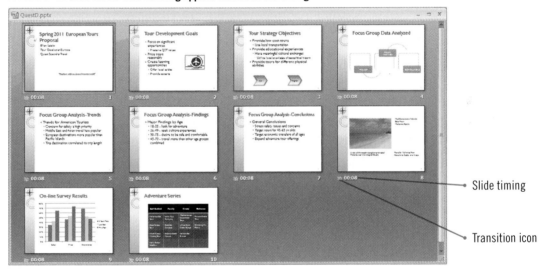

Slide timing

Transition icon

## Rehearsing slide show timings

You can set different slide timings for each slide. For example, you can have the title slide appear for 20 seconds, the second slide for 1 minute, and so on. You can set timings by clicking the Rehearse Timings button in the Set Up group on the Slide Show tab. Slide Show view opens and the Rehearsal toolbar shown in Figure D-8 opens. It contains buttons to pause between slides and to advance to the next slide. After opening the Rehearsal toolbar, practice giving your presentation. PowerPoint keeps track of how long each slide appears and sets the timing accordingly. You can view your rehearsed timings in Slide Sorter view. The next time you run the slide show, you can use the timings you rehearsed.

**FIGURE D-8:** Rehearsal toolbar

Total elapsed time for all slides

Move to the next slide

Click to pause

Time elapsed while viewing current slide

Click to reset the clock to zero for the current slide

# Setting Slide Animation Effects

Animation effects let you control how the objects and main points in your presentation appear on the screen during a slide show. You can set custom animation effects or use one of several standard animation effects. For example, you can apply a Fade by 1st Level Paragraphs animation effect to bulleted text so that each first level bullet appears separately from the others. Using animation effects allows you to control how information flows and what information is emphasized. You can animate text, graphics, sounds, hyperlinks, SmartArt diagrams, charts and individual chart elements. The standard animation effects include Fade, Wipe, and Fly In and can be applied to any selected object. Custom animation effects are organized into four categories, which provide you a wide range of animation choices, such as Ease In and Flicker. ▓▓▓▓ Ellen wants you to animate the text and graphics of several slides in the presentation using animation effects.

## STEPS

1. **Verify that the Animations tab is selected on the Ribbon, double-click Slide 2 to view it in Normal view, then click the body text object**
   The bullets in the text object can be animated to appear one at a time during a slide show.

2. **Click the Animate list arrow in the Animations group, then click By 1st Level Paragraphs in the Fade section**
   As you click the animation option a Live Preview of the Box In transition and the Fade animation effect plays.

   > **QUICK TIP**
   > Animation effects can be serious and business-like or humorous. Choose appropriate effects for your presentation content and audience.

3. **Click the Slide Show button 🖵 on the status bar, then press [Esc] when you see Slide 3**
   The Fade animation effect, which begins after the slide transition effect, is active on Slide 2. You can also animate other objects on a slide by setting custom animations.

4. **Make sure Slide 3 is selected, click the grouped arrow object on the slide, then click the Custom Animation button in the Animations group**
   The Custom Animation task pane opens.

   > **QUICK TIP**
   > If you want the parts of a grouped object to animate individually, then you must ungroup the objects before you animate them.

5. **Click the Add Effect button in the Custom Animation task pane, then point to Entrance**
   A submenu of Entrance animation effects appears next to a menu of four animation categories, Entrance, Emphasis, Exit, and Motion Paths as shown in Figure D-9. An Entrance animation effect causes an object to enter the slide with an effect; an Emphasis animation effect causes an object already visible on the slide to have an effect; an Exit animation effect causes an object to leave the slide with an effect; and a Motion Paths animation effect causes an object to move on a specified path on the slide.

6. **Click More Effects**
   The Add Entrance Effect dialog box opens. All of the effects in this dialog box allow an object to enter the slide using a special effect.

   > **QUICK TIP**
   > To change the order in which objects are animated on the slide, select the object in the Custom Animation task pane, then click the appropriate Re-Order arrow at the bottom of the pane.

7. **Scroll down to the Exciting section, click Glide, then click OK**
   The arrow object now has the glide effect applied to it as shown in Figure D-10. Notice that the arrow object now has an animation tag and is listed in the Custom Animation task pane as the first object to be animated on the slide. **Animation tags** identify the order in which objects are animated during slide show.

8. **Click the Custom Animation task pane Close button ☒, click the Slide Show tab on the Ribbon, then click the From Beginning button in the Start Slide Show group to run the Slide Show from Slide 1**
   The special effects make the presentation more interesting to view.

9. **When you see the black slide, press [Spacebar], then save your changes**

FIGURE D-9: Custom Animation task pane open

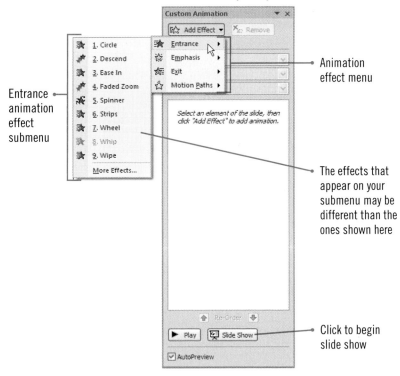

Entrance animation effect submenu

Animation effect menu

The effects that appear on your submenu may be different than the ones shown here

Click to begin slide show

FIGURE D-10: Screen showing animated arrow object

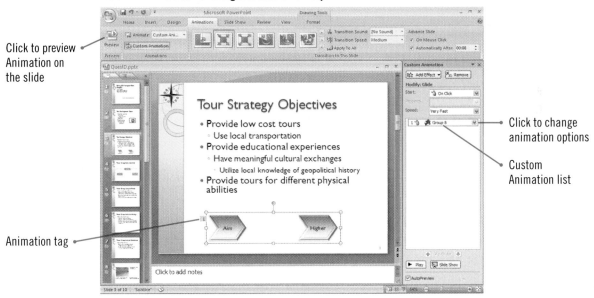

Click to preview Animation on the slide

Click to change animation options

Custom Animation list

Animation tag

## Presentation checklist

You should always rehearse your slide show. If possible, rehearse your presentation in the room and with the computer that you will use. Use the following checklist to prepare for the slide show:

- Is **PowerPoint** or **PowerPoint Viewer** installed on the computer?
- Is your **presentation file** on the hard drive of the computer you will be using? Try putting a shortcut for the file on the desktop. Do you have a backup copy of your presentation file on a removable storage device?
- Is the **projection device** working correctly? Can the slides be seen from the back of the room?

- Do you know how to control **room lighting** so that the audience can see both your slides and their handouts and notes? You may want to designate someone to control the lights if the controls are not close to you.
- Will the **computer** be situated so you can advance and annotate the slides yourself? If not, designate someone to advance them for you.
- Do you have enough copies of your **handouts**? Bring extras. Decide when to hand them out, or whether you prefer to have them waiting at the audience members' seats when they enter.

# Inspecting a Presentation

Reviewing your presentation can be an important step, not only to find and fix errors, but also to locate and delete private company or personal information and document properties you do not want to share with others. If you share presentations with others, especially over the Internet, it is a good idea to inspect the presentation file using the Document Inspector. The **Document Inspector** looks for hidden data and personal information that is stored in the file itself or in the document properties. Document properties, also known as **metadata**, includes specific data about the presentation, such as the author's name, sub-ject matter, title, who saved the file last, and when the file was created. Other types of information the Document Inspector can locate and remove include: presentation notes, comments, ink annotations, invis-ible on-slide content, off-slide content, and custom XML data. QST has strict rules about revealing personal and company information in documents. You decide to view and add some document properties, inspect your presentation file, and learn about the Mark as Final command.

## STEPS

**QUICK TIP**
Click the Document Properties list arrow, then click Advanced Properties to open the Properties dialog box to see or change more document properties.

1. **Click the Office button, point to Prepare, then click Properties**

   The Document Properties pane opens showing the file location and the title of the presentation. Now enter some descriptive data for this presentation file.

2. **Enter the data shown in Figure D-11, then click the Properties pane Close button**

   This data provides detailed information about the presentation file that you can use to identify and organ-ize your file. You can also use this information as search criteria to locate the file at a later time. You now use the Document Inspector to search for information you might want to delete in the presentation.

3. **Click, point to Prepare, click Inspect Document, click Yes to save the changes to the document, then read the dialog box**

   The Document Inspector dialog box opens. The Document Inspector searches the presentation file for six different types of information that you might want removed from the presentation before sending it.

**QUICK TIP**
If you need to save a presentation to run in an earlier version of PowerPoint, check for unsupported fea-tures using the Run Compatibility Checker feature.

4. **Make sure all of the check boxes are selected, then click Inspect**

   The presentation file is reviewed and the Document Inspector dialog box displays the results shown in Figure D-12. Notice that there are three items found: document properties in the Document Properties pane, an off slide object that you created and didn't use, and some reminder notes you wrote yourself in the Notes pane on Slides 8, 9, and 10. You decide to leave the document properties alone but delete the off-slide object, and the notes in the Notes pane for all of the slides.

5. **Click the Off-Slide Content Remove All button, click the Presentation Notes Remove All button, then click Close**

   All of those items are removed from the presentation.

6. **Click, point to Prepare, click Mark as Final, then click OK in the alert dialog box**

   A dialog box opens. Be sure to read the dialog box to understand what happens to the file and how to recog-nize a marked-as-final presentation. You decide to proceed with this operation.

**QUICK TIP**
Presentations marked as final in PowerPoint 2007 are not read-only if they are opened in earlier ver-sions of PowerPoint.

7. **Click OK, click the Home tab on the Ribbon, click the Slide 1 thumbnail in the Slides pane, then click anywhere in the title text object**

   Notice that the commands on the Ribbon are dimmed as shown in Figure D-13. Because you marked the file as final, the file is read-only. A **read-only** file is one that can't be edited or modified in any way. Anyone who has received a read-only presentation can edit the presentation by removing the mark as final status. You still want to work on the presentation, so you remove the mark as final status.

8. **Click, point to Prepare, click Mark as Final, then save your changes**

   The commands on the Ribbon are active again, and the file can now be modified.

**FIGURE D-11:** Document Properties pane

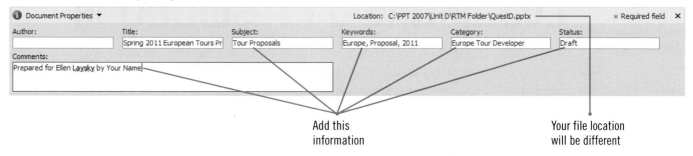

Add this
information

Your file location
will be different

**FIGURE D-12:** Document Inspector dialog box

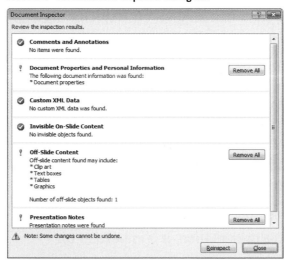

**FIGURE D-13:** Marked-as-final presentation

Commands on
the Ribbon are
dimmed and not
available to use

Icon indicates the
presentation is
marked as final

## Digitally sign a presentation

So what is a digital signature and why would you want to use one in PowerPoint? A digital signature is similar to a hand-written signature in that it authenticates your document; however, a digital signature, unlike a hand-written signature, is created using computer cryptography and is not visible within the presentation itself. There are three primary reasons you would add a digital signature to a presentation: one, to authenticate the signer of the document; two, to assure that the content of the presentation has not been changed since it was signed; and three, to assure the origin of the signed document. To add a digital signature, click the Office button, point to Prepare, click Add a Digital Signature, then follow the dialog boxes.

# Evaluating a Presentation

As you create a presentation, keep in mind that a good design requires preparation. An effective presentation is focused and visually appealing—easy for the speaker to present and simple for the audience to understand. The visual elements (colors, graphics, and text) can strongly influence the audience's attention and interest and can determine the success of your presentation. See Table D-3 for general information on the impact a visual presentation has on an audience. *You know Ellen will critique your presentation, so you take the time to evaluate your presentation's effectiveness.

## STEPS

1. **Click the Slide Show button 🖥 on the status bar, then press [Spacebar] when the slide show finishes**

2. **Click the Slide Sorter button 🔠 on the status bar**
   You decide that Slide 8 should come after Slide 10.

3. **Drag Slide 8 to the right side of Slide 10, then save your changes**
   Slide 8 is moved to the end of the presentation. The final presentation is shown in Slide Sorter view. Compare your screen to Figure D-14.

4. **Double-click Slide 1, then evaluate your presentation according to the guidelines below**
   Figure D-15 shows a poorly designed slide. Contrast this slide with your presentation as you review the following guidelines.

### When evaluating a presentation, it is important to:

- **Keep your message focused**
  Don't put every point you plan to say on your presentation slides. Keep the audience anticipating further explanations to the key points shown in the presentation.

- **Keep your text concise**
  Limit each slide to six words per line and six lines per slide. Use lists and symbols to help prioritize your points visually. Your presentation text provides only the highlights; use notes to give more detailed information. Your presentation focuses attention on the key issues and you supplement the information with further explanation and details during your presentation.

- **Keep the design simple, easy to read, and appropriate for the content**
  A design theme makes the presentation consistent. If you design your own layout, keep it simple and use design elements sparingly. Use similar design elements consistently throughout the presentation; otherwise, your audience may get confused.

- **Choose attractive colors that make the slide easy to read**
  Use contrasting colors for slide background and text to make the text readable. If you are giving an on-screen presentation, you can use almost any combination of colors that look good together.

- **Choose fonts and styles that are easy to read and emphasize important text**
  As a general rule, use no more than two fonts in a presentation and vary the font size, using nothing smaller than 24 points. Use bold and italic attributes selectively.

- **Use visuals to help communicate the message of your presentation**
  Commonly used visuals include clip art, photographs, charts, worksheets, tables, and movies. Whenever possible, replace text with a visual, but be careful not to overcrowd your slides. White space on your slides is OK!

**FIGURE D-14:** The final presentation in Slide Sorter view

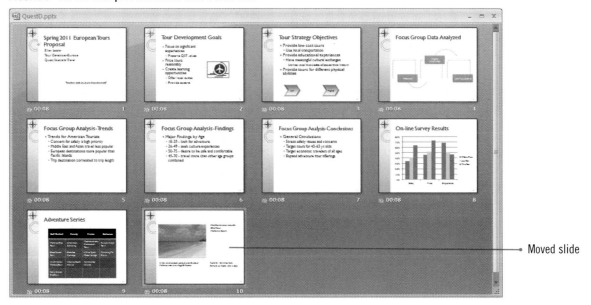

Moved slide

**FIGURE D-15:** A poorly designed slide

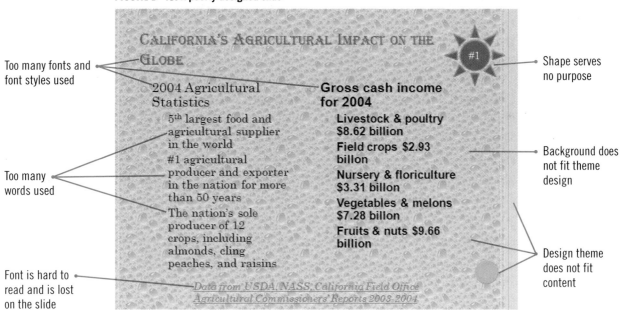

Too many fonts and font styles used

Shape serves no purpose

Too many words used

Background does not fit theme design

Design theme does not fit content

Font is hard to read and is lost on the slide

**TABLE D-3:** Audience impact from a visual presentation

| impact | description |
| --- | --- |
| Visual reception | 75% of all environmental stimuli is received through visual reception |
| Learning | 55% of what an audience learns comes directly from visual messages |
| Retention | Combining visual messages with verbal messages can increase memory retention by as much as 30% |
| Presentation goals | You are twice as likely to achieve your communication objectives using a visual presentation |
| Meeting length | You are likely to decrease the average meeting length by 26% when you use a visual presentation |

*Source: Presenters Online, www.presentersonline.com*

# Creating a Design Template

When planning the design of your presentation, keep in mind that you are not limited to using just the standard themes PowerPoint provides or the ones you find on the Web. You can customize your presentation using a template. A **template** is a type of presentation file that contains custom design information made to the slide master, slide layouts, and theme. You can create a new template from a blank presentation, or you can modify an existing PowerPoint presentation that you have access to and save it as a template. If you modify an existing presentation, you can keep, change, or delete any color, graphic, or font as necessary. When you are finished creating a new presentation or modifying an existing presentation, you can save it as a template file, which adds the .potx extension to the filename. You can then use your template presentation as the basis for new presentations. You are finished working on your presentation for now. You want to save the presentation as a template so you and others can use it.

## STEPS

1. **Click the** Office button **, point to** Save As, **click** Other Formats, **click the** Save as type list arrow, **then click** PowerPoint Template (*.potx)

   Because this is a template, PowerPoint automatically opens the Templates folder on your hard drive as shown in Figure D-16.

2. **Use the Favorite Link or Folders pane to locate the drive and folder where you store your Data Files, click to select the filename (currently QuestD.potx) in the File name list box, type** QuestD Template, **then click** Save

   The presentation is saved as a PowerPoint template to the drive and folder where you store your Data Files, and the new template presentation appears in the PowerPoint window. The filename in the title bar has a .potx extension which identifies this presentation as a template.

3. **Click the** Slide Sorter button **on the status bar, click** Slide 3, **press and hold** [Shift], **click** Slide 10, **release** [Shift], **then click the** Cut button **in the Clipboard group**

   Slides 3 through 10 are deleted.

4. **Double-click** Slide 2, **press and hold** [Shift], **click the** body text object, **click the** title text object, **right-click the** clip art object, **release** [Shift], **then click** Cut

   The clip art object and the text in the text objects are deleted. Sometimes templates have sample text.

5. **Type** Slide Title Here, **click the** content placeholder, **type** Bulleted list, **press** [Enter], **press** [Tab], **type** Bulleted list, **click the** Layout button **in the Slides group, then click** Title and Content

   Sample text replaces the text, and the slide layout changes to the Title and Content slide layout.

6. **Click the** Slide 1 thumbnail **in the Slides tab, press** [Shift], **select the three text objects on the slide, then press** [Delete]

   The WordArt object and the text in the text objects are deleted.

7. **Click the** title text placeholder, **type** QST Template, **click the** subtitle placeholder, **type** Subtitle text here, **then save your changes**

8. **Click the** View tab, **then click the** Slide Sorter button **in the Presentation Views group**

   Figure D-17 shows the final template presentation in Slide Sorter view.

9. **Save your work, print the template presentation as** handouts (2 per page), **close the presentation, then exit PowerPoint**

**FIGURE D-16:** Save As dialog box showing Templates folder

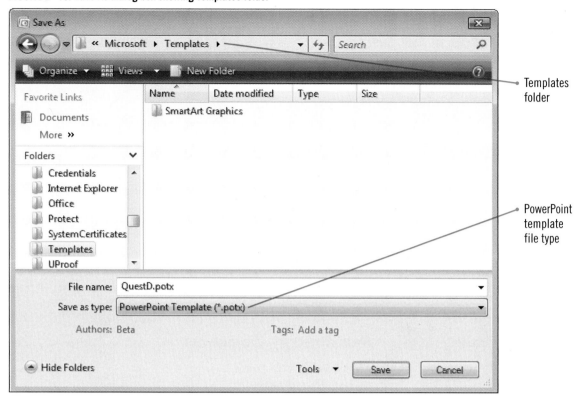

Templates folder

PowerPoint template file type

**FIGURE D-17:** Completed template presentation in Slide Sorter view

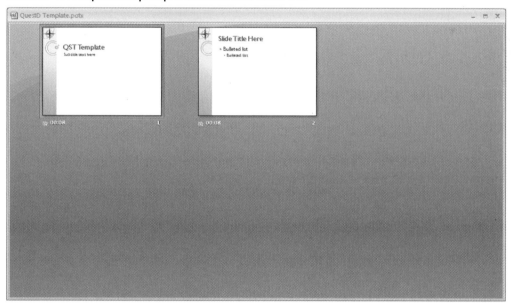

## Applying a theme from another presentation

When you apply a theme from one presentation to another, you automatically apply the master layouts, colors and fonts over the existing presentation's theme. To apply a theme from another presentation, open the presentation you want to apply the theme to, click the Design tab, then click the Themes group More button.

Click Browse for Themes, use the Favorite Links or Folders pane to navigate to the presentation whose theme you want to apply. The presentation you select can be a regular presentation or a template with the .potx extension. Click the presentation name, then click Apply.

# Practice

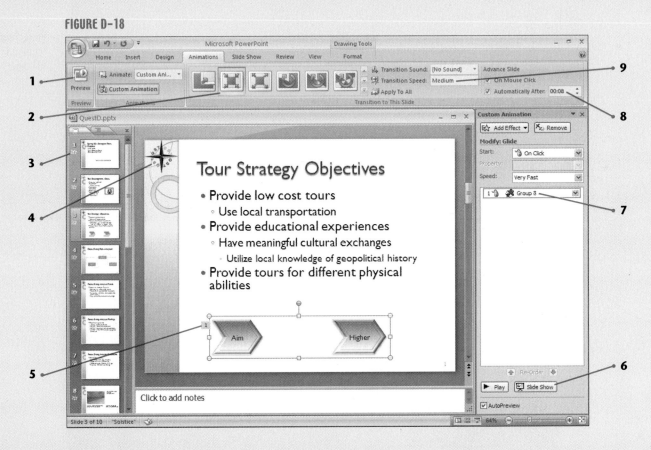

If you have a SAM user profile, you may have access to hands-on instruction, practice, and assessment of the skills covered in this unit. Log in to your SAM account (http://sam2007.course.com/) to launch any assigned training activities or exams that relate to the skills covered in this unit.

## ▼ CONCEPTS REVIEW

**Label each element of the PowerPoint window shown in Figure D-18.**

FIGURE D-18

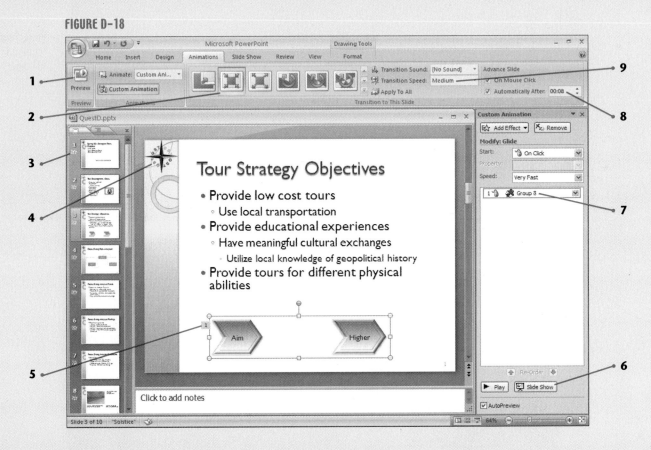

**Match each term with the statement that best describes it.**

10. **Animation tag**
11. **Background**
12. **Transitions**
13. **Masters**
14. **Metadata**
15. **Annotate**

a. Visual effects that determine how a slide moves in and out of view during a slide show
b. Slides that store theme and placeholder information
c. To draw on a slide during a slide show
d. Includes document properties such as the author's name
e. Identifies the order in which objects are animated
f. The area behind text and graphics

## Select the best answer from the list of choices.

**16. Which of the following statements about masters is *not* true?**

    **a.** Masters store information

    **b.** Changes made to the slide master are reflected in the handout and notes masters as well

    **c.** Each slide layout in the presentation has a corresponding slide layout in the Slide Master view

    **d.** The design theme is placed on the master slide

**17. According to the book, an object placed on the slide master defines which item?**

    **a.** A background graphic

    **b.** A logo

    **c.** A shape

    **d.** A master placeholder

**18. What is the effect called that determines how a slide moves in and out of view during a slide show?**

    **a.** Theme

    **b.** Animation

    **c.** Timing

    **d.** Transition

**19. What is the effect called that controls how an object appears on the screen during a slide show?**

    **a.** Transition

    **b.** Animation

    **c.** Path

    **d.** Template

**20. The Document Inspector can do all of the following *except*,**

    **a.** look for hidden data

    **b.** delete metadata

    **c.** remove on-slide content

    **d.** locate presentation notes

**21. A PowerPoint file that *can't* be edited or modified defines what type of file?**

    **a.** A marked as final file

    **b.** A template file

    **c.** An inspected file

    **d.** A file saved in another file format

**22. According to the book, which standard should you follow to evaluate a presentation?**

    **a.** Slides should include most of the information you wish to present

    **b.** The message should be outlined in a concise way.

    **c.** Use many different design elements to keep your audience from getting bored.

    **d.** Replace visuals with text as often as possible.

**23. Which of the following statements about templates is *not* true?**

    **a.** The file extension .potx is applied to the PowerPoint file when you save it as a template.

    **b.** You can create a template from a new presentation.

    **c.** A template is a type of presentation that contains custom design information.

    **d.** A template is designed to create custom slide layouts.

## ▼ SKILLS REVIEW

**1. Understand masters.**

    **a.** Open the presentation PPT D-3.pptx from the drive and folder where you store your Data Files, then save the presentation as **MediaCom**.

    **b.** Open the Slide Master view using the View tab, then click the Civic Slide Master thumbnail.

    **c.** Insert the picture PPT D-4.jpg, then resize the picture so it is 0.8" wide.

    **d.** Drag the picture to the upper right corner of the slide within the design frame of the slide, then deselect the picture.

    **e.** Switch to Normal view, then save your changes.

### 2. Customize the background style.

    **a.** Switch to Slide 2, click the Design tab, then open the background styles gallery.

    **b.** Change the background style to Style 3.

    **c.** Open the Format Background dialog box.

    **d.** Set the Transparency to 25%, then apply the background to all of the slides.

    **e.** Close the dialog box, switch to Slide Master view, then open the Civic Slide Master slide.

    **f.** Select the inserted picture, then use the Picture Tools Format tab to make its background transparent.

    **g.** Switch to Normal view, then save your changes.

### 3. Use slide show commands.

    **a.** Begin the slide show on Slide 1, then proceed to Slide 4.

    **b.** Use the Felt Tip Pen to circle the words Early Adopters, Mass Adopters, and Late Adopters.

    **c.** Use the Pen Options menu button to erase all ink on the slide, then change the pointer back to the Arrow.

    **d.** Right-click the slide and go to Slide 8, use the Highlighter pointer to highlight each bullet on the slide.

    **e.** Press [Home], then advance through the slide show, don't save any ink annotations, then save your work.

### 4. Set slide show transitions and timings.

    **a.** Go to Slide 1, then apply the Wheel Clockwise, 8 Spokes transition in the Wipes group to all of the slides.

    **b.** Change the transition speed to slow, then switch to Slide Sorter view.

    **c.** Change the slide timing to 5 seconds, then apply to all of the slides.

    **d.** Click Slide 10, then apply the Applause sound.

    **e.** Click Slide 1, then switch to Normal view.

    **f.** View the slide show, then save your work.

**FIGURE D-19: Completed presentation**

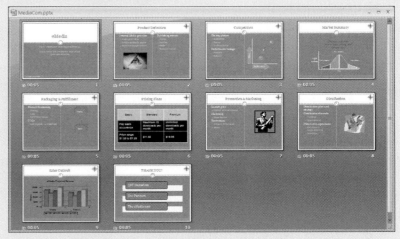

### 5. Set slide show animation effects.

    **a.** Go to Slide 2, then open the Custom Animation task pane.

    **b.** Apply the Emphasis Flash Bulb effect to the title text object, then apply the Entrance Unfold effect to both bulleted text objects.

    **c.** On Slide 3 apply the Emphasis Shimmer effect to the title text object, then apply the Entrance Rise Up effect to the bulleted text object.

    **d.** On Slide 4 apply the Entrance Flip effect to the title text object, then apply an Entrance animation effect of your choice from the Exciting group to the six individual objects in the graphic.

    **e.** Apply animation effects to the rest of the slides in the presentation. Animate all of the text objects and the other objects.

    **f.** Edit the animations effects as needed, then save your changes.

    **g.** Compare your presentation to Figure D-19.

**6. Inspect a presentation.**

  **a.** Open the Document Properties pane, type **Internet Product** in the Subject text box, then type **Review** in the Status text box

  **b.** Close the Document Properties pane, then open the Document Inspector dialog box.

  **c.** Make sure the Off-Slide Content check box is selected, then inspect the presentation.

  **d.** Delete the off-slide content, and the presentation notes, then close the dialog box.

  **e.** Save your changes.

**7. Evaluate a presentation.**

  **a.** Go to Slide 1, then run a slide show.

  **b.** Evaluate the presentation using the points described in the lesson as criteria.

  **c.** Move Slide 6 below Slide 8.

  **d.** Save your work, then print the slides of your presentation.

**8. Create a template.**

  **a.** Save the presentation as a template (.potx) with the name **MediaCom Template** to the drive and folder where your Data Files are stored.

  **b.** Delete all slides except Slide 1 and Slide 2.

  **c.** Delete the picture and text on Slide 2, type **Slide Title Here** in the title text placeholder, type **Bulleted List 1** in the left content placeholder, then type **Bulleted List 2** in the right content placeholder.

  **d.** Delete the subtitle text object on Slide 1, then type **QST MediaCom Template** in the title text object in place of the current text.

  **e.** Delete the slide transitions and animations on both slides.

  **f.** Save your work, then print the presentation as handouts, two slides per page.

  **g.** Close the presentation, then exit PowerPoint.

## ▼ INDEPENDENT CHALLENGE 1

You are a travel consultant for Turner Travel, located in Portland, Oregon. You have been working on a sales presentation that is going to be accessed by customers on the company Web site. You need to finish up what you have been working on by adding transitions, timings, and animation effects to the sales presentation.

  **a.** Open the file PPT D-5.pptx from the drive and folder where you store your Data Files, and save the presentation as **TurnerTravel**.

  **b.** Add your name as the footer on all slides and handouts.

  **c.** Apply the Fade Through Black slide transitions to all of the slides.

  **d.** Apply the Entrance Glide animation to the title text on each slide.

  **e.** Apply the Emphasis Flicker animation to the bulleted text objects on each slide.

  **f.** Apply the Entrance Thread animation to the table on Slide 8.

  **g.** Apply a 10 second slide timing to each slide, then change the transition speed to Medium.

  **h.** Spell check the presentation, then save it.

  **i.** View the slide show, and evaluate your presentation. Make changes if necessary.

  **j.** Print the slides as handouts (six slides per page), then close the presentation, and exit PowerPoint.

# ▼ INDEPENDENT CHALLENGE 2

You are a development engineer at FarNorth Sports, Inc., an international sports product design company located in Winnipeg, Manitoba, Canada. FarNorth Sports designs and manufactures items such as bike helmets, bike racks, and kayak paddles, and markets these items primarily to countries in North America and Western Europe. You need to finish the work on a quarterly presentation that outlines the progress of the company's newest technologies by adding animations, customizing the background, and using the Document Inspector.

a. Open the file PPT D-6.pptx from the drive and folder where you store your Data Files, and save the presentation as **FarNorth**.

b. Apply an appropriate design theme, then apply a new slide background style. Make sure the new background style is appropriate for the design theme you have chosen.

c. Apply the Box Out slide transition to all slides, then animate the following objects: the text on Slide 2, the clip art object on Slide 3, the table on Slide 4, and the chart on Slide 6. View the slide show to evaluate the effects you added and make adjustments as necessary.

d. Run the Document Inspector with all options selected, identify what items the Document Inspector finds, close the Document Inspector dialog box, then review the slides to find the items.

e. Add a slide at the end of the presentation that identifies the items the Document Inspector found.

f. Run the Document Inspector again and remove all items except the document properties.

**Advanced Challenge Exercise**

- Click the Rehearse Timings button on the Slide Sorter toolbar.
- Set slide timings for each slide in the presentation.
- Save new slide timings.

g. Add your name as a footer to the handouts, save your work, then run a slide show to evaluate your presentation.

h. Print the presentation as handouts (four slides per page), then close the presentation and exit PowerPoint.

# ▼ INDEPENDENT CHALLENGE 3

You work for JB & Associates Financial, a full service investment and pension firm. Your boss wants you to create a presentation on small business pension plan options to be published on the company Web site. You have completed adding the information to the presentation, now you need to add a design theme, format some information, add some animation effects, and add slide timings.

a. Open the file PPT D-7.pptx from the drive and folder where you store your Data Files, and save the presentation as **SBPlans**.

b. Apply an appropriate design theme.

c. Apply animation effects to the following objects: the shapes on Slide 3 and the text and clip art on Slide 5. View the slide show to evaluate the effects you added and make adjustments as necessary.

d. Convert the text on Slide 4 to a Basic Radial SmartArt graphic (Found in the Cycle category).

e. Apply the Polished style to the SmartArt graphic, then change the colors of the graphic to Colorful Range – Accent Colors 2 to 3

f. Switch to Slide 3, align the Sector and Quality arrow shapes to one another, then align the Allocation and Maturity arrow shapes to one another.

g. Adjust the aligned arrow shapes so they are centered on the Buy/Sell oval shape, then apply a 15 second timing to Slides 3–7 and a 5 second timing to Slides 1 and 2.

## Advanced Challenge Exercise

- Open the Slide Master view, select the last slide layout, then click the Insert Layout button.
- Click the Insert Placeholder button arrow, click Table, then drag a placeholder in the blank area of the master slide layout. (*Hint*: Draw the table placeholder so it takes up most of the blank space in the layout.)
- Return to Normal view, apply the new Custom Layout to Slides 6 and 7. Adjust the placeholder in Slide Master view if necessary.

**h.** Add your name as a footer to the handouts, save your work, then run a slide show to evaluate your presentation.

**i.** Print the presentation as handouts (four slides per page), then close the presentation and exit PowerPoint.

# ▼ REAL LIFE INDEPENDENT CHALLENGE

You work for the operations supervisor at the Southern State University student union. Create a presentation that you can eventually publish to the college Web site that describes all of the services offered at the student union.

**a.** Plan and create the slide presentation that describes the services and events offered at the student union. To help create content, use the student union at your school or use the Internet to locate information on college student unions. The presentation should contain at least six slides.

**b.** Use an appropriate design theme.

**c.** Add clip art and photographs available in the Clip Organizer to help create visual interest.

**d.** Save the presentation as **SSU Services** to the drive and folder where you store your Data Files. View the slide show and evaluate the contents of your presentation. Make any necessary adjustments.

**e.** Add transitions, animation effects, and timings to the presentation. View the slide show again to evaluate the effects you added.

**f.** Add your name as a footer to the handouts. Spell check, save, inspect, and print the presentation as handouts (four slides per  page). Compare your finished presentation to Figure D-20.

**g.** Create a template from this presentation. Delete unnecessary slides and objects, type appropriate sample text if necessary, then save the presentation as **SSU Services Template** to the drive and folder where you store your Data Files.

**h.** Close the presentation and exit PowerPoint.

**FIGURE D-20**

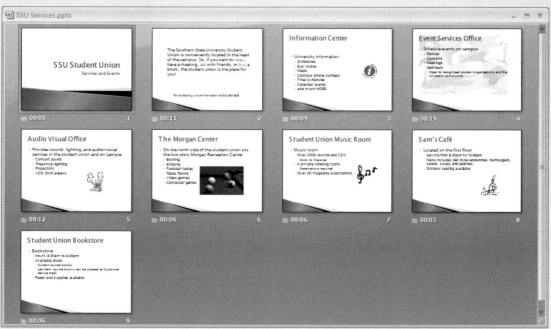

PowerPoint 2007

Open the file PPT D-8.pptx, then save the presentation as a template (.potx) with the filename **Island Travel Template** to the drive and folder where you store your Data Files. Change the presentation to look like Figures D-21 and D-22. Be sure to remove all unnecessary information, objects, and slides from the template presentation. Add your name as a footer to the slides.

**FIGURE D-21**

**FIGURE D-22**

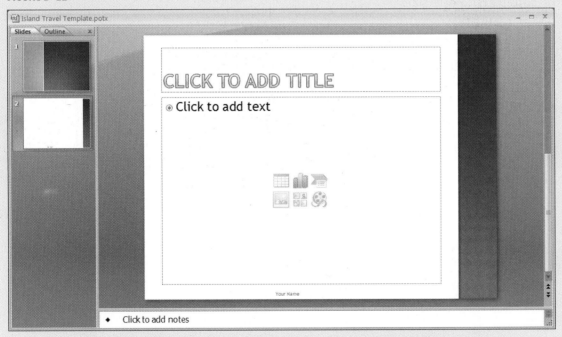

# Working with Advanced Tools and Masters

**Files You Will Need:**

PPT E-1.pptx
PPT E-2.pptx
PPT E-3.pptx
PPT E-4.pptx
PPT E-5.pptx
PPT E-6.pptx

Once you have learned the basics of creating a presentation and running a slide show, you are ready to learn more advanced features of PowerPoint. Learning to use advanced features like Connector shapes, the Format Painter tool, and customized slide layouts helps you create impressive presentations. Knowing how to modify masters allows you the freedom to customize the slides, handouts, and notes of your presentation.  As the assistant to Ellen Latsky, the European tour developer for Quest Specialty Travel, you have been working on a tour proposal presentation, which Ellen will give later in the year. After receiving some initial feedback from Ellen, you revise the presentation by enhancing some shapes, customizing animations, and customizing the master views.

**OBJECTIVES**

Draw and format connectors

Use advanced formatting tools

Customize animation effects

Create custom slide layouts

Format master text

Change master text indents

Adjust text objects

Customize Handout and Notes
   Masters

# Drawing and Formatting Connectors

PowerPoint has a number of connector tools that enable you to create three different types of connector lines or arrows—straight, elbow (bent), or curved. For example, use the connector tools to connect shapes with a line or arrow. Use the Curve tool to create a freeform curved line. Once you have drawn a line or connector, you can format it using Quick Styles, outline color, and effects. ▰▰▰▰ The Curved Arrow connector tool will work well to complete the diagram on Slide 4.

## STEPS

1. **Start PowerPoint, open the presentation** PPT E-1.pptx **from the drive and folder where you store your Data Files, save the presentation as** QuestE, **click the** View tab **on the Ribbon, click the** Arrange All button **in the Window group, then click the** Slide 4 thumbnail **in the Slides tab**
   Slide 4 of the presentation appears.

2. **Click the** Home tab **on the Ribbon, click the** Shapes button **in the Drawing group, in the Lines section click the** Curved Arrow Connector button ⎘, **then position** ╂ **on the top connection site** ▣ **of Shape 1**
   Notice that Shape 1 has six possible connection sites to anchor a line or arrow. See Figure E-1.

**TROUBLE**
If you accidentally release the mouse before you reach a connection site, an endpoint is created at the end of the connector. Drag the connector endpoint to the correct connection site.

3. **Drag the pointer to the** ▣ **on the bottom of** Shape 2
   Red handles (circles) appear at either end of the arrow connector, indicating that it is attached to the two shapes. The arrow has an adjustment handle (yellow diamond) which allows you to alter the path of the arrow.

4. **Position the** ⬉ **pointer over the arrow head, then drag the arrow to the** ▣ **on the left side of** Shape 2
   The arrow now flows from the top of Shape 1 to the left side of Shape 2.

5. **Click the** Shapes button, **right-click** ⎘ **in the Shapes gallery, then click** Lock Drawing Mode
   Locking the drawing mode allows you to draw the same shape over and over without having to select its button in the Shapes Gallery each time.

6. **Drag from the left** ▣ **on** Shape 2 **to the bottom** ▣ **on** Shape 3, **drag from the bottom** ▣ **on** Shape 3 **to the right** ▣ **on** Shape 4, **drag from the right** ▣ **on** Shape 4 **to the top** ▣ **on** Shape 1, **then press** [Esc]
   You created three more arrows. Pressing [Esc] unlocks the drawing mode.

7. **Right-click the** bottom-right arrow, **then click** Format Shape
   The Format Shape dialog box opens so you can format the connector arrow.

**QUICK TIP**
If you rearrange shapes that are joined with connector lines, the connector lines remain attached and move with the shapes.

8. **Type** 2 **in the Width text box, in the Arrow settings section click the** End type list arrow, **click the** Arrow icon, **click the** End size list arrow, **then click the** Arrow R Size 8 icon
   The style of the arrow changes to a more distinct style.

9. **In the left pane click** Shadow, **click the** Presets list arrow, **click the** Offset Diagonal Bottom Right icon, **click the** Distance down arrow **once, then in the left pane click** Line Color
   The shadow gives the arrow some depth. You can also change the color of the arrow.

10. **Click the** Color list arrow, **click** Red, Accent 3 **in the Theme Colors section, click** Close, **click in a blank area of the slide, then save the presentation**
    Compare your screen to Figure E-2.

**FIGURE E-1:** Shape showing connection sites

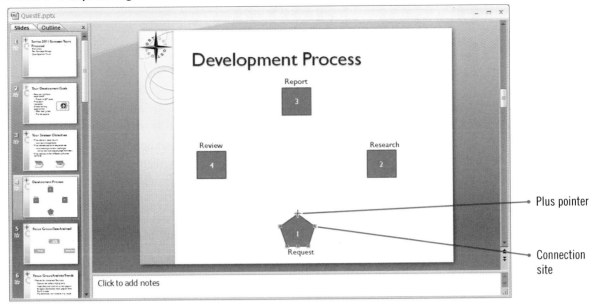

Plus pointer

Connection site

**FIGURE E-2:** Slide showing formatted connector arrow

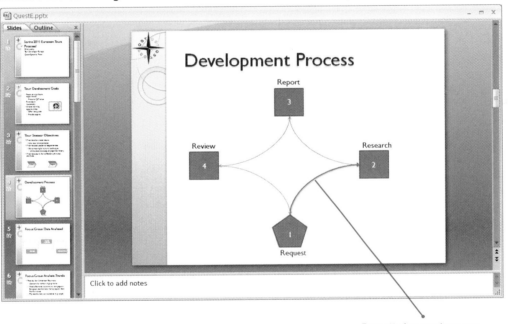

Formatted connector arrow

## Drawing a freeform shape

A freeform shape can consist of straight lines, freehand (or curved) lines, or a combination of the two. To draw a freeform shape, click the Shapes button in the Drawing group on the Ribbon, then click the Freeform button in the Lines section. Drag the pointer to draw the desired shape, then double-click when you are done. To draw a straight line with the Freeform tool, click where you want to begin the line, drag the pointer, then double-click to deactivate the Freeform tool. To edit a freeform object, right-click the object, then click Edit Points on the shortcut menu.

# Using Advanced Formatting Tools

With PowerPoint's advanced formatting tools, you can change attributes such as fill texture, 3-D effects, and shadow for text and shapes. If you have multiple objects that you want to format, you can use the Format Painter to pick up the attributes from one object and apply them to another object. ▰▰▰▰ You decide to use the advanced formatting tools to enhance the diagram on Slide 4.

## STEPS

1. **Click the red arrow, double-click the Format Painter button ⬧ in the Clipboard group, then position the Format Painter pointer ⬧ over one of the blue arrows**

   The Format Painter tool "picks up" the attributes of an object and copies them to the next object you select. Double-clicking the Format Painter button allows you to apply the same formatting to multiple objects on the slide without having to reselect the tool.

2. **Click each of the three blue arrows, then press [Esc]**

   Now all of the arrow connectors are formatted alike as shown in Figure E-3.

3. **Right-click Shape 1, click Format Shape on the shortcut menu to display the Format Shape dialog box, click the Picture or texture fill option button, then click the Texture list arrow**

   The Format Shape dialog box opens and the texture gallery appears.

4. **Click the Brown marble square, drag the dialog box title bar to move the dialog box off of Shape 1, then click 3-D Format in the left pane**

   The brown marble texture fills the shape. The 3-D Format options appear in the dialog box.

5. **In the Bevel section click the Top list arrow, click the Slope icon, in the Surface section click the Lighting list arrow, then in the Special section click the Two Point icon**

   The lighting effect defines the bevel effect better.

6. **In the Depth section type 20 in the Depth text box, then click 3-D Rotation in the left pane**

   Changing the depth lengthens the effect from the default of 0 points to 20 points.

7. **Click the Presets list arrow, in the Perspective section click the Perspective Left icon in the top row, then click Close**

   The shape changes perspective and you can see the effect and the depth of the effect better. The number in the shape is hard to see, but you can apply formatting to make the characters more visible.

8. **Click the Font list arrow in the Font group, then click Arial Black**

   The text in Shape 1 is now easy to read.

9. **Double-click ⬧ in the Clipboard group, click each of the three remaining shapes, then click ⬧ again to turn off the Format Painter**

   Now all the shapes on the slide have the same fill, font, and 3D effects.

10. **Click in a blank area of the slide, then save your changes**

    Compare your screen with Figure E-4.

**FIGURE E-3:** Slide showing formatted connector arrows

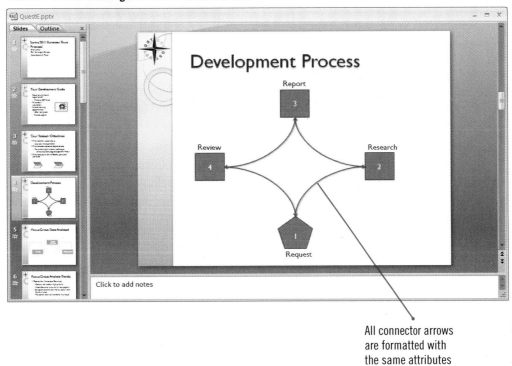

All connector arrows
are formatted with
the same attributes

**FIGURE E-4:** Slide showing formatted shapes

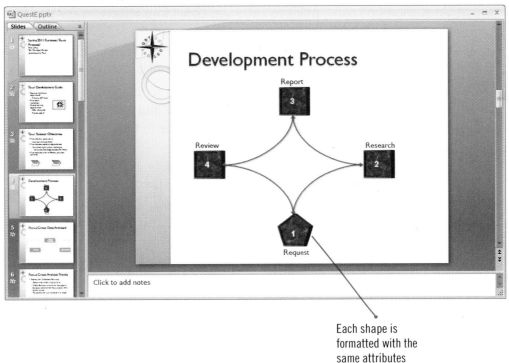

Each shape is
formatted with the
same attributes

## Creating columns in a text box

In PowerPoint 2007, you have the ability to create columns within text objects when the information you are working with fits better in a column format. Select the text object, click the Columns button in the Paragraph group on the Home tab, then click either Two Columns, Three Columns, or More Columns. The More Columns option allows you to set up to 16 columns and customize the spacing between columns. You can display the ruler to set specific widths for the columns and further customize the columns.

# Customizing Animation Effects

Animating objects allows you to focus on key information and control how information flows on the slide during a slide show. The simplest way to animate an object is to apply a standard animation effect using the Animate list arrow in the Animations group; however, you can apply and customize other animation effects using the Custom Animation task pane which includes animation effects not found in the Animate list on the Ribbon. You can customize effect options including starting time, direction, and speed. You decide to apply animation effects to the arrows and shapes on Slide 4 and then customize the effects to highlight the shapes.

## STEPS

1. **Click Shape 1, click the Animations tab on the Ribbon, then click the Custom Animation button in the Animations group**

   The Custom Animation task pane opens.

2. **Click Add Effect in the Custom Animation task pane, point to Emphasis, click More Effects, in the Subtle section click Flash Bulb, then click OK**

   As soon as you select an animation effect, the effect is previewed on the slide and an animation tag appears next to the shape.

3. **Click the red arrow between Shape 1 and Shape 2, click Add Effect in the Custom Animation task pane, point to Entrance, click More Effects, in the Basic section click Strips, then click OK**

   An animation effect is applied to the connector arrow from Shape 1 to Shape 2. Compare your screen with Figure E-5.

> **TROUBLE**
>
> If you want to delete the animation effect, select the effect in the Custom Animation task pane, then click Remove.

4. **Apply the Emphasis Flash Bulb animation effect to Shape 2, apply the Entrance Strips animation effect to the arrow between Shape 2 and Shape 3, then apply the Flash Bulb and Strips animation effects in alternating order to the rest of the lines and shapes in the diagram**

   When you are finished, each shape has the Flash Bulb animation effect and each arrow has the Strips animation effect. There are a total of eight animation effects on the slide.

5. **Click the Play button at the bottom of the Custom Animation task pane**

   Three of the arrows do not move in the correct direction. The direction of an animation effect is set by default but can be changed.

6. **Click the arrow between Shape 1 and Shape 2, click the Direction list arrow in the Custom Animation task pane, click Right Up, click the arrow between Shape 2 and Shape 3, click the Direction list arrow click Left Up, click the arrow between Shape 4 and Shape 1, click the Direction list arrow, click Right Down, then click Play**

   The animation effects applied to the arrows now play correctly. You can also adjust the speed of the animations.

7. **Press [Ctrl], in the Custom Animation task pane click items 2, 4, 6, and 8 in the animation list, release [Ctrl], click the Speed list arrow, click Fast, then click Play**

   All the animations play the way you want them too. Compare your screen to Figure E-6.

8. **Click the Custom Animation task pane Close button ☒, then save your changes**

**FIGURE E-5:** Slide showing applied animation effects

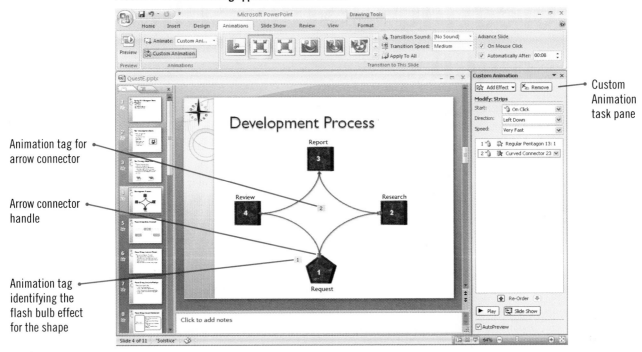

Custom Animation task pane

Animation tag for arrow connector

Arrow connector handle

Animation tag identifying the flash bulb effect for the shape

**FIGURE E-6:** Slide showing completed animation effects

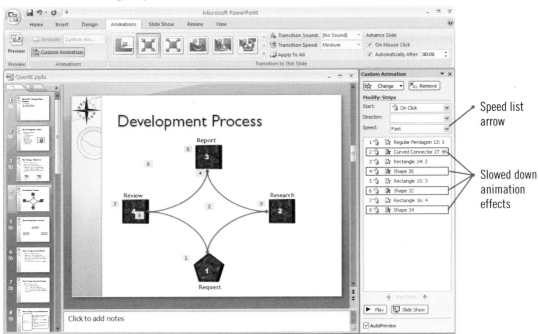

Speed list arrow

Slowed down animation effects

## Understanding animation timings

Each animated object on a slide has a starting time in relation to the other animated objects. There are three different starting time options: Start On Click, Start With Previous, and Start After Previous. The Start On Click timing option starts the animation effect when you click the mouse. A small mouse icon appears next to the animation effect in the animation list when this timing option is applied. The Start With Previous timing option begins the animation effect at the same time as the previous effect in the animation list, so two or more animation effects play at once. This timing option does not display an icon in the animation list. The Start After Previous timing option, which displays a clock icon in the animation list, begins the animation effect immediately after the previous effect in the animation list finishes playing without clicking the mouse.

# Creating Custom Slide Layouts

The standard slide layouts supplied in PowerPoint are adequate to create the majority of slides for your presentation. However, if you are consistently modifying a standard slide layout for presentations, having a custom slide layout that you can reuse would be helpful. To create a custom slide layout, you choose from eight different placeholders to draw on the slide, including text, chart, and media placeholders. You create and save custom slide layouts in Slide Master view, which then become a part of the presentation. 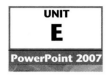 You need to create a custom slide layout for the presentation that displays picture thumbnails on the slide that you can use as navigation buttons during a slide show.

## STEPS

1. **Click the View tab on the Ribbon, click the Slide Master button in the Presentation Views group, right-click a blank area of the slide, then click Ruler**

   Slide Master view opens and the ruler displays.

2. **Click the last slide layout in the left pane, then click the Insert Layout button in the Edit Master group**

   A new slide layout is added to the presentation and appears in the Slide pane with a title text placeholder and footer placeholders as shown in Figure E-7. The new slide layout contains all of the slide background elements associated with the current theme. The default placeholders are not needed.

3. **In the Master Layout group, click the Title check box, click the Footers check box, then click the Insert Placeholder button arrow**

   The default placeholders are removed from the slide layout. The eight available placeholder options appear in the placeholder gallery.

4. **Click Picture, then position ✛ on the slide so the pointer is lined up at the 2" marks on both the vertical and horizontal rulers**

   As you move the pointer on the slide its position is identified on the rulers by dotted lines.

5. **Drag a box down and to the right until the pointer is lined up with the 0" marks on the rulers**

   A 2" picture placeholder appears on the slide. You can duplicate the placeholder.

6. **Click the Home tab on the Ribbon, click the Paste button arrow in the Clipboard group, click Duplicate, then duplicate the picture placeholder two more times**

   There are four picture placeholders on the slide.

QUICK TIP

To position place-holders precisely on the slide, use Guides and the Align com-mands to help you.

7. **Drag each placeholder to a position on the slide as shown in Figure E-8, then click the Slide Master tab on the Ribbon**

   The placeholders are arranged on the slide layout.

8. **Click the Title check box in the Master Layout group, then click the Rename button in the Edit Master group**

   The title text placeholder is added back to the slide layout, and the Rename Layout dialog box opens.

QUICK TIP

The new Picture slide layout also appears in the Layout gallery.

9. **Type Picture, click Rename, then position the pointer over the slide layout thumbnail**

   The new name of the custom slide layout appears in the ScreenTip.

10. **Right-click a blank area of the slide, click Ruler, click the Normal button 🔲 on the status bar, then save your changes**

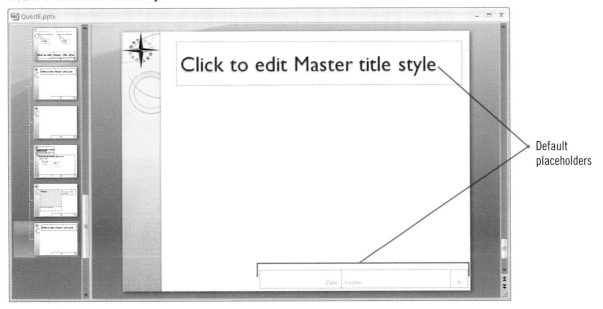

Default placeholders

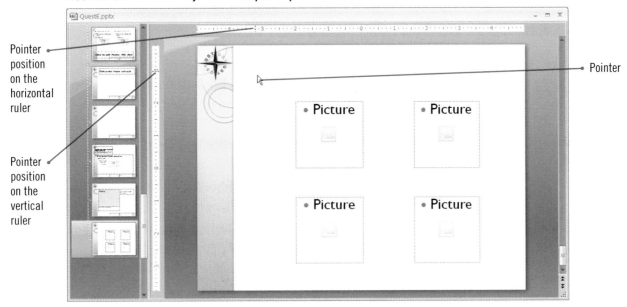

Pointer position on the horizontal ruler

Pointer position on the vertical ruler

Pointer

## Restoring the Slide Master layout

If the Slide Master is missing a placeholder, you can click the Master Layout button in the Master Layout group to reapply the place-holder. Clicking the Master Layout button opens the Master Layout dialog box, as shown in Figure E-9. Click the placeholder check box to reapply the placeholder. To restore a slide layout in Slide Master view, click the Insert Placeholder button arrow in the Master Layout group, click the desired type of placeholder, then draw the place-holder on the Slide Master layout.

FIGURE E-9: Master Layout dialog box

PowerPoint 2007

# Formatting Master Text

To ensure that you use a consistent blend of fonts and font styles throughout the presentation, you should format slide text using standard theme fonts or make changes to the text placeholders in Slide Master view. A font theme defines two fonts—a major font (for headings) and a minor font (for body text). The fonts used in a theme can be the same font or two contrasting fonts. You can also make specific changes to master text, by opening the Slide Master view and changing the text color, style, size, and bullet type. When you change a bullet type, you can use a character symbol from a font, a picture from the Clip Gallery (or other source), or an image that you scan into your computer. You decide to make a few formatting changes to the master text placeholder of your presentation.

## STEPS

1. **Click the Design tab on the Ribbon, click the Fonts button in the Themes group, slowly move your pointer over the visible font themes in the gallery, click the down scroll arrow twice, then click Equity**

   The font theme for the whole presentation changes from the Solstice theme to the Equity theme. When you change a theme, whether it's the font theme, color theme, effects theme, or design theme, you actually change the Slide Master. You like the new font theme, but decide to make some minor changes in Slide Master view.

2. **Press [Shift], click the Normal button 🖳 on the status bar, release [Shift], then click the Solstice Slide Master thumbnail (first thumbnail) in the left pane**

   Slide Master view appears with the Slide Master displayed in the Slide pane.

3. **Right-click Click to edit Master text styles in the master text placeholder, click the Bullets button list arrow 📇 on the Mini toolbar, then click Bullets and Numbering**

   The Bullets and Numbering dialog box opens. The Bulleted tab is selected; the Numbered tab is used to create sequentially numbered or lettered bullets.

4. **Click Customize, click the Font list arrow, then click Webdings**

   The available bullet choices change.

5. **Scroll to the top of the dialog box, click the symbol shown in Figure E-10, then click OK**

   The new symbol appears in the Bullets and Numbering dialog box.

6. **Click the Color list arrow, in the Theme Colors section click Indigo, Accent 6, click the Size down arrow until 65 appears, then click OK**

   The color and size of the new bullet in the first level of the master text placeholder is modified.

7. **Click the Normal button 🖳 on the status bar, then click the Slide 2 thumbnail in the Slides pane**

   You see how the changes affect the body text bullets in Normal view. Compare your screen to Figure E-11.

8. **Save your changes**

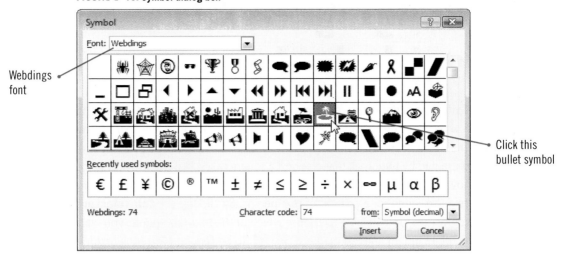

Webdings font

Click this bullet symbol

FIGURE E-11: Slide showing new bullets

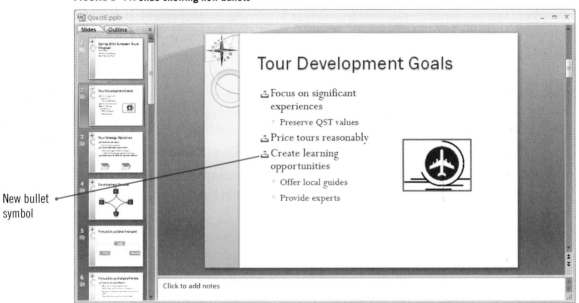

New bullet symbol

## Exceptions to the Slide Master

If you change the format of text on a slide and then apply a different theme to the presentation, the slide that you formatted retains the text formatting changes you made rather than taking the new theme formats. These format changes that differ from the Slide Master are known as **exceptions**. Exceptions can only be changed on the individual slides where they occur. For example, you might change the font and size of a particular text object on a slide to make it stand out and then decide later to add a different theme to your presentation. The text you formatted before you applied the theme is an exception, and it is unaffected by the new theme. Another way to override the Slide Master is to remove the background graphics on one or more slides. You might want to do this to get a clearer view of your slide text. Click the Design tab, then click the Hide Background Graphics check box in the Background group to select it.

# Changing Master Text Indents

Master text and content placeholders have nine levels of text, called **indent levels**. You can modify indent levels using PowerPoint's ruler. For example, you can change the space between a bullet and text of an indent level or change the position of the whole indent level. The position of each indent level on the ruler is represented by two small triangles and a square called **indent markers**. You can modify an indent level by moving these indent markers on the ruler. You can also set tabs on the horizontal ruler, which identifies where a text indent or a column of text begins. By clicking the **tab selector** located at the far left of the horizontal ruler, you are able to choose which of the four tab options you want to use. Table E-1 describes PowerPoint's indent and tab markers. To better emphasize the text in the master text placeholder, you change the first two indent levels.

## STEPS

1. **Press [Shift], then click the Normal button on the status bar, release [Shift], then click the Solstice Slide Master thumbnail (first thumbnail) in the left pane**
   Slide Master view opens.

2. **Click anywhere in the first line of text in the master text placeholder, click the View tab on the Ribbon, then click the Ruler check box in the Show/Hide group**
   The horizontal and vertical rulers for the master text placeholder appear. The indent markers, on the horizontal ruler, are set so that the first line of text in each level—in this case, the bullet—begins to the left of subsequent lines of text. This is called a **hanging indent**.

**TROUBLE**
If you accidentally drag an indent marker past the ½" mark, click the Undo button on the Quick Access toolbar.

3. **Position the pointer over the Hanging Indent marker, then drag to the ½" mark on the ruler**
   The space between the first indent level bullet and text increases. Compare your screen to Figure E-12.

4. **Click anywhere in the second line of text in the master text placeholder, then drag the Left indent marker to the ⅞" position shown in Figure E-13**
   The whole indent level moves to the right.

5. **Click the Normal button on the status bar, then click the Slide 7 thumbnail in the Slides pane**
   Slide Master view closes and Slide 7 appears, showing the indent changes in the body text object. A left tab stop on the ruler will allow you to move a word and align it with text above it.

6. **Click to the left of the word combined in the body text object to place the insertion point, then click under the 2 in the horizontal ruler**
   A left-aligned tab appears in the ruler.

7. **Press [Tab]**
   The word "combined" moves to the right and is aligned with the text above it as shown in Figure E-14.

8. **Click the Ruler check box in the Show/Hide group, then save your changes**
   The rulers close and are no longer visible.

**FIGURE E-12:** First-level text with moved hanging indent marker

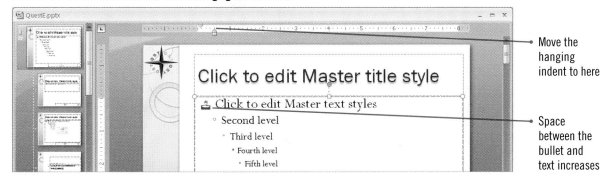

Move the hanging indent to here

Space between the bullet and text increases

**FIGURE E-13:** Slide showing moved second-level indent

Left indent marker

Indent level moves to the right

**FIGURE E-14:** Slide showing left tab stop

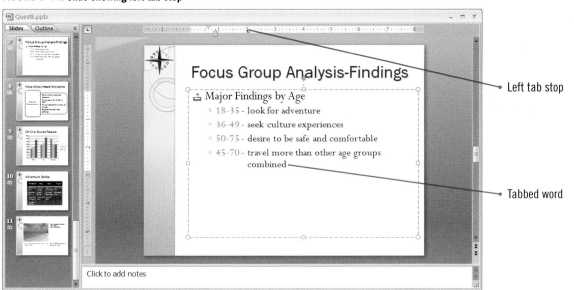

Left tab stop

Tabbed word

**TABLE E-1:** Indent and Tab Markers

| symbol | name | function |
| --- | --- | --- |
| ▽ | First line indent marker | Controls the position of the first line of text in an indent level |
| △ | Hanging indent marker | Controls the position of the hanging indent |
| ▭ | Left indent marker | Controls the position of subsequent lines of text in an indent level |
| L | Left-aligned tab | Aligns tab text on the left |
| ⊥ | Center-aligned tab | Aligns tab text in the center |
| ⌟ | Right-aligned tab | Aligns tab text on the right |
| ⊥ | Decimal-aligned tab | Aligns tab text on a decimal point |

# Adjusting Text Objects

You have complete control over the placement of text in PowerPoint, whether the text is in a shape or in a text object. All text in PowerPoint is created within a text box, which has **margins** that determine the distance between the edge of the text and all four edges of the text box. The space between lines of text or bullets can also be modified. There are two types of text spacing in PowerPoint: paragraph spacing and leading (rhymes with "wedding"). **Paragraph spacing** is the space before and after paragraphs (bullet levels). **Leading** refers to the amount of space between lines of text within the same paragraph (bullet level). Using the text alignment feature, you can move text within text boxes or shapes. You decide to move the text margin in the shapes on Slide 3 and then change paragraph spacing of the text object on Slide 7.

## STEPS

1. **Click the Home tab on the Ribbon, click the Slide 3 thumbnail in the Slides tab, right-click a blank area of the slide, then click Ruler**
   Slide 3 appears in the slide pane with the rulers showing.

2. **Right-click the text Aim in the left arrow, click Format Shape on the shortcut menu, then drag the Format Shape dialog box to the right so you can see the indent markers on the ruler**
   When you right-click the text in the shape, the individual object is selected within the grouped object and the indent markers for the text appear in the ruler.

3. **Click Text Box in the left pane, in the Internal margin section click the Left up arrow until 0.3" appears, then click Close**
   Compare your screen to Figure E-15. The text margin moves to the right in the arrow and the text is centered in the shape.

4. **Right-click the text Higher in the right arrow, click Format Shape on the shortcut menu, then click Text Box in the left pane**
   The Format Shape dialog box opens.

5. **Click the Left up arrow until 0.3" appears, click the Wrap text in shape check box to remove the check mark, then click Close**
   The text margin is changed in the arrow shape. In order for the text not to automatically wrap within the shape, you turned the wrapping feature off.

6. **Click the Slide 7 thumbnail in the Slides tab, select the four second-level bullets in the body text object, click the Line Spacing button  in the Paragraph group, then click Line Spacing Options**
   The Paragraph dialog box opens.

7. **In the Spacing section type 24 in the Before text box, type 12 in the After text box, then click OK**
   The spacing before and after each bullet on Slide 7 increases.

8. **Click the Align Text button  in the Paragraph group, click More Options, in the Text layout section click the Vertical alignment list arrow, click Middle Centered, then click Close**
   All of the text is aligned to the middle center of the text box. Compare your screen to Figure E-16.

9. **Right-click a blank area of the slide, click Ruler to close the ruler, then save your changes**

**FIGURE E-15: Slide showing changed text margin**

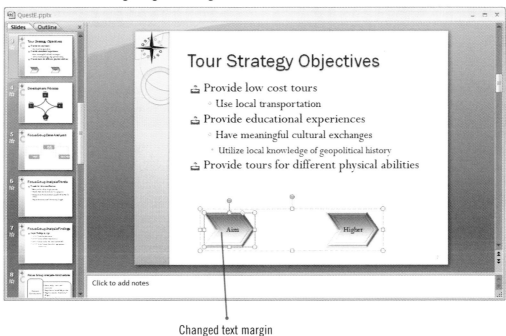

Changed text margin

**FIGURE E-16: Slide showing changed line spacing**

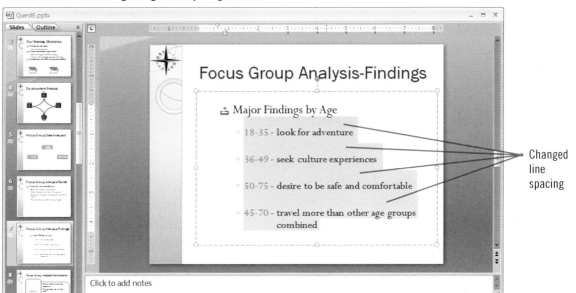

Changed line spacing

## More on text spacing

The differences between paragraph spacing and leading can be confusing if you aren't used to working with text layouts, so let's look at the pages in this book for help. This paragraph you are reading has space between the lines of text; that space is called line spacing or leading. Now, look at the numbered steps of this lesson. The space between each numbered step is an example of paragraph spacing. So, when you add a hard return to create a new paragraph, that space is paragraph spacing. Paragraph spacing is often larger than leading, which helps distinguish paragraphs from individual lines of text within a paragraph.

# Customizing Handout and Notes Masters

It is often helpful to provide your audience with supplemental materials to use during a presentation. Creating handouts for your audience provides them a way to follow along and take notes during your presentation and keep for future use. As the presenter, creating notes pages that you can refer to while giving the presentation can be extremely useful, especially when your presentation is complex or detailed. Before you create handouts or notes pages you might want to customize them to fit your specific needs. ░░░░░ Ellen Latsky has asked you to prepare some supplemental materials for this presentation. You customize the Handout Master by changing the slides per page and the background style. Then you change the Notes Master by changing the page setup and the notes page orientation. Finally, you print both handouts and notes pages.

## STEPS

1. **Click the** View tab **on the Ribbon, then click the** Handout Master button **in the** **Presentation Views group**
   The presentation's Handout Master view appears, showing a page with six large empty placeholders that represent where the slides will appear when you print handouts. There are four small placeholders, one in each corner of the slide, which are the header, footer, date, and number placeholders. Notice that the date placeholder displays today's date.

2. **Click the** Background Styles button **in the Background group, then click** Style 9
   When you print handouts on a color printer, they will have a gradient fill background.

3. **Click the** Slides Per Page button **in the Page Setup group, then click** 3 Slides
   Three slide placeholders appear on the left side of the handout as shown in Figure E-17.

**QUICK TIP**
To change the orientation of the slides on the handout, click the Slide Orientation button in the Page Setup group.

4. **Click the** Header placeholder, **drag the** Zoom Slider **to 100%, type** European Tour **Proposal, press [Pg Dn], click the** Footer placeholder, **then type** Your Name
   Now your handouts are ready to print.

5. **Click the** Fit slide to current window button 🔲 **on the status bar, click the** Office **button, click** Print, **in the Print what list box click** Handouts, **in the Slides per page list box click** 3, **then click** OK
   Handouts of the presentation print using the options you've set.

6. **Click the** Close Master View button **in the Close group, click the** View tab **on the Ribbon, then click the** Notes Master button **in the Presentation Views group**
   Notes Master view opens showing four corner placeholders—one each for the header, footer, date, and number—a large notes text box placeholder, and a large Slide Master image placeholder.

7. **Click the** Notes Page Orientation button **in the Page Setup group, then click** Landscape
   The page orientation changes to landscape. Notice that all of the text placeholders are now stretched out. Compare your screen to Figure E-18.

8. **Click the** Office button, **click** Print, **in the Print what list box click** Notes Pages, **then click** OK
   Notes pages of the presentation print in landscape orientation.

9. **Click the** Close Master View button **in the Close group, save your work, then exit** **PowerPoint**

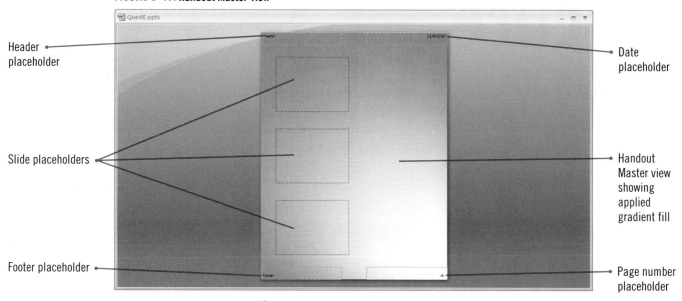

Header placeholder

Slide placeholders

Footer placeholder

Date placeholder

Handout Master view showing applied gradient fill

Page number placeholder

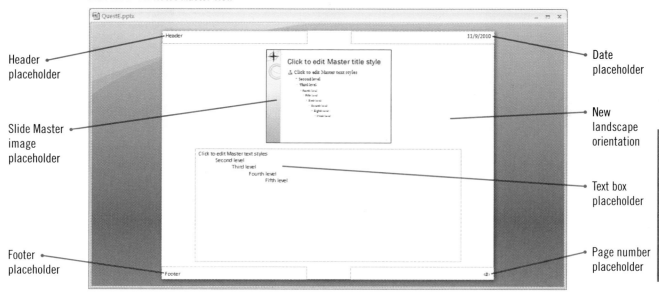

Header placeholder

Slide Master image placeholder

Footer placeholder

Date placeholder

New landscape orientation

Text box placeholder

Page number placeholder

**PowerPoint 2007**

## Creating handouts in Microsoft Office Word

Sometimes it's helpful to use a word processing program like Microsoft Office Word to create detailed handouts or notes pages. You might also want to create a Word document based on the outline of your presentation. To send your presentation to Word, click the Office button, point to Publish, then click Create Handouts in Microsoft Office Word. The Send to Microsoft Office Word dialog box opens and provides you with five document layout options from which to choose. There are two layouts that include notes entered in the Notes pane. Select a layout, then click OK. Word opens and a new document opens with your inserted presentation, using the layout you selected. To send just the text of your presentation to Word, click the Outline only document layout.

# Practice

If you have a SAM user profile, you may have access to hands-on instruction, practice, and assessment of the skills covered in this unit. Log in to your SAM account (http://sam2007.course.com/) to launch any assigned training activities or exams that relate to the skills covered in this unit.

## ▼ CONCEPTS REVIEW

**Label each of the elements of the PowerPoint window shown in Figure E-19.**

FIGURE E-19

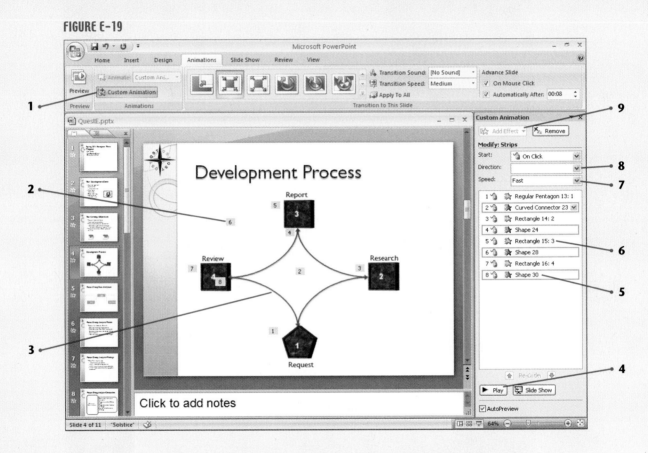

**Match each of the terms with the statement that describes its function.**

10. **Format Painter tool**  a. Identifies where the text indent or column of text begins
11. **Tab**  b. A text level in a text object, usually started with a bullet
12. **Indent level**  c. Picks up attributes from an object and applies them to another object
13. **Hanging indent**  d. The space between lines of text
14. **Leading**  e. The space after a hard return
15. **Paragraph spacing**  f. The first line of text begins to the left of subsequent lines of text

## Select the best answer from the list of choices.

**16. What appears at either end of a line or arrow that indicates it's attached to two shapes?**

   **a.** Red handles                            **c.** Attachment sites

   **b.** Anchor points                          **d.** Connection handles

**17. What is a connection site?**

   **a.** An attachment point for a placeholder in a custom layout

   **b.** The anchor point of a text box

   **c.** The end of a connector arrow

   **d.** The attachment point on a shape for a connector

**18. The small triangles and square that represent the position of each level in a text placeholder are:**

   **a.** Ruler marks.                            **c.** Indent markers.

   **b.** Indent levels.                          **d.** Tabs.

**19. Which of the following statements about connectors is not correct?**

   **a.** The line connector has a rotate handle in the middle of it to adjust the line's path.

   **b.** You can attach a connector to different points on a shape.

   **c.** You can draw more than one connector at the same time by locking the drawing mode.

   **d.** Rearranging shapes connected with connectors moves the connectors to better connection sites.

**20. In PowerPoint, tabs:**

   **a.** Determine the location of margins.         **c.** Identify where a text indent begins.

   **b.** Determine spacing between lines of text.    **d.** Can be only left- or center-aligned.

**21. The Format Painter button:**

   **a.** Changes the order of shapes on a slide.

   **b.** Is the feature you use to paint objects in PowerPoint.

   **c.** Picks up and applies formatting attributes from one object or slide to another.

   **d.** Allows you to change the type of shape.

# ▼ SKILLS REVIEW

**1. Draw and format connectors.**

   **a.** Start PowerPoint and open the presentation PPT E-2.pptx, then save it as **BookShop** to the drive and folder where you store your Data Files.

   **b.** Go to Slide 4, click the Shapes button in the Drawing group, right-click Elbow Arrow Connector, then click Lock Drawing Mode.

   **c.** Position the pointer over the left connection site of the Plant shape, then drag to the top connection site of the Regional Warehouse shape.

   **d.** Position the pointer over the right connection site of the Plant shape, drag to the top connection site of the Individual Stores shape, then press [Esc].

   **e.** Click the Shapes button, click Line, position the pointer over the right connection site of the Regional Warehouse shape, then drag to the left connection site of the Individual Stores shape.

   **f.** Select all three connectors, right-click one of the connectors, click Format Object, make the connectors 2 pt wide and change the line color to Black, click Close, then deselect the objects.

   **g.** Right-click the connector between Regional Warehouse shape and the Individual Stores shape, click Format Shape, click the Dash Type list arrow, click Dash Dot, then click Close.

   **h.** Change the Elbow Arrow connectors' arrow heads End type to Diamond Arrow and their End size to Arrow R Size 9.

   **i.** Save the presentation.

**2. Use advanced formatting tools.**

   **a.** Go to Slide 1.

   **b.** Right-click the text object in the lower-right corner of the slide, then click Format Shape.

   **c.** Click the Gradient fill option button, click the Preset colors list arrow, then click Moss.

   **d.** Click Line Style in the left pane, then click the Width up arrow until 3 pt appears.

    **e.** Click Shadow in the left pane, click the Presets list arrow, click Offset Bottom, click the Distance up arrow until 5 pt appears, then click Close.

    **f.** Double-click the Format Painter button in the Clipboard group to pick up the format of the selected text box on the title slide, apply it to each of the diamond objects on Slide 4, then press [Esc].

    **g.** Save your changes.

**3. Customize animation effects.**

    **a.** Click the Animations tab, click the Plant shape, click the Custom Animation button, then click Add Effect.

    **b.** Point to Entrance, click More Effects, click Diamond, then click OK.

    **c.** Select the arrow connectors, add the Strips Entrance effect, then select the right arrow connector.

    **d.** Click the Direction list arrow, click Right Down, then click Play.

    **e.** Select the Regional Warehouse and Individual Stores shapes, add the Dissolve In Entrance effect, add the Flash Bulb Emphasis effect, then click Play.

    **f.** Select the dotted line, add the Ease In Entrance effect, then click Play.

    **g.** Select the arrow connectors, change the animation speed to Fast, then click Play.

    **h.** Close the task pane, then save your changes.

**4. Create custom slide layouts.**

    **a.** Switch to Slide Master view, then click the last slide layout in the left pane.

    **b.** Display the ruler and the drawing guides, then insert a new layout.

    **c.** Add a 3" square Media placeholder, move the vertical guide left to 4.49, move the horizontal guide up to 0.98, then move the Media placeholder to the intersection of the guides.

    **d.** Move the vertical guide right to 0.47 to the left of the zero mark, add a 4" × 3" Table placeholder, then move the placeholder to the intersection of the guides.

    **e.** Name the custom slide layout Media Table, turn off guides, then save your work.

**5. Format master text.**

    **a.** Click the Flow Slide Master in the left pane, then make the first-level bulleted item in the master text placeholder bold.

    **b.** Change the bullet symbol of the first-level bullet to a character bullet. In the Wingdings character set, select character code 38, the sixth bullet from the left in the first row.

    **c.** Use the Bullets and Numbering dialog box to set the size of the bullet to 75% of the text.

    **d.** Change the bullet color to the Theme Color Green, Accent 5.

    **e.** Change the bullet symbol color of the second indent level to the Theme Color Dark Teal, Text 2.

    **f.** Save your changes.

**6. Change Master text indents.**

    **a.** Move the hanging indent marker of the first-level bullet to the ½" mark on the ruler and left indent marker of the second-level bullet as shown in Figure E-20.

**FIGURE E-20**

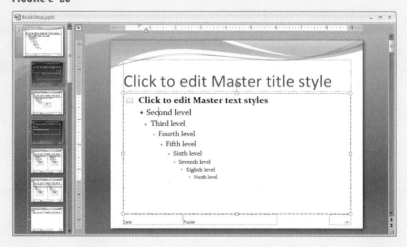

    **b.** Hide the rulers, switch to Normal view, then save the presentation.

**7. Adjust text objects.**

    **a.** Press [Shift], right-click anywhere in the body text object on Slide 2, then click Format Shape on the shortcut menu.

    **b.** Click Text Box in the left pane, then change the vertical alignment of the text to Top Centered.

    **c.** Adjust the internal margin on the left and right sides to 0.5".

    **d.** Click the Resize shape to fit text option button, then click Close.

# ▼ SKILLS REVIEW (CONTINUED)

e. Figure E-21 shows you the completed presentation.

f. Save your changes.

8. **Customize Handout and Notes Masters.**

a. Switch to Handout Master view.

b. Change the slides per page to 4 slides, then change the handout orientation to Landscape.

c. In the header text placeholder type **BookShop**, then in the footer text placeholder type **Your Name**.

d. Close Handout Master view, then switch to Notes Master view

e. Change the background style to Style 5, in the header text placeholder type **Product Report**, then in the footer text placeholder type **Your Name**.

f. Close Notes Master view, save your changes, then print the presentation as handouts, 2 slides per page.

g. Close the presentation and exit PowerPoint.

**FIGURE E-21**

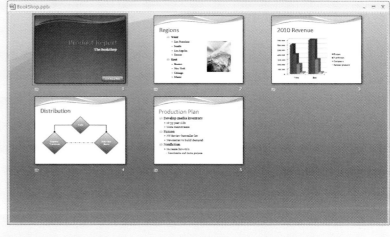

# ▼ INDEPENDENT CHALLENGE 1

You work in marketing at ZZ101 Records in Los Angeles, California. ZZ101 Records is a record label that specializes in alternative music and hip hop. As a growing record company, your business is looking for investment capital to expand its business markets and increase sales. It is your responsibility to develop a presentation that the owners can present to potential investors. You have been working on the content of the presentation and now you are ready to add custom animations and customize Slide Master text.

a. Open the presentation PPT E-3.pptx from the drive and folder where you store your Data Files, then save it as **ZZ101**.

b. Preview the presentation in Slide Show view.

c. Bold the first-level indent text, then change the bullet style in the first-level indent. See Figure E-22. (*Hint*: The bullet is a Webdings font (Character code 43) and is 85% of text size.)

d. Convert the text on Slide 4 to a SmartArt graphic using the Vertical Box List SmartArt graphic layout, then apply the Moderate Effect SmartArt Style to the graphic.

e. Select Slide 6, create at least two shapes connected by connectors and format all of the objects using advanced formatting techniques you learned in the lesson.

f. Use the Custom Animation task pane to apply animation effects to objects and text on at least three slides, then preview the presentation in Slide Show view.

g. Add your name to the notes and handouts footers, save the presentation, then print the slides of your final presentation as handouts in pure black and white.

h. Close the presentation and exit PowerPoint.

**FIGURE E-22**

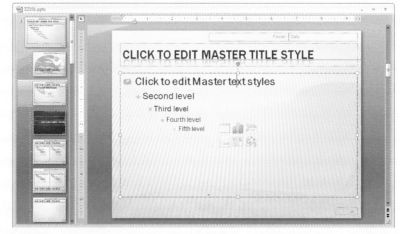

# ▼ INDEPENDENT CHALLENGE 2

You are the owner of The Reef Catering in Melbourne, New South Wales, Australia. You have built your business on private parties, wedding receptions, and special events over the last five years. To expand, you decide to pursue the business and hotel markets. Use PowerPoint to develop a presentation that you can use to gain corporate catering accounts.

a. Open the presentation PPT E-4.pptx from the drive and folder where you store your Data Files, then save it as **Reef**.

b. View the Oriel Slide Master slide. Change the Font theme to Foundry, then change the bullet in the first-level indent level to an arrow bullet.

c. Search PowerPoint clip art and add a koala bear to the Oriel Slide Master and the Title Slide Layout. Format the clip art as necessary.

d. Connect the shapes on Slide 4 using arrow connectors. Draw an Elbow arrow connector between each shape formatted with a 3 pt dash line and an Arrow R Size 7 end arrow style.

e. Switch to Slide 2 and change the text alignment and line spacing to create the best look.

f. Change the left internal margin of each shape on Slide 4 to 0".

g. Create a new custom slide layout using three different placeholders, then save the new layout as **Custom1**.

h. View the presentation in Slide Show view. Add your name to the handouts footer.

i. Save and print the presentation as handouts, 2 slides per page.

## Advanced Challenge Exercise

■ Switch to Slide 5, then select the body text object.

■ Click the Home tab on the Ribbon, then click the Columns button in the Paragraph group.

■ Click Two Columns.

■ Save the presentation as **Reef ACE** to the drive and folder where you store your Data Files, then print the presentation as handouts, 2 slides per page.

j. Close the presentation and exit PowerPoint.1

# ▼ INDEPENDENT CHALLENGE 3

You are a computer game designer for The Zone, an Internet interactive game developer. One of your responsibilities is to develop new interactive game concepts and present the information at a company meeting. Complete the presentation provided, which promotes two new interactive Internet game concepts you've developed. Use the following game ideas in your presentation or create two of your own.

• **US Forces I** is an interactive World War II game where you play an American serviceman. You have the option to play with and against others online to achieve one of six different objectives.

• **TopSecret** is an interactive contemporary action/adventure game where you create a secret government agent who has to battle against evil forces to save nations or the world from destruction.

a. Open the presentation PPT E-5.pptx from the drive and folder where you store your Data Files, then save it as **Zone**. If you develop your own material, open a new presentation, storyboard the ideas for the presentation, then create at least six slides. What do you want your audience to know about the product idea?

b. Apply a theme. Modify the theme as necessary, such as changing background objects, font theme, color theme, or effect theme.

c. Use clip art, photos, shapes, and other objects as necessary to enhance the presentation.

d. Edit any text and add any additional information to create a professional presentation.

e. Format the bullet and text in the Master text and title placeholders on the master slide layout to fit the subject matter.

f. Create a custom slide layout, name it **Concept**, then apply it to at least one slide in the presentation.

# ▼ INDEPENDENT CHALLENGE 3 (CONTINUED)

**g.** Change the page orientation of the Notes Master view to Landscape, add your name to the notes and handouts footer, then save the presentation.

**h.** View the presentation in Slide Show view.

**i.** Print the notes pages in pure black and white.

### Advanced Challenge Exercise

- Click the Office button, point to Publish, then click Create Handouts in Microsoft Office Word.
- Click the Blank lines below slides option button, then click OK.
- Save the document as **Zone Handouts** to the drive and folder where you store your Data Files.
- Print the handouts, close the document, then exit Word.

**j.** Close the presentation and exit PowerPoint.

# ▼ REAL LIFE INDEPENDENT CHALLENGE

You work for the operations manager at the Southern State University student union. You have been working on a presentation that you eventually will publish to the college Web site that describes all of the services offered at the student union. Complete work on the presentation by working with masters and animation effects.

**a.** Open the presentation PPT E-6.pptx from the drive and folder where you store your Data Files, then save it as **SSU Union**.

**b.** Apply animation effects to all the objects in the presentation. Customize the animation speed and property as necessary.

**c.** Create a custom slide layout and apply it to a slide.

**d.** Format the bullet and text in the Master text and title placeholders on the master slide layout to fit the subject matter.

**e.** Modify master text indents on the master slide layout.

**f.** Change the page orientation of Handout Master view to Landscape, add your name to the notes and handouts footer, and save the presentation.

**g.** Adjust the alignment and line spacing of at least one text object.

**h.** View the presentation in Slide Show view.

**i.** Print the final presentation as notes pages in pure black and white.

**j.** Close the presentation and exit PowerPoint.

# ▼ VISUAL WORKSHOP

Create a slide that looks like the example in Figures E-23. Be sure to use connector lines. Add your name to the handout footer, then save the presentation as **Development**. Print the Slide view of the presentation. In addition, submit the final presentation as a printed handout.

**FIGURE E-23**

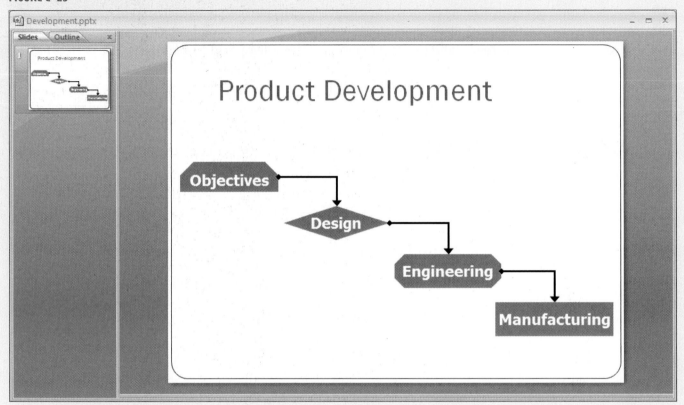

# Enhancing Charts

**Files You Will Need:**

PPT F-1.pptx
PPT F-2.xlsx
PPT F-3.xlsx
PPT F-4.pptx
PPT F-5.xlsx
PPT F-6.xlsx
PPT F-7.pptx
PPT F-8.pptx
PPT F-9.pptx
PPT F-10.xlsx
PPT F-11.xlsx
PPT F-12.pptx
PPT F-13.xlsx
PPT F-14.xlsx

A PowerPoint presentation is first and foremost a visual communication tool. Slides that deliver information with relevant graphics have a more lasting impact on an audience than slides with plain text. The most effective way to display numerical data is to show the data graphically in a chart. You can show numerical data in many different ways including columns, bars, lines, or pie wedges. Deciding which type of chart best illustrates your data is important to consider when choosing a chart type. For example, a pie chart is designed to display data from one data series in proportion to the sum of all of the data series; whereas, a column chart is designed to display data changes over time or for demonstrating comparisons among data points. In this unit, you continue to work on the Quest Specialty Travel (QST) presentation that includes charts. You customize the chart layout, format chart elements, and animate the chart. Finally, you insert an Excel chart and link an Excel worksheet to the presentation.

**OBJECTIVES**

Work with charts in PowerPoint

Change chart design and style

Customize a chart layout

Format chart elements

Animate a chart

Embed an Excel chart

Link an Excel worksheet

Update a linked Excel worksheet

# Working with Charts in PowerPoint

One of the best ways to enhance a presentation is to insert graphic elements such as a chart. When you have numerical data that you want to compare, a chart helps the audience visualize and understand the information. Because Excel is now fully integrated with PowerPoint, you can easily create fantastic-looking charts on the presentation slides. ▆▆▆▆ As you continue to develop the QST presentation, you plan to include charts on several slides.

## DETAILS

### Overview of charting in PowerPoint:

**QUICK TIP**
If you open a presentation with a chart that was created in Microsoft Graph, PowerPoint will recognize it and allow you to open and edit it using Excel.

- **Create charts using Excel from PowerPoint**

  If you have Microsoft Office 2007 installed on your computer, PowerPoint uses Excel, by default, to create charts. If you don't have Excel, Microsoft Graph opens and displays a chart and a datasheet with sample data on your slide. You can enter your own data in the Graph datasheet or import data from another source. When you create a chart directly from a presentation slide using the Chart button, a sample chart is placed on the slide and a separate Excel window opens beside the PowerPoint window displaying the chart's data in a worksheet. Displaying both program windows at the same time provides you with the ability to work directly on the chart in the Excel window and see the changes on the slide in the PowerPoint window. See Figure F-1.

- **Embed or link a chart**

  You have some options to choose from when considering how you want to insert an Excel chart (or any other object) to your presentation. There are two ways in which you can add a chart to a slide: you can embed it or link it. An embedded chart is an object created in another program and inserted in a slide. An embedded chart becomes a part of the presentation like a picture or a piece of clip art. The embedded chart's data is stored in an Excel worksheet that is incorporated into the presentation file. You can embed a chart in PowerPoint by creating it using the Chart button or by copying a chart from Excel and pasting it on a slide. A linked chart is different in that the chart that is displayed on the slide is not saved with the presentation. A linked chart is an object that is created in another program and is saved in a separate file. If you want to make changes to a linked Excel chart, you must open the saved Excel file that holds the chart.

**QUICK TIP**
A chart template does not save theme or style information, only chart type information.

- **Modify charts using styles and layouts**

  Because document themes and theme effects are alike for all Office programs, you can apply a specific theme or effect to a chart in Excel and PowerPoint will recognize the formatting. By using themes and effects, you don't have to format individual elements of a chart to match the colors and graphics in your PowerPoint file. You can, however, refine individual elements, such as the chart area, plot area, data series, or the legend of your chart. There are a number of chart layouts that you can apply to quickly change the layout of your chart. The chart layout specifies where chart elements, such as axes titles, data labels, and the legend, are displayed within the chart area. You cannot create your own chart layouts and styles, but you can create a template of a customized chart, which you can use later to apply to another chart.

**QUICK TIP**
If you do not have Excel 2007 installed on your computer, you will not be able to utilize any of the advanced charting capabilities in the 2007 Microsoft Office system.

- **Add advanced formatting to charts**

  You have a number of formatting options to choose from if you want to modify specific elements of a chart. The predefined styles will not always give you exactly the formatting options you want for a chart. For example, you may want to alter the way data labels look or how axes are displayed. You can specify the axes scales and adjust the interval between the values or categories. You can also add tick marks and specify the intervals between data points. **Tick marks** are small lines of measurement that intersect an axis and identify the categories, values, or series in a chart. Trendlines and error bars added to a chart provide more information about the data. A **trendline** is a graphical representation of an upward or downward trend in a data series, also used to predict future trends. **Error bars** identify potential error amounts relative to each data marker in a data series. Figure F-2 displays some advanced formatting items.

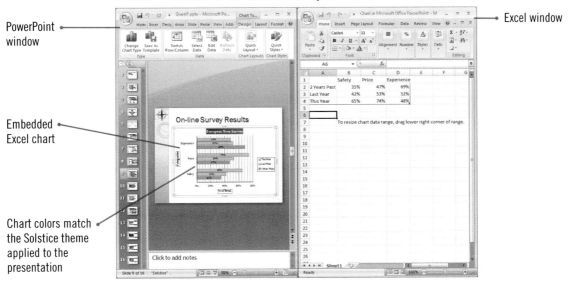

PowerPoint window

Excel window

Embedded Excel chart

Chart colors match the Solstice theme applied to the presentation

FIGURE F-2: Formatted chart

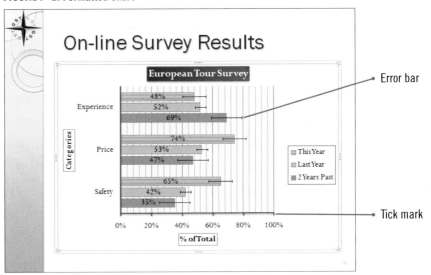

Error bar

Tick mark

## Data series and data series markers

Each column or row of data in the worksheet is called a data series. Each data series has corresponding data markers in the chart, which are graphical representations such as bars, columns, or pie wedges. Figure F-3 shows how each data series marker in the chart corresponds to the data in the chart. Notice the correlation between the data in the Safety column of the datasheet and the data series markers in the chart.

FIGURE F-3: Chart and worksheet

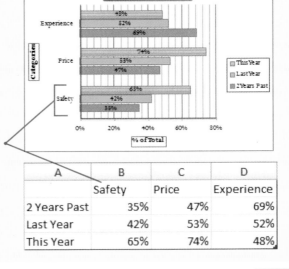

Safety data series

|  | Safety | Price | Experience |
|---|---|---|---|
| 2 Years Past | 35% | 47% | 69% |
| Last Year | 42% | 53% | 52% |
| This Year | 65% | 74% | 48% |

# Changing Chart Design and Style

Being able to use Excel to create charts in PowerPoint offers you many advantages including the ability to format charts using Excel's Chart tools to customize the design, layout, and formatting. After you create a chart, you can immediately change the way it looks by individually changing different chart elements or by applying a predefined chart layout or style. The chart layout options are in the Quick Layout gallery. For example, you can select a chart layout that adds a chart title and moves the legend to the bottom of the chart. You can also easily change the color and effects of chart elements by applying one of the styles found in the Chart Quick Styles gallery.  The chart that includes survey results needs some work. You change the chart layout, style, and type of the chart on Slide 9.

## STEPS

1. **Start PowerPoint, open the presentation** PPT F-1.pptx **from the drive and folder where you store your Data Files, save the presentation as** QuestF, **click the** View tab **on the Ribbon, click the** Arrange All button **in the Window group, then click the** Slide 9 thumbnail **in the Slides tab**
   Slide 9 appears in the Slide pane.

2. **Click the** chart, **then click the** Chart Tools Design tab **on the Ribbon**
   The chart is selected and ready to edit.

3. **Click the** More button ⬇ **in the Chart Layouts group, then click** Layout 9 **in the Quick Layout gallery**
   This particular layout option adds a chart title and value and category axis titles to the chart as shown in Figure F-4.

4. **Click the** Chart Title, **type** European Tour Survey, **click the** Vertical (Value) Axis Title, **type** % of Total, **click the** Horizontal (Category) Axis Title, **then type** Categories
   The new chart labels help identify aspects of the chart.

5. **Click the** More button ⬇ **in the Chart Styles group, then click** Style 36
   The Style 36 option changes the colors of the data series markers to better match the presentation colors. This new style option also adds a light background color behind the data series markers, for better contrast with the graph.

6. **Click the** Change Chart Type button **in the Type group**
   The Change Chart Type dialog box opens.

7. **Click** Bar **in the left pane, make sure that** Clustered Bar **is selected, then click** OK
   The data series markers change from columns to bars and rotate 90 degrees.

8. **Click a blank area of the slide, then click the** Save button 🖫 **on the Quick Access toolbar**
   Compare your screen to Figure F-5.

**FIGURE F-4:** Chart showing new layout

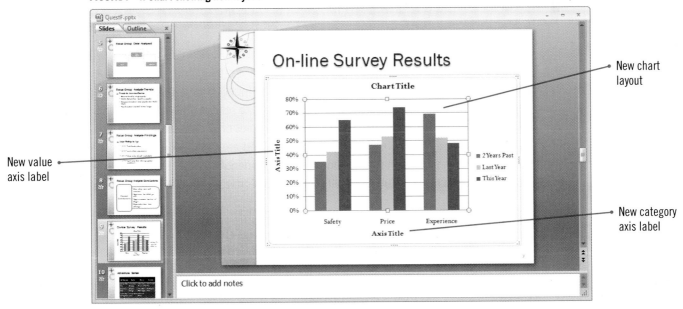

New value
axis label

New chart
layout

New category
axis label

**FIGURE F-5:** Chart showing new style and labels

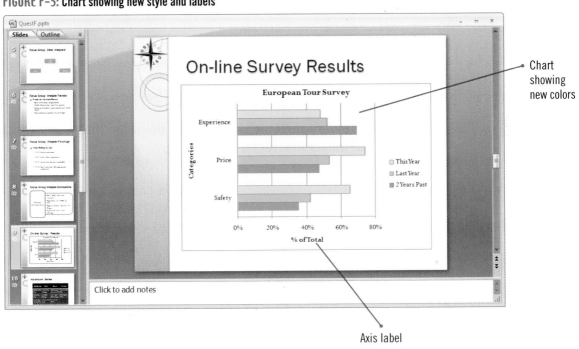

Chart
showing
new colors

Axis label

## Save a chart as a template

If you create a customized chart that you want to reuse, you can save it as a template (*.crtx) to the Charts Template folder. Then, instead of re-creating the chart type, you can simply apply the chart template to an existing chart or create a new chart based on the template. To save a chart as a template, select the chart you want to save, then click the Save As Template button in the Type group on the Chart Tools Design tab. To apply a chart template to an existing chart, click the Change Chart Type button in the Type group, click Templates, then click the chart template.

# Customizing a Chart Layout

One of the many advantages of using Excel to create charts in PowerPoint is the ability you have to customize chart elements, such as labels, axes, gridlines, and the chart background. For example, you can change the plot area color so the data markers are distinctly set off or you can add gridlines to a chart to make it easier to read. Gridlines help make the data easier to read in the chart and extend from the horizontal or vertical axes across the plot area. There are two types of gridlines: major gridlines and minor gridlines. **Major gridlines** identify major units on the axis and are usually identified by a tick mark. **Minor gridlines** identify minor units on the axis and can also be identified by a tick mark. You decide to improve the appearance of the Survey Results chart by customizing some elements of the chart.

## STEPS

1. **Click the chart, click the Chart Tools Layout tab on the Ribbon, then click the Gridlines button in the Axes group**

   The Gridlines menu opens. The chart already has major gridlines on the vertical axis.

2. **Point to Primary Vertical Gridlines, then click Major & Minor Gridlines on the gallery**

   This adds minor vertical gridlines to the chart as shown in Figure F-6. Notice that the major gridlines are darker in color than the minor gridlines and are identified by a tick mark on the value axis at each unit of value.

3. **Click the Data Table button in the Labels group, then click Show Data Table with Legend Keys**

   You like seeing the data on the chart because it helps define the data markers, but using the data table takes up too much room on the slide and significantly decreases the size of the chart.

4. **Click the Data Table button in the Labels group, click None, click the Data Labels button in the Labels group, then click Center**

   The data table closes and data labels appear in the center of each data marker.

5. **Click the Axis Titles button in the Labels group, point to Primary Horizontal Axis Title, then click More Primary Horizontal Axis Title Options**

   The Format Axis Title dialog box opens.

6. **Click Border Color in the left pane, click the Solid line option button, click the Color list arrow, click the Brown, Accent 5 color box, then click Close**

   A brown border appears around the value axis title. The category axis title would also look good with a border around it.

7. **Click the Vertical (Category) Axis Title, then press [F4]**

   A brown border appears around the category axis title. Pressing [F4] repeats the last formatting action.

8. **Click a blank area of the slide, then save your presentation**

   Compare your screen to Figure F-7.

FIGURE F-6: Chart showing new minor gridlines

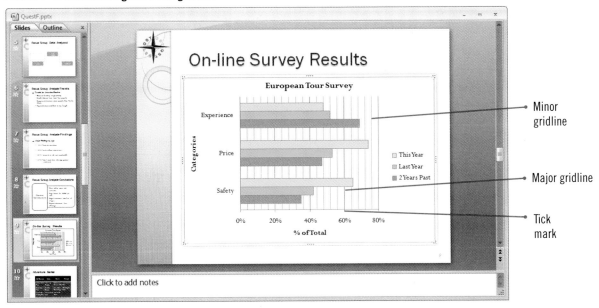

Minor gridline

Major gridline

Tick mark

FIGURE F-7: Chart showing added and formatted elements

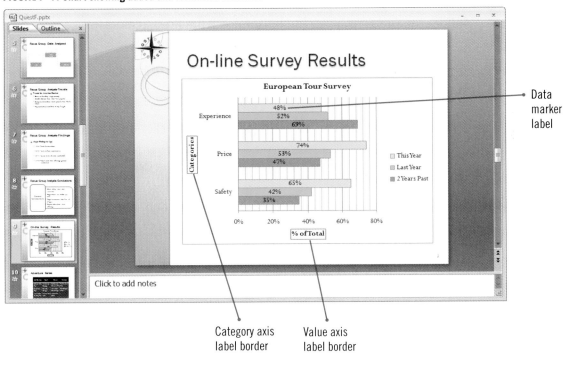

Data marker label

Category axis label border

Value axis label border

## Using the Research task pane

Sometimes when you are developing a presentation, you need help formulating your ideas or researching a subject. PowerPoint has an extensive set of online tools found in the Research task pane that gives you immediate access to many different kinds of information. The Research task pane provides the following research tools: an English dictionary, an English, French, and Spanish thesaurus, a word and phrase translator, four research Web sites (including an encyclopedia), and two business research Web sites. To open the Research task pane, click the Research button in the Proofing group on the Review tab. The Research options link at the bottom of the Research task pane provides additional research books and research sites that you can add to the Research task pane.

# Formatting Chart Elements

Quick Styles in PowerPoint provide you with a number of choices to modify all the elements in a chart. Even with all the Quick Style choices, you still may want to format individual elements to make the chart easy to look at and comprehend. ░░░░ Overall, you like what you have done to the European Tour survey chart so far, but you decide to format some individual elements of the chart to better fit the QST presentation design.

## STEPS

1. **Click the Chart, click the Chart Area list arrow in the Current Selection group, then click Series "This Year"**

   All of the This Year data markers are selected in the chart.

2. **Click the Chart Tools Format tab on the Ribbon, click the Shape Fill button in the Shape Styles group, point to Gradient, then click More Gradients**

   The Format Data Series dialog box opens.

3. **Drag the dialog box title bar to the left to move the dialog box off the chart, type –25 in the Series Overlap text box, then click Fill in the left pane**

   A small space is applied between the data markers for each data series in the chart. You can enter a value from –100% to 100% in the Series Overlap text box. A negative number adds space between each data marker while a positive number overlaps the data markers.

4. **Click the Gradient fill option button, click the Preset colors list arrow, click Gold (4th row), then click Close**

   The This Year data series markers change to a gold color. Compare your screen to Figure F-8.

5. **Click the chart title, then click the More button ⊟ in the Shape Styles group**

   The Shapes Style gallery opens.

6. **Click Moderate Effect – Accent 6 (5th row), then click any one of the numbers on the value axis**

   Applying the new style to the chart title makes it stand out. Clicking any of the numbers on the value axis selects the entire axis.

7. **Click the More button ⊟ in the Shape Styles group, click Moderate Line – Accent 5, click any one of the words on the Vertical (Category) Axis, then click Moderate Line – Accent 5 in the Shape Styles group**

   The new style applies a brown color and shadow to the axis and better defines the plot area.

8. **Right-click the chart legend, click Format Legend in the submenu, click Border Color in the left pane, then click the Solid line option button**

   A solid border line appears around the legend.

9. **Click the Color list arrow, click Indigo, Accent 6 (top row), then click Close**

10. **Click a blank area of the slide, then save the presentation**

    Compare your screen to Figure F-9.

FIGURE F-8: Chart showing modified data markers

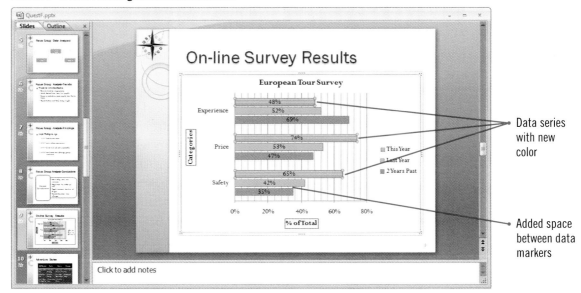

FIGURE F-9: Completed chart

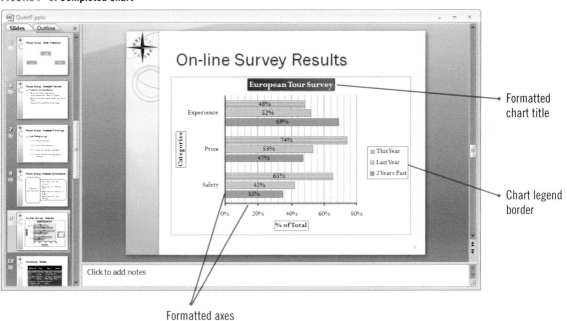

Formatted axes

## Saving in PDF and XPS file formats

In certain situations, for example when sharing sensitive or legal materials with others, you may find it necessary to save your presentation file in a fixed layout format. A **fixed layout format** is a specific file format that "locks" the file from future change and allows others only the ability to view or print the presentation. To be able to save or export a presentation in a fixed layout format directly from PowerPoint, you first must download and install the Save as PDF or XPS add-in from the Microsoft Office 2007 Web site. (You may also choose another software solution that enables you to create a fixed layout format file.) Once you have the add-in installed, click the Office button, point to Save As, then click PDF or XPS. The Save As dialog box opens. Select the appropriate file type and other options to save your presentation in a fixed layout format. To view a fixed layout format presentation, you need appropriate viewer software that you can download from the Internet.

# Animating a Chart

You can animate elements of a chart, much in the same way you animate text and graphics. You can animate the entire chart as one object or you can animate the data markers. There are two options for animating data markers individually: by series or by category. Animating data markers individually by series displays data markers of each data series (or the same colored data markers). Animating data markers individually by category displays the data markers of each category in the chart. If you choose to animate the chart's data markers as a series, the entire data series animates as a group; the same is true for animating data markers by category. And, of course, you have complete control over the animation speed and the animation playing order. If you animate the chart background, individual data series markers, and other objects or text on the slide, it may be difficult for your audience to distinguish the key information on the slide.  You decide to animate only the data series markers of the chart.

## STEPS

1. **Click the Animations tab on the Ribbon, then click the Custom Animation button in the Animations group**
   The Custom Animation task pane opens.

2. **Click the chart, click the Add Effect button in the Custom Animation task pane, point to Entrance, then click More Effects**
   The Add Entrance Effect dialog box opens.

3. **In the Basic section, click Fly In, then click OK**
   The Fly In animation effect is added to the chart, and the chart is added to the animations list as Chart 5. Compare your screen to Figure F-10.

4. **Click the Chart 5 list arrow in the animations list in the Custom Animation task pane, then click Effect Options**
   The Fly In dialog box opens.

5. **Click the Chart Animation tab, click the Group chart list arrow, click By Element in Series, click the Start animation by drawing the chart background check box to remove the check mark, then click OK**
   The Fly In dialog box closes. Then, each data series marker, by series, flies in from the bottom of the slide beginning with the 2 Years Past data series. Notice that there are nine animation tags on the chart, one for each data series marker. The chart background, which would have been animated by default, is not animated.

6. **Click the Direction list arrow in the Custom Animation task pane, click From Left, click the Speed list arrow, then click Fast**
   The direction of the animation effect now comes from the left and is slowed down slightly.

7. **Click the Chart 5 list arrow in the animations list, click Effect Options, in the Settings section, click the Smooth start check box, then click the Smooth end check box**
   Changing the smooth start and smooth end options slows the start and finish of the animation effect for each data series marker.

8. **Click the Timing tab, click the Start list arrow, click After Previous, type 2.5 in the Delay text box, then click OK**
   Watch closely at how the changed settings affect the progression of the data series markers animation. Using the After Previous setting and a 2.5 second delay between animations ensures that each data series marker is emphasized. Compare your screen to Figure F-11.

9. **Close the Custom Animation task pane, then save the presentation**

**FIGURE F-10:** Screen showing added animation effect

You may not see the Add-Ins tab on your computer

Animation tag

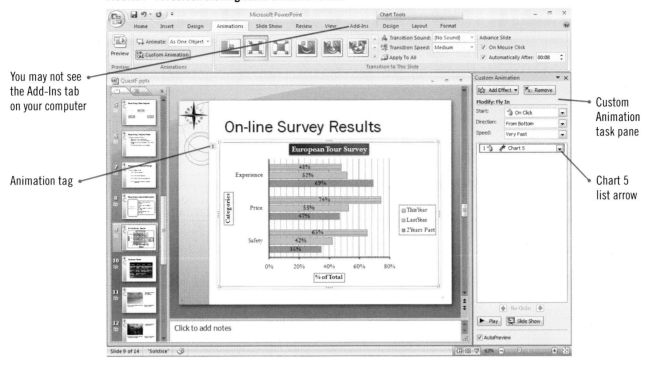

Custom Animation task pane

Chart 5 list arrow

**FIGURE F-11:** Finished chart

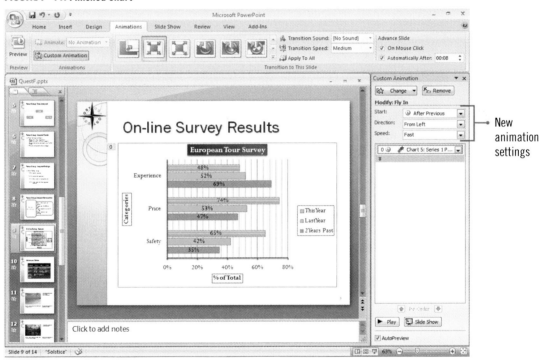

New animation settings

## Adding voice narrations

If your computer has speakers, a sound card, and a microphone, you can record a voice narration and then play it during your slide show. If you have a narration and other sounds that play automatically on the same slide, the voice narration takes precedence over the other sounds and will not play until you click them. To record a narration, click the Record Narration button in the Set Up group on the Slide Show tab. If you want the recording to be linked to the presentation, click the Link narrations in check box. If you do not select this option, the recording will be embedded in the presentation. If the Record Narration command is not available, then you do not have the necessary hardware.

# Embedding an Excel Chart

When a chart is the best way to present information on a slide, you can create one within PowerPoint or you can embed an existing Excel chart directly to the slide. When you use another program to create an object, the program, Excel in this case, is known as the **source program**. The object you create with the source program is saved to a file called the **source file**. When you insert a chart into a presentation, the presentation file in which the chart is inserted becomes the **destination file**.  Ellen wants to include supporting data from last year's sales numbers, so you insert an Excel chart on a new slide.

## STEPS

> **QUICK TIP**
> You can also press [Ctrl][D] to duplicate a slide.

1. **With Slide 9 still selected, click the** Home tab **on the Ribbon, click the** New Slide button list arrow **in the Slides group, then click** Duplicate Selected Slides
   A new slide with a duplicate chart appears in the Slide pane and in the Slides tab.

2. **Select the slide title** On-line Survey Results, **type** Quarterly Sales Figures, **click the chart, then press** [Backspace]
   The slide has a new title and the duplicate chart is deleted.

3. **Click the** Insert tab **on the Ribbon, then click the** Object button **in the Text group**
   The Insert Object dialog box opens. Using this dialog box, you can create a new chart or locate an existing one to insert on a slide.

> **QUICK TIP**
> You can also open the chart in Excel, copy it, and then paste it into your slide.

4. **Click the** Create from file option button, **click** Browse, **locate the file** PPT F-2.xlsx **in the drive and folder where you store your Data Files, click** OK, **then click** OK **in the Insert Object dialog box**
   The chart containing the quarterly sales data appears and is embedded on the slide. Notice that the chart is not completely visible. You can open the chart and use Excel's commands to alter it.

5. **Double-click the** chart **to open Microsoft Office Excel**
   The chart appears inside an Excel worksheet on the slide. Excel commands and tabs appear on the Ribbon under the PowerPoint title bar as shown in Figure F-12.

> **QUICK TIP**
> If the chart you want to insert is in another presentation, you can open both presentations and then copy and paste the chart from one presentation to the other.

6. **Drag the Excel worksheet window lower-middle** sizing handle **until the axis labels at the bottom of the chart are visible, then drag the window right-middle** sizing handle **until the legend is visible**
   The entire chart is in the visible viewing area.

7. **Click the** Chart Tools Design tab **on the Ribbon, click the** Chart Styles More button, **then click** Style 40 (row 5 last column)
   The chart style changes with new data marker colors and a new plot area color.

8. **Right-click the** Vertical (Value) Axis, **click the** Bold button **B** **on the Mini toolbar, click the** category axis, **then press** [F4]
   Both the value and category axes labels are bold and now easier to read.

9. **Click outside the chart to exit Excel, drag the** chart **so its upper-left corner is under the word Quarterly, then drag the lower-right** sizing handle **down and to the right**
   Compare your screen to Figure F-13.

10. **Click a blank area of the slide, then save the presentation**

**FIGURE F-12:** Inserted Excel chart

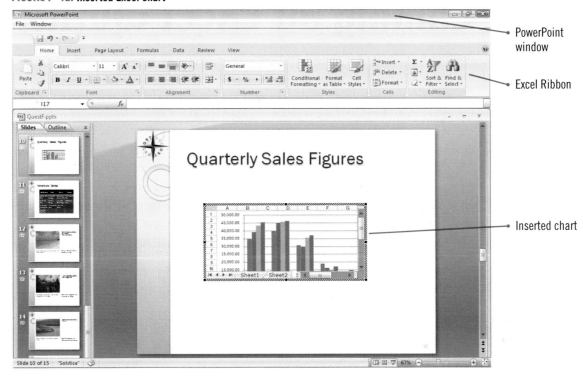

- PowerPoint window
- Excel Ribbon
- Inserted chart

**FIGURE F-13:** Formatted Excel chart

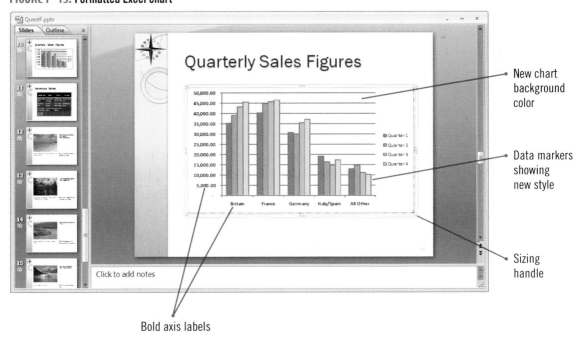

- New chart background color
- Data markers showing new style
- Sizing handle
- Bold axis labels

### Embedding a worksheet

You can embed all or part of an Excel worksheet in a PowerPoint slide. To embed an entire worksheet, go to the slide where you want to place the worksheet. Click the Insert tab on the Ribbon, then click the Object button in the Text group. The Insert Object dialog box opens. Click the Create from file option button, click Browse, locate and double-click the worksheet filename, then click OK. The worksheet is embedded in the slide. Double-click it to edit it using Excel commands as needed to work with the worksheet. To insert only a portion of a worksheet, open the Excel workbook and copy the cells you want to include in your presentation.

# Linking an Excel Worksheet

Another way to connect objects to your presentation is to establish a **link**, or connection, between the source file and the destination file. Unlike embedded objects, a linked object is stored in its source file, not on the slide or in the presentation file. So when you link an object to a PowerPoint slide, a representation (picture) of the object, not the object itself, appears on the slide. Any changes made to the source file using the source program of a linked object are automatically reflected in the linked representation in your PowerPoint presentation. Some of the objects that you can link to PowerPoint include bitmap images, Microsoft Excel worksheets, and PowerPoint slides from other presentations. Use linking when you want to be sure your presentation contains the latest information and when you want to include an object, such as an accounting spreadsheet, that may change over time. See Table F-1 for suggestions on when to embed an object and when to link an object. ▓▓▓▓ You need to link and format an Excel worksheet to the presentation. The worksheet was created by the Quest Specialty Travel Accounting Department earlier in the year.

## STEPS

**QUICK TIP**
If you plan to do the steps in this lesson again, make a copy of the Excel file PPT F-3.xlsx to keep the original data intact.

1. **Click the Home tab on the Ribbon, click the New Slide button, then type Quest Specialty Travel**
   The new Slide 11 is created and appears in the Slide pane with the title Quest Specialty Travel.

2. **Click the Insert tab on the Ribbon, then click the Object button in the Text group**
   The Insert Object dialog box opens.

3. **Click the Create from file option button, click Browse, locate the file PPT F-3.xlsx in the drive and folder where you store your Data Files, click OK, click the Link check box, then click OK**
   The Excel worksheet appears on the slide. The worksheet would be easier to see if it were larger.

4. **Drag the lower-right sizing handle down and to the right, drag the lower-left sizing handle down and to the left, then position the worksheet in the middle of the slide**
   The worksheet should be about as wide on the slide as shown in Figure F-14. If the worksheet has a background fill color, it would be set off from the slide and help to focus audience's attention.

**QUICK TIP**
Another way to link objects like a worksheet is to create a hyperlink. Copy the object in its source program, click the Paste button list arrow in PowerPoint, then click Paste as Hyperlink.

5. **Right-click the worksheet, then click Format Object on the shortcut menu**
   The Format Object dialog box opens.

6. **Drag the dialog box to the left out of the way if it is blocking the worksheet, in the Fill section click the Color list arrow, click Automatic, then click Preview**
   A dark teal color is applied behind the worksheet. The color is too dark for the presentation.

7. **In the Fill section, type 50 in the Transparency text box, then click Preview**
   The intensity of the background color is at 50 % and looks better.

8. **In the Line section click the Color list arrow, click Automatic, click the Weight up arrow once, click OK, then click a blank area of the slide**
   The worksheet appears with the new background color and border. Compare your screen to figure F-15.

9. **Save the presentation, then close the presentation**
   The PowerPoint file closes but PowerPoint remains open.

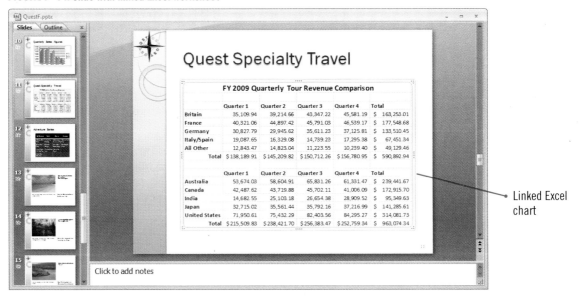

Linked Excel chart

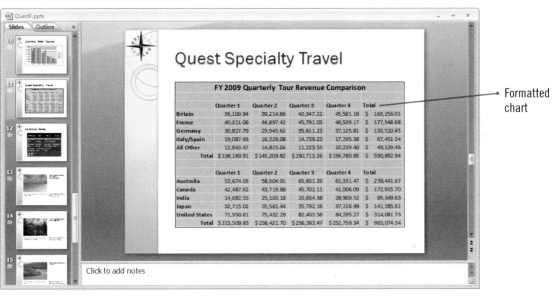

Formatted chart

PowerPoint 2007

TABLE F-1: Embedding Versus Linking

| situation | action |
| --- | --- |
| When you are the only user of an object and you want the object to be a part of your presentation | Embed |
| When you want to access the object in its source program, even if the original file is not available | Embed |
| When you want to update the object manually while working in PowerPoint | Embed |
| When you always want the latest information in your object | Link |
| When the object's source file is shared on a network or when other users have access to the file and can change it | Link |
| When you want to keep your presentation file size small | Link |

# Updating a Linked Excel Worksheet

To edit or change the information in a linked object, you must open the object's source file in its source program. For example, you must open Microsoft Word to edit a linked Word table, or you must open Microsoft Excel to edit a linked Excel worksheet. You can open the source program by double-clicking the linked object in the PowerPoint slide, as you did with embedded objects, or by starting the source program directly using any method you prefer. When you work on a linked object in its source program, your PowerPoint presentation can be either open or closed. ⬛⬛⬛ You have just received an e-mail that some of the data in the Excel worksheet is incorrect. You decide to start Excel and change the data in the source file and then update the linked object in the presentation.

## STEPS

**QUICK TIP**

To edit or open a linked object in your presentation, the object's source program and source file must be available on your computer or network.

1. **Click the** Start button ⬤ **on the Taskbar, point to** All Programs, **click** Microsoft Office, **click** Microsoft Office Excel 2007, **click the** Office button ⬤, **click** Open, **locate the file** PPT F-3.xlsx **in the drive and folder where you store your Data Files, then click** Open

   The worksheet PPT F-3.xlsx opens up in the Microsoft Excel window.

2. **Click cell** B4, **press** [Shift], **click cell** E8, **release** [Shift], **right-click cell** E8, **then click the** Accounting Number Format button $\boxed{\$ \; ▾}$ **on the Mini toolbar**

   All of the selected cells now have the accounting format and display the dollar symbol.

3. **Click cell** B12, **drag to cell** E16, **press** [F4], **then click cell** B14

   The same accounting number format is applied to these cells.

4. **Type** 18630.51, **click cell** E8, **type** 13427.34, **then press** [Enter]

   The Quarter 1 value for India and the Quarter 4 value for All Other in the worksheet change. All totals that include these values in the Total cells are updated accordingly. Compare your screen to Figure F-16.

5. **Click cell** F9, **press** [Ctrl], **click cell** F17, **click the** Bold button $\boxed{\text{B}}$ **in the Font group, click the Excel window** Close button $\boxed{\times}$, **then click** Yes **to save your changes**

   The bold attribute is added to these cells to highlight the overall totals, and the Excel window closes.

**QUICK TIP**

The destination file can remain open when you update links. After you change the source file and switch back to the destination file, the linked object is updated.

6. **In the PowerPoint program window click the** Office button ⬤, **then click** 1 QuestF.pptx **in the Recent documents list**

   A Microsoft Office PowerPoint Security Notice dialog box opens, telling you that the presentation contains links and asking if you want to update them. This message appears whenever you open a presentation that contains linked objects that have been changed.

7. **Click** Update Links

   The Excel worksheet in the QuestF.pptx presentation file is now updated with the new data.

8. **Click the** View tab **on the Ribbon, click** Arrange All **in the Window group, click** Slide 11 **in the Slides tab, then click the** linked worksheet

   Compare your screen to Figure F-17. The linked Excel worksheet shows the new numbers and the formatting changes you made. PowerPoint automatically makes all of the changes when you update the links.

9. **Save the presentation, add your name as the footer to the handouts, print handouts 4 per page, then exit PowerPoint**

FIGURE F-16: Modified Excel worksheet

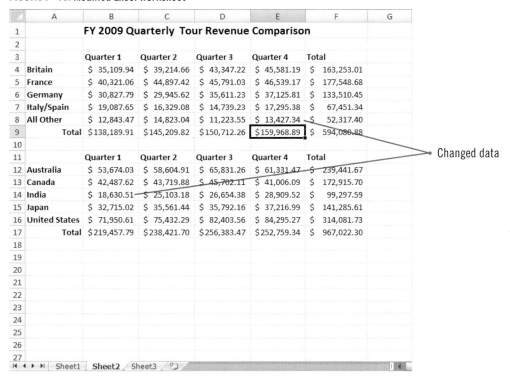

FIGURE F-17: Slide showing updated linked worksheet

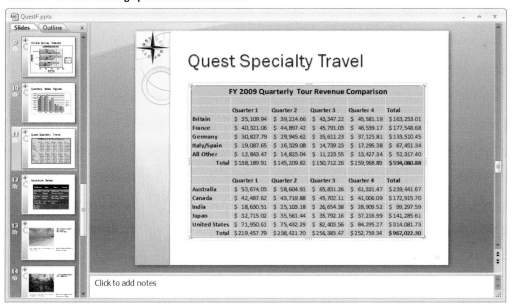

## Using Paste Special

Paste Special is used to paste text or objects into PowerPoint using a specific file format. For example, you may want to paste some text as a picture or as plain text without formatting. Copy the text, then in PowerPoint click the Paste button list arrow, click Paste Special, then select the appropriate file format option. You can also link an object or selected information from another program to PowerPoint using the Paste Special command. This technique is useful when you want to link part of an Excel worksheet or a chart from a workbook that contains both a worksheet and a chart. To link just the chart, open the Microsoft Excel worksheet, then copy the chart. Leaving Excel and the source file open, click the Paste button list arrow, click Paste Special, click the Paste link option button, then click OK.

# Practice

If you have a SAM user profile, you may have access to hands-on instruction, practice, and assessment of the skills covered in this unit. Log in to your SAM account (http://sam2007.course.com/) to launch any assigned training activities or exams that relate to the skills covered in this unit.

## ▼ CONCEPTS REVIEW

**Label each of the elements of the PowerPoint window shown in Figure F-18.**

FIGURE F-18

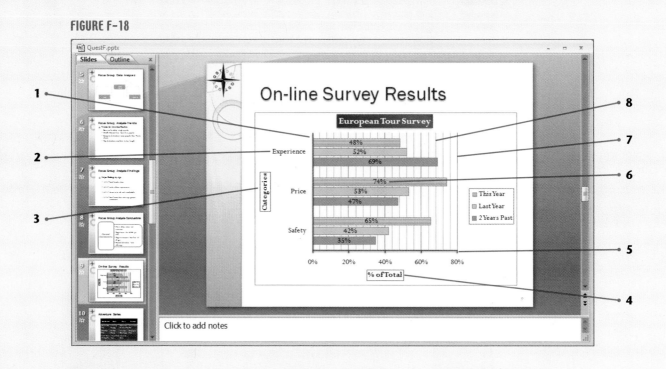

**Match each of the terms with the statement that describes its function.**

9. Create and then reuse to make a customized chart type
10. The file that contains the Excel chart that you embed into a PowerPoint file
11. The PowerPoint file where you embed an Excel chart
12. The connection between a source file and a destination file
13. The specific file format that locks the file from future change

a. Fixed layout format
b. Destination file
c. Template
d. Link
e. Source file

## Select the best answer from the list of choices.

14. **Which of the statements below is not true about working with charts in PowerPoint?**
    a. Microsoft Graph is used to create a chart if Excel is not available.
    b. A linked chart is saved in the presentation.
    c. Document themes and effects are consistent between PowerPoint and Excel.
    d. An embedded chart's data is stored in an Excel worksheet.

15. **Which of the following is not true about charts?**
    a. A column chart displays a data series in proportion to the sum of all the data series.
    b. Cones and bubbles are examples of different chart types.
    c. Both Excel and PowerPoint use the same chart types.
    d. You can update a linked chart in its source program.

16. **What is a data series?**
    a. A graphical representation of a data series marker
    b. A range of data
    c. All of the data elements in a chart
    d. A column or row of data

17. **Which animation method would you use to display each data series marker independently with the same color?**
    a. By series
    b. Individually by category
    c. Individually by series
    d. By category

18. **You use a(n) _____ program to create an object that you insert into PowerPoint.**
    a. Support
    b. Linked
    c. Destination
    d. Source

19. **Small lines that intersect an axis and identify categories are called:**
    a. category markers.
    b. tick marks.
    c. plot layout lines.
    d. chart wedges.

20. **Changes made to a _____ object's source file are automatically reflected in the destination file.**
    a. embedded
    b. inserted
    c. linked
    d. Microsoft Graph

# ▼ SKILLS REVIEW

1. **Change chart design and style.**
   a. Start PowerPoint, open the presentation PPT F-4.pptx, then save it as **Italia Publishing** to the drive and folder where you store your Data Files.
   b. Select Slide 3, then select the chart.
   c. Open the Chart Tools Design tab, then apply Layout 7 from the Chart Layouts group.
   d. Change the axis label on the value axis to **Millions** and then change the category axis label to **Divisions**.
   e. Apply Style 37 from the Chart Styles group.
   f. Change the chart type to Clustered Cylinder. (*Hint*: A cylinder is a type of column chart.)

2. **Customize a chart layout.**

   **a.** Open the Chart Tools Layout tab, then change the horizontal gridlines to major gridlines and the vertical gridlines to major gridlines.

   **b.** Click the Chart Floor button in the Background group, click More Floor Options, click the Solid fill option button, type **35** in the Transparency text box, then click Close.

   **c.** Click the Chart Wall button in the Background group, then click None.

   **d.** Right-click the value axis label, click the Shape Outline button list arrow on the Mini toolbar, then click Blue-Gray, Accent 1.

   **e.** Select the category axis title, then press [F4].

   **f.** Click a blank area of the chart, then save your changes.

3. **Format chart elements.**

   **a.** Click the Chart Area list arrow in the Current Selection group, then click Series "2nd Qtr."

   **b.** Click the Format Selection button in the Current Selection group, then drag the Gap Width slider to the left to about 150%.

   **c.** Click Fill in the left pane, then change the fill to a Gradient fill, click the Direction list arrow, then click Linear Down.

   **d.** Click 3-D Format in the left pane, click the Material list arrow, click Dark Edge, then click Close.

   **e.** Right-click the value axis, then click Format Axis.

   **f.** Under Axis Options click the Major unit Fixed option button, then type **15** in the text box.

   **g.** Click the Major tick mark type list arrow, click Cross, click Close, then save your changes.

4. **Animate a chart.**

   **a.** Open the Animations tab, then click the Custom Animation button in the Animations group.

   **b.** Apply the Descend Entrance animation effect that is in the Moderate group to the chart.

   **c.** Click the animation list arrow (Object 4), click Effect Options, then click the Chart Animation tab.

   **d.** Change the animation to By Element in Series, click the check box to not draw the chart background, then click OK.

   **e.** Close the Custom Animation task pane, then save your changes.

5. **Embed an Excel chart.**

   **a.** Select Slide 4, then click the Insert tab.

   **b.** Click the Object button in the Text group, click the Create from file option button, click Browse, locate and open the file PPT F-5.xlsx from the drive and folder where you store your Data Files, then click OK.

   **c.** Double-click the chart, then drag the sizing handles so the entire chart is visible. You should see the value axis title and the category axis title as well as the legend.

   **d.** Click the chart, click the Chart Tools Design tab, then change the chart style to Style 36.

   **e.** Change the horizontal gridlines to display only major gridlines.

   **f.** Right-click the legend, click the Shape Outline button list arrow on the Mini toolbar, click Black, Text 1, then click outside the chart.

   **g.** Resize the chart so it fills most of the slide.

   **h.** Click a blank area of the slide, then save your changes.

6. **Link an Excel worksheet.**

   **a.** Add a new slide after the current slide with the Title Only layout.

   **b.** Type **Italia Publishing**, click the Insert tab, then click the Object button in the Text group.

   **c.** Click the Create from file option button, locate the file PPT F-6.xlsx in the drive and folder where you store your Data Files, then link it to the slide.

   **d.** Resize the worksheet object by dragging its sizing handles.

   **e.** Right-click the worksheet, click Format Object, click the Color list arrow, then click Automatic.

   **f.** Change the transparency to 40%, click OK, then save your changes.

**7. Update a linked Excel worksheet.**

a. Right-click the worksheet, point to Linked Worksheet Object, then click Edit.

b. Select cells B5 to F9, click the Accounting Number Format button list arrow in the Number group, then click Euro.

c. Click cell F9, then click the Bold button in the Font group.

d. Click cell D5, type **72492.38**, click cell E7, then type **87253.11**.

e. Click the Excel window Close button, then click Yes to save your changes. The changes appear in the linked worksheet. Figure F-19 shows the completed presentation.

f. Add your name to the handout footer, save your work, print the handouts 4 per page, close the presentation, and exit PowerPoint.

**FIGURE F-19**

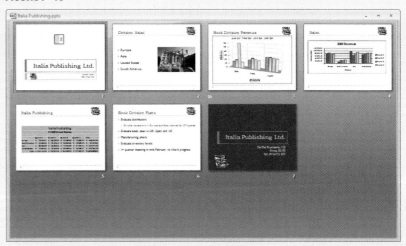

# ▼ INDEPENDENT CHALLENGE 1

You work for Business Builders Inc., a business consulting company that helps small and medium businesses organize or restructure themselves to be more efficient and profitable. You are one of four senior consultants who work directly with clients. To prepare for an upcoming meeting with executives at ComSystems, a mobile phone communications company, you create a brief presentation outlining typical investigative and reporting techniques, past results versus the competition, and the company's business philosophy. Use PowerPoint to customize a chart on Slide 5 of the presentation.

a. Start PowerPoint, open the presentation PPT F-7.pptx from the drive and folder where you store your Data Files, then save it as **Bz Builders**.

b. Select the chart on Slide 5, then apply Layout 3 from the Chart Layouts gallery.

c. Apply Style 26 from the chart Styles gallery, then type **AMPI Rating Comparison** in the chart title text box.

d. Change the chart type to Clustered Bar, then add minor vertical gridlines to the chart.

e. Open the Format Axis dialog box for the value axis, click Number in the left pane, click Number in the Category list, then type **1** in the Decimal Places text box.

f. Show data labels using the Inside End option.

**Advanced Challenge Exercise**

■ Select the Value axis, open the Format Axis dialog box for the Value axis, in the Axis Options section click the Major unit Fixed option button, then type **0.5**.

■ In the Axis Options section click the Minor unit Fixed option button, then type **0.1**.

■ Select the category axis, open the Format Axis dialog box, click Alignment in the left pane, then type **–25** in the Custom angle text box.

g. Change the data labels to the Inside End option, then spell check and save your presentation.

h. Add your name as a footer to the slides and handouts, print the slides of the presentation, then submit your presentation plan and printouts.

i. View the presentation in Slide Show view, save the presentation, close the presentation, then exit PowerPoint.

# ▼ INDEPENDENT CHALLENGE 2

One of your responsibilities working in the Delaware State Schools system is to provide program performance data for educational programs designed for disabled children in the state. You need to develop and give a presentation describing the program's results at a national education forum held this year in Cincinnati, Ohio. You have been working on the presentation and now you need to use PowerPoint to put the finishing touches on a chart.

a. Start PowerPoint, open the presentation PPT F-8.pptx from the drive and folder where you store your Data Files, then save it as **Delaware Schools**.

b. Select Slide 7, select the chart, then change the chart style to Style 27.

c. Open the Chart Tools Layout tab click the 3-D Rotation button, then in the Rotation section click the X down arrow once.

d. Open the Chart Tools Format tab, select the Reading data series, then change the shape fill to the gradient Linear Down (Dark Variation).

e. Change the Writing data series to the Woven mat texture shape fill, then change the Math data series to Linear Up (Light Variation).

f. Open the Custom Animation task pane, apply the Wipe Entrance effect to the chart, then slow the speed down to Fast.

g. Open the Effect Options dialog box for animation effect, change the animation so the data markers appear by category, then click the check box so the chart background does not animate.

h. Spell check and save the presentation.

i. Add your name as a footer to the slides and handouts, then print the final slide presentation.

j. View the presentation in Slide Show view, save and close the presentation, then exit PowerPoint.

# ▼ INDEPENDENT CHALLENGE 3

RNM Industries is a large company that develops and produces technical medical equipment and machines for operating and emergency rooms throughout the United States. You are one of the business managers in the company, and one of your assignments is to prepare a presentation for the stockholders on the profitability and efficiency of each division in the company. Use PowerPoint to develop the presentation.

a. Open the file PPT F-9.pptx from the drive and folder where you store your Data Files, then save it as **RNM Industries**.

b. Apply the Flow theme, then add at least two graphics to the presentation.

c. Add a new slide titled Company Divisions, then create a SmartArt graphic that identifies the company's seven divisions: Administration; Accounting; Sales and Marketing; Research and Development; Product Testing; Product Development; and Manufacturing.

d. Format the new SmartArt graphic using SmartArt Styles and colors.

e. Select the Division Performance slide, then insert the Excel file PPT F-10.xlsx from the drive and folder where you store your Data Files.

f. Double-click the chart, then drag the corner sizing handles so all of the chart is visible.

**Advanced Challenge Exercise**

- Right-click the value axis, then click Format Axis.
- Click the Axis labels list arrow, then click Low.
- Click the Minor tick mark type list arrow, click None, then click Close.

g. Apply the Style 42 chart style to the chart, deselect the chart, then increase the size of the chart and center it in the slide.

h. Select the Division Budgets slide, then link the Excel file PPT F-11.xlsx from the drive and folder where you store your Data Files.

# ▼ INDEPENDENT CHALLENGE 3 (CONTINUED)

**i.** Open the linked worksheet in Excel, select cells B5 through F12, click the Accounting Number Format button in the Number group, then close Excel.

**j.** Right-click the linked chart, click Format Object, then change the fill color to Automatic at 60% transparency.

**k.** Resize the worksheet to fill the slide, add your name as a footer to the slides and handouts, then print the final slide presentation.

**l.** View the presentation in Slide Show view, close the presentation and exit PowerPoint.

# ▼ REAL LIFE INDEPENDENT CHALLENGE

You are on staff at your college newspaper. One of your jobs is to review computer games and post a presentation on the paper's Web site. The presentation identifies the top computer games based on student testing and other reviews. Use PowerPoint to create a presentation that includes research and your own information. Use the basic presentation provided as a basis to develop this presentation.

As you create this presentation, follow these guidelines:

* Include three computer games in your presentation.
* Each game has at least one defined mission or task.
* Consumer satisfaction of each game is identified on a scale of 1.0 to 10.0.
* There are three categories of games: Adventure, Action, and Strategy.

If you have access to the Web, you can research the following topics to help you develop information for your presentation

* Consumer or industry reviews of computer games
* Computer game descriptions and pricing

**a.** Connect to the Internet, then use a search engine to locate Web sites that have information on PC computer games. Review at least two Web sites that contain information about computer games. Print the home pages of the Web sites you use to gather data for your presentation.

**b.** Open the presentation PPT F-12.pptx from the drive and folder where you store your Data Files, then save it as **PC Game Review**.

**c.** Add your name as the footer on all slides and handouts.

**d.** Your presentation should contain at least eight slides, including a title slide.

**e.** (Before you complete this step make a copy of the Data File PPT F-13.xlsx.) Link the Excel chart PPT F-13.xlsx from the drive and folder where you store your Data Files on the Game Reviews slide.

**f.** Resize the chart on the slide, then open the linked chart in Excel.

**g.** Click the Sheet 1 tab at the bottom of the Excel window, provide a name for each game, click the Sheet 2 tab, then save your changes.

**h.** Right-click the chart legend click Delete in the Shortcut menu, click the Page Layout tab, click the Colors button in the Themes group, then click Aspect.

**i.** Save your changes, then exit Excel.

**j.** Create at least one SmartArt diagram that briefly explains the story line of one of the games.

**k.** Create a table that lists the price of each game.

**l.** Enhance the presentation with clip art or other graphics, an appropriate design theme, and other items that improve the look of the presentation.

**m.** Modify the Slide Master as necessary and create a new slide layout, if necessary, to use in the presentation.

**n.** Spell check, save the presentation, then view the presentation in Slide Show view.

**o.** Add your name as a footer to the slides and handouts, print the slides of the presentation as handouts (4 slides per page).

**p.** Close the presentation and exit PowerPoint.

# ▼ VISUAL WORKSHOP

Create a slide that looks like the example in Figure F-20. Start a new presentation, then insert the Excel worksheet PPT F-14.xlsx from the drive and folder where you store your Data Files. Format the worksheet using PowerPoint's formatting features. Save the presentation as **Chase Products Inc.** Add your name as a footer on the slides, then save and print the presentation slides.

**FIGURE F-20**

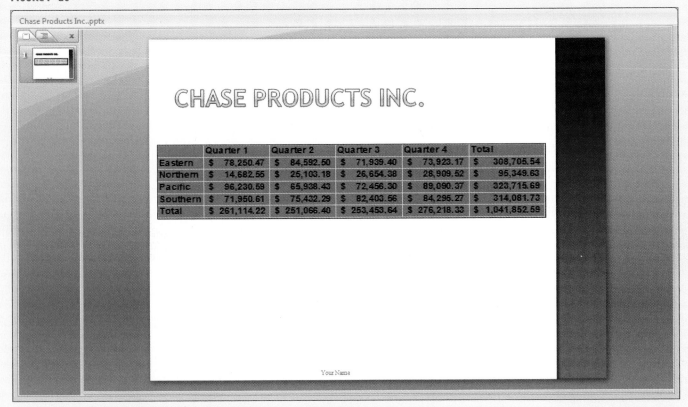

# Inserting Illustrations, Objects, and Media Clips

**Files You Will Need:**

PPT G-1.pptm
PPT G-2.jpg
PPT G-3.jpg
PPT G-4.jpg
PPT G-5.jpg
PPT G-6.jpg
PPT G-7.jpg
PPT G-8.jpg
PPT G-9.jpg
PPT G-10.pptx
PPT G-11.docx
PPT G-12.pptx
PPT G-13.pptm
PPT G-14.jpg
PPT G-15.wav
PPT G-16.jpg
PPT G-17.docx
PPT G-18.pptx
PPT G-19.pptx
PPT G-20.pptx
PPT G-21.pptx
PPT G-22.pptm

PowerPoint provides you with many different types of graphics to improve your presentation. From customized tables and professional-looking diagrams to movies and sounds, you have a wide range of options when it comes to developing your presentation. You also have other advanced tools, such as hyperlinks, macros, and action buttons that help correlate, simplify, and assimilate information. In this unit, you will work on a short presentation for a specific tour that will be linked to the primary European Tours presentation that you have been working on for Ellen Latsky at Quest Specialty Travel. You will use PowerPoint's advanced features to customize a table and a SmartArt graphic, then you will insert a movie and sound that complements the information. Finally, you will use a macro to insert some pictures, create action buttons, and link one presentation to another one.

**OBJECTIVES**

Create custom tables

Design a SmartArt graphic

Format a SmartArt graphic

Insert an animation

Insert a sound

Use macros

Add action buttons

Insert a hyperlink

# Creating Custom Tables

A table is a great way to display and organize related information. In PowerPoint 2007, you have the ability to create dynamic-looking tables. Tables you create in PowerPoint automatically display the style as determined by the theme assigned to the slide, including color combinations and shading, line styles and colors, and other attributes. It is easy to customize the layout of a table or change how data is organized. You can delete and insert rows or columns, merge two or more cells together, or split one cell into more cells. ▰▰▰▰ You open a short presentation on Black Forest tours in Germany that you have been working on and finish customizing a table.

## STEPS

1. **Start PowerPoint, open the presentation** PPT G-1.pptm **from the drive and folder where you store your Data Files, save the presentation as** QuestG, **then click** OK **in the privacy warning alert dialog box**

   The presentation opens. Notice that this presentation has the file extension .pptm instead of .pptx. The .pptm file extension identifies the PowerPoint file as having macros attached to it. A **macro** is an action or a set of actions that you use to automate tasks.

2. **Click the** Options button **in the Security Warning message bar, read the Microsoft Office Security Options dialog box, click the** Enable this content option button, **click OK, click the** View tab **on the Ribbon, then click the** Arrange All button **in the Window group**

   You have just enabled the macros attached to this presentation. As a rule, you should not enable macros from unfamiliar sources or those you do not trust because they could contain viruses.

3. **Click the** table **on Slide 1, click the** Table Tools Design tab **on the Ribbon, click the** Pen Style button ▬ **in the Draw Borders group, then click the** dash-dot style (4th **line style from the top)**

   The pointer changes to ✎, which indicates that you are in drawing mode.

4. **Click the** white vertical column line **that divides the Pricing and Extras columns in the table, then click the** vertical column line **for each row in that column to the bottom of the table**

   See Figure G-1.

QUICK TIP
You can also press [Esc] to end drawing mode.

5. **Click the** Draw Table button **in the Draw Borders group, click the** Table Tools Layout tab **on the Ribbon, click the** Hostel/Barn cell, **then click the** Split Cells button **in the Merge group**

   Clicking the Draw Table button ends drawing mode and the pointer changes back to ⬚. The Split Cells dialog box opens. The default table is 2 columns and 1 row, and the Number of columns text box is selected.

QUICK TIP
To change the text direction in a text box or a table, select the text, click the Text Direction button in the Paragraph group, then click the appropriate option.

6. **Type** 1, **click the** Number of rows up arrow once, **then click** OK

   You split the cell so a new row is created.

7. **Drag to select the word** Barn, **press** [Ctrl][X] **to cut the word, click the** new row, **press** [Ctrl][V] **to paste the word, then delete the slash next to Hostel**

   The words Hostel and Barn are now in two separate rows within the Accommodations column.

8. **Repeat Steps 5–7 for the House/Farm cell and the Hotel/Inn cell**

   Compare your screen with Figure G-2.

9. **Click outside the table, click the** Save button 🖫 **on the Quick Access toolbar, then click** OK **in the privacy warning alert dialog box**

**FIGURE G-1:** Table with new column line style

New column style

Pen pointer

**FIGURE G-2:** Formatted table

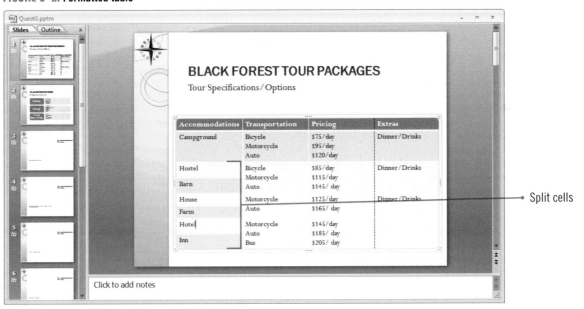

Split cells

## Drawing tables

If you have limited space or a certain size table you want on a slide, you can draw it. Choose the slide where you want the table, click the Insert tab on the Ribbon, click the Table button in the Table group, then click Draw Table. The pointer changes to a pencil. Using the pencil to define the boundaries of the table, drag in the area of the slide where you want the table. A dotted outline appears as you draw. Next, you can create rows and columns. Click the Table Tools Design tab on the Ribbon, click the Draw Table button in the Draw Borders group, then using the pencil pointer draw lines for columns and rows. Be sure to draw within the boundary line of the table.

# Designing a SmartArt Graphic

The introduction of the SmartArt graphic in PowerPoint 2007 has dramatically improved your ability to create vibrant content on slides. You no longer have to struggle to combine your content with graphic illustrations. SmartArt allows you to easily combine your content with an illustrative diagram, improving the overall quality of your presentation and therefore, content understanding and retention by your audience. Now, in a matter of minutes you can create a SmartArt graphic using slide content that would otherwise have been placed in a simple bulleted list. You continue working on the Black Forest tours presentation by changing the graphic layout, adding a shape and text to the SmartArt graphic, and then changing its color and style.

## STEPS

**TROUBLE**
If the Text Pane does not open automatically, click the Text Pane button in the Create Graphic group.

1. **Click Slide 2 on the Slides tab, click the Locations shape in the SmartArt graphic, then click the SmartArt Tools Design tab on the Ribbon**

   The Locations shape is selected and displays sizing handles and a rotate handle. Each shape in the SmartArt graphic is separate and distinct from the other shapes and can be individually edited, formatted, or moved within the boundaries of the SmartArt graphic. The SmartArt Text Pane is also open.

2. **Click the Add Bullet button in the Create Graphic group, then type Kehl-Kork in the Text Pane**

   A new bullet appears in the Text Pane and in the upper-right shape of the graphic. Compare your screen with Figure G-3.

3. **Click the More button ⊽ in the Layouts group, then click Picture Accent List (1st column)**

   The SmartArt graphic layout changes.

4. **Click the Add Shape button list arrow in the Create Graphic group, click Add Shape After, then click next to the new bullet in the Text pane to place the insertion point**

   A new shape in the same style appears and a new bullet appears in the Text Pane.

5. **Type Other Offers, press [Enter], press [Tab], type Walking France, press [Enter], type Biking Austria, press [Enter], type Biking England, press [Enter], then type Walking Germany**

6. **Click the More button ⊽ in the SmartArt Styles group, click Polished in the 3-D section, then click the Change Colors button in the SmartArt Styles group**

   A gallery of color themes appears showing the current theme applied to the graphic under Accent 1.

7. **In the Colorful section, click Colorful Range - Accent Colors 5 to 6**

   Each shape now has its own color.

8. **Click the Text Pane Close button ✕, then click the Right to Left button in the Create Graphic group**

   The graphic flips and appears as a mirror image. You prefer the original view of the graphic.

9. **Click the Right to Left button in the Create Graphic group, click a blank area of the slide, then save your changes**

   Compare your screen to Figure G-4.

**FIGURE G-3:** SmartArt graphic with added text

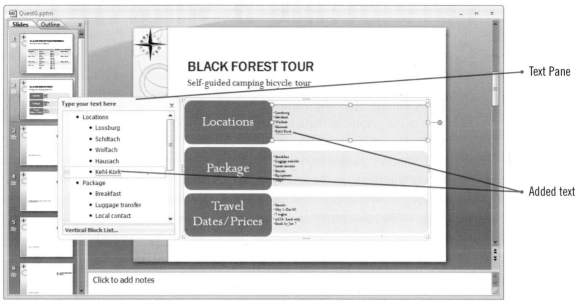

Text Pane

Added text

**FIGURE G-4:** SmartArt graphic with new design

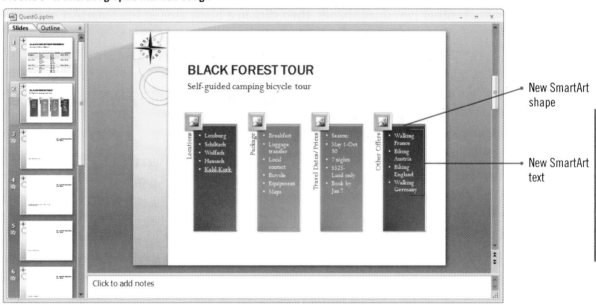

New SmartArt shape

New SmartArt text

## Creating organizational charts

An organizational chart graphically illustrates the management structure of a business or organization. Organizational chart layouts are now incorporated within the SmartArt feature under the Hierarchy group. You can create organizational charts using SmartArt when your organizational chart has fewer than 30 shapes and you want to add effects or animate the chart. The Layout button in the Create Graphic group on the SmartArt Tools Design tab allows you to change the branch layout for the selected shape.

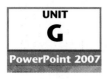

# Formatting a SmartArt Graphic

Though you can use styles and themes to format a SmartArt graphic, you still may need to refine individual aspects of the graphic to make it look the way you want it to look. You can use the commands on the SmartArt Tools Format tab to change shape styles, fills, outlines, and effects. You can also convert text within the SmartArt graphic to WordArt and format the text using any of the WordArt formatting commands. Individual shapes in the SmartArt graphic can be made larger or smaller, or altered into a different shape altogether. ▒▒▒▒ You continue working on the SmartArt graphic on Slide 2 by modifying four picture shapes, adding pictures to the picture shapes, and adjusting the text in the graphic.

1. **Click the SmartArt graphic, click the SmartArt Tools Format tab on the Ribbon, move the pointer over the small shape behind the picture icon above the word Locations until it changes to ⌖, then click the shape**
   The small shape behind the picture icon is selected.

2. **Click the Change Shape button in the Shapes group, then click Round Diagonal Corner Rectangle (the last shape in the Rectangles section)**
   The form of the small shape changes.

3. **Click the small shape above the word Package, press [F4], repeat this action for the other two small shapes, then click in a blank area of the SmartArt graphic**
   All four small shapes now have a new shape as shown in Figure G-5.

4. **Click the left-most picture icon above the word Locations**
   The Insert Picture dialog box opens.

5. **Locate the file PPT G-2.jpg from the drive and folder where you store your Data Files, then click Insert**
   A small thumbnail picture is placed in the picture shape.

6. **Click the picture icon above the word Package, insert the file PPT G-3.jpg, click the picture icon above the word Prices, insert the file PPT G-4.jpg, click the picture icon above the words Other Offers, then insert the file PPT G-5.jpg**
   All four shapes have pictures in them.

7. **Click a blank area inside the SmartArt graphic, drag the left sizing handle to the left to the edge of the white space on the slide, then drag the right sizing handle to the right edge of the slide**
   The SmartArt graphic fills the white area on the slide.

8. **Click a blank area of the slide, then save your work**
   Compare your screen with Figure G-6.

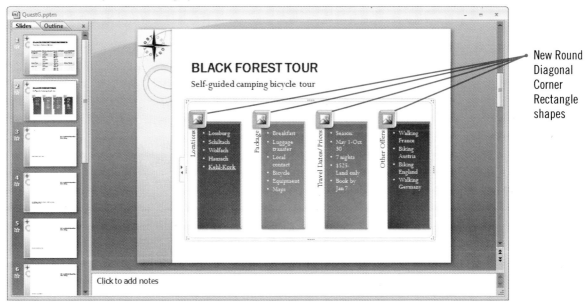

New Round Diagonal Corner Rectangle shapes

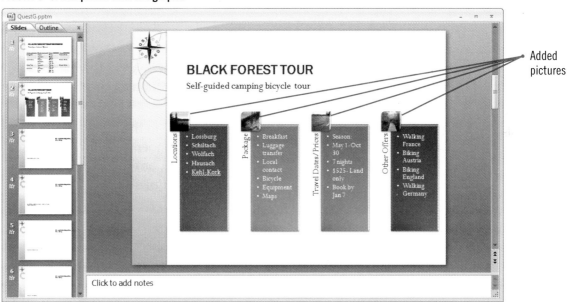

Added pictures

**PowerPoint 2007**

## Changing page setup and slide orientation

When you need to customize the size and orientation of your presentation you can do so using the commands in the Page Setup group on the Design tab on the Ribbon. Click the Page Setup button to open the Page Setup dialog box. In the Page Setup dialog box, you can change the width and height of the slides to twelve different settings, including On-screen Show, Letter Paper, 35mm Slides, and Banner. You can also set a custom slide size by determining the height and width of the slides. If the presentation would work better in Portrait rather than Landscape mode, you can click the Slide Orientation button in the Page Setup group on the Design tab to change the orientation of the presentation. The orientation setting for the slides is separate from the orientation setting for the notes, handouts, and outline. You can set the slide orientation in the Page Setup dialog box or by clicking the Slide Orientation button in the Page Setup group.

# Inserting an Animation

In your presentations, you may want to use special effects to illustrate a point or capture the attention of your audience. You can do this by inserting an animation or a movie. An **animation** contains multiple images that stream together or move when you run a slide show to give the illusion of motion. Animations are stored as Graphics Interchange Format (GIF) files. PowerPoint comes with a number of animated GIFs, which are stored in the Microsoft Clip Organizer. The **Clip Organizer** contains various drawings, photographs, clip art, sounds, animated GIFs, and movies that you can insert into your presentation. A **movie** is live action captured in digital format by a movie camera. You continue to develop your presentation by inserting an animation of a bicyclist in the forest.

## STEPS

1. **Click** Slide 1 **in the Slides tab**

2. **Click the** Insert tab **on the Ribbon, click the** Movie button list arrow **in the Media Clips group, then click** Movie from Clip Organizer
   The Clip Art task pane opens and displays animations.

3. **Type** bicycle **in the Search for text box, then click** Go
   PowerPoint searches for bicycle animations.

**TROUBLE**
If you do not see the GIF file in Figure G-7, choose a different GIF or ask your instructor or technical support person for help.

4. **Click the** down scroll arrow **until you see the thumbnail of the bicyclist shown in** Figure G-7, **then click the** thumbnail
   The animation appears in the center of the slide.

5. **Click the Clip Art task pane** Close button ✕
   The Clip Art task pane closes and the Picture Tools Format tab is open on the Ribbon.

6. **Right-click the** animation, **then click** Size and Position **on the shortcut menu**
   The Size and Position dialog box opens.

7. **In the Scale section double-click the number** 100 **in the Height text box, type** 150, **click the** Position tab **in the dialog box, select the** number **in the Horizontal text box, type** 8.12, **press** [Tab] **twice, type** 6 **in the Vertical text box, then click** Close
   The animation moves to a new location on the slide and increases in size.

8. **Click the** Brightness button **in the Adjust group, click** +20 %, **then click a blank area of the slide**
   The animation is a little brighter and fits better with the other slide elements. Compare your screen with Figure G-8. The animation won't begin unless you view it in Slide Show view.

**QUICK TIP**
An animated GIF file will also play if you publish the presentation as a Web page and view it in a browser such as Internet Explorer.

9. **Click the** Slide Show button 🖳 **on the status bar, watch the animation for a few seconds, press** [Esc], **then save your work**

**FIGURE G-7:** Clip Organizer showing animation files

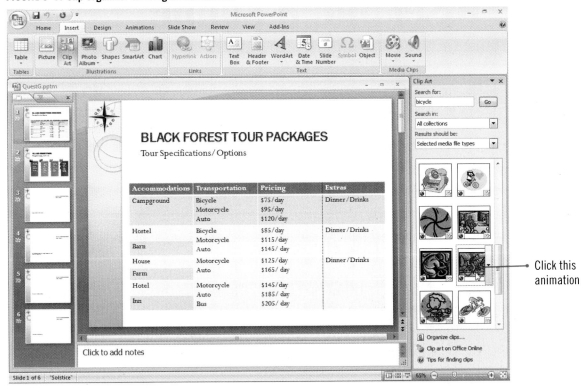

Click this animation

**FIGURE G-8:** Slide showing formatted animation

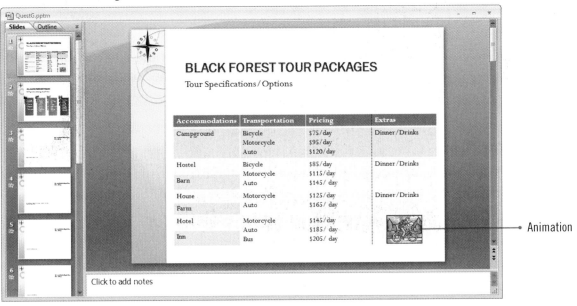

Animation

## Inserting movies

You can insert movies from the Microsoft Clip Organizer, the Microsoft Web site, or from other sources. To insert a movie from your computer hard drive or a removable disk, click the Insert tab on the Ribbon, click the Movie button list arrow in the Media Clips group, then click Movie from File. Navigate to the location of the movie you want, then insert it. If you're using the Clip Art task pane, search for the file you want, then insert it. After you insert a movie, you can edit it using the Picture Tools Format tab. You can also open the Custom Animation task pane and apply an effect to the movie. From the Custom Animation task pane, you can indicate whether to continue the slide show or to stop playing the movie.

# Inserting a Sound

PowerPoint allows you to insert sounds in your presentation in the same way you insert animations or movies. You can add sounds to your presentation from files on a disk, the Microsoft Clip Organizer, the Internet, or a drive on a network. The primary use of sound in a presentation is to provide emphasis to a slide or an element on the slide. For example, if you are creating a presentation about a raft tour of the Colorado River, you might insert a rushing water sound on a slide showing a photograph of people rafting. If you try to insert a sound that is larger than 100 KB, PowerPoint will automatically link the sound file to your presentation. You can change this setting in the Advanced section of the PowerPoint Options dialog box. You insert a wind sound on Slide 1 of the presentation to enhance the animation on the slide.

## STEPS

1. **Click the Insert tab on the Ribbon, click the Sound button list arrow in the Media Clips group, then click Sound from Clip Organizer**
   The Clip Art task pane opens and displays all the sound files installed with PowerPoint. PowerPoint sounds are Windows Audio (.wav) files, but you can also install other types of sound files, such as (.aiff), (.au), (.mid), (.mp3), and (.wma).

2. **Type wind in the Search for text box, then click Go**
   PowerPoint searches for wind sounds.

3. **Click the sound file labeled Strong Wind**
   A dialog box opens asking if you want the sound to play automatically or if you want it to play only when you click the icon during the slide show.

### QUICK TIP
The sound icon you see may be different from the one illustrated in Figure G-9 depending on your sound card software.

4. **Click Automatically**
   A small sound icon appears in the center of the slide, as shown in Figure G-9. The sound will play automatically during a slide show.

### TROUBLE
If you do not hear a sound, your computer may not have a sound card installed. See your instructor or technical support person for help.

5. **Drag the sound icon to the lower-right corner of the slide, click the Sound Tools Options tab, click the Loop Until Stopped check box in the Sound Options group, click the Preview button in the Play group, listen to the sound a few seconds until you hear a pause at the loop, then click the Preview button**
   You know the sound has looped when you hear a brief pause and then the sound begins again.

6. **Click the Slide Show Volume button in the Sound Options group, click Low, click the Preview button in the Play group, listen to the sound for a few seconds, then click the Preview button**
   The sound volume is slightly softer.

7. **Click the Slide Show button 🖵 on the status bar, watch the slide for a few seconds, then press [Esc]**
   Notice that the sound icon appears during the slide show.

8. **Click the Results should be list arrow, click the All media types check box, click Go, then click Clip Art task pane Close button ☒**
   The default settings are now restored to the Clip Art task pane.

9. **Click a blank area of the slide, then save your changes**
   Compare your screen to Figure G-10.

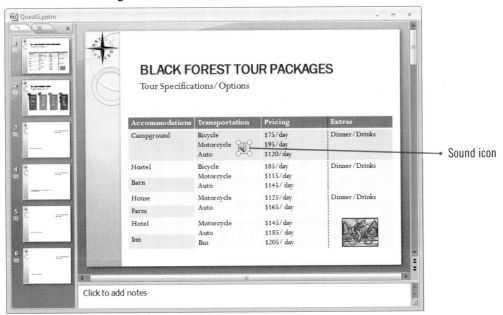

Sound icon

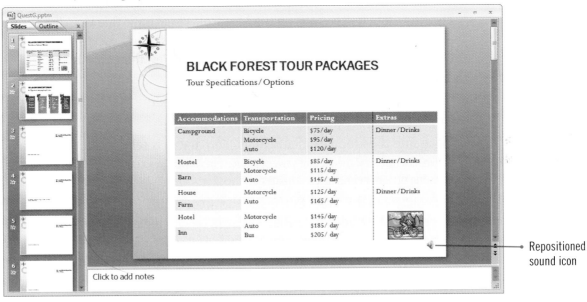

Repositioned sound icon

**PowerPoint 2007**

## Playing music from a CD

You can play a CD audio track during your slide show. Insert the CD into the CD drive, click the Insert tab on the Ribbon, click the Sound button list arrow, then click Play CD Audio Track. The Insert CD Audio dialog box opens. Select the beginning and ending track number and the timing options you want. See Figure G-11. When you are finished in the Insert CD Audio dialog box, click OK. A CD icon appears on the slide. You can indicate if you want the CD to play automatically when you move to the slide or only when you click the CD icon during a slide show. The CD must be in the CD-ROM drive before you can play an audio track.

**FIGURE G-11:** Insert CD Audio dialog box

# Using Macros

As you learned in the first lesson of this unit, a macro is a recording of an action or a set of actions that you use to automate tasks. The contents of a macro consist of a series of command codes that you create in the Visual Basic for Applications programming language using Microsoft Visual Basic, which you can access through the Developer tab in PowerPoint. You can use macros to automate almost any action that you perform repeatedly when creating presentations, which saves you time and effort. Any presentation with the .pptm file extension is saved with a macro. ░░░░░ You use macros that you already created to format and place four pictures.

**STEPS**

1. **Click Slide 3 in the Slides tab, click the Office button ⊕, click PowerPoint Options at the bottom of the menu, click the Show Developer tab in the Ribbon check box, then click OK**
   The Developer tab appears on the Ribbon.

2. **Click the Developer tab on the Ribbon, then click the Visual Basic button in the Code group**
   The Visual Basic window opens displaying two small windows as shown in Figure G-12. Each window represents a separate macro. Each macro is designed to reduce the size of a picture and place it in a specific place on the slide. The difference between the two macros is that the Module2 macro unlocks the aspect ratio of a picture so that any size picture can be reduced within the designated parameters.

3. **Click the Close button ▣ on the Microsoft Visual Basic title bar, click the Insert tab on the Ribbon, click the Picture button in the Illustrations group, locate the file PPT G-6.jpg from the drive and folder where you store your Data Files, then click Insert**
   An oversized picture covers most of the slide.

4. **Click the Developer tab on the Ribbon, then click the Macros button in the Code group**
   The Macro dialog box opens displaying the two macros attached to this presentation file.

5. **Make sure the Module1.PictureReduction macro is selected, then click Run**
   The macro runs and the picture's size is reduced to fit within a certain area on the slide. The macro also positions the picture to precise coordinates on the slide.

6. **Click Slide 4 in the Slides tab, insert the picture file PPT G-7.jpg from the drive and folder where you store your Data Files, click the Developer tab on the Ribbon, click the Macros button in the Code group, click Module2.PictureReduction in the list, then click Run**
   This macro resizes and positions a picture with a portrait orientation.

7. **Insert the picture file PPT G-8.jpg on Slide 5, apply the Module1.PictureReduction macro to the picture, insert the picture file PPT G-9.jpg on Slide 6, then apply the Module1.PictureReduction macro to the picture**
   Compare your screen to Figure G-13.

8. **Click the Picture Tools Format tab on the Ribbon, click the Drop Shadow Rectangle style in the Picture Styles group, then apply this same picture style to the pictures on Slides 3, 4, and 5**
   Each of the pictures you inserted into the presentation is now formatted with the same drop shadow.

9. **Click ⊕, click PowerPoint Options, click the Show Developer tab in the Ribbon check box, click OK, then save your work**

FIGURE G-12: Visual Basic window

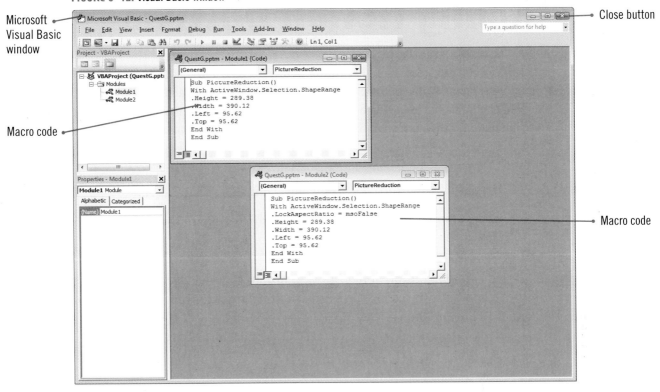

FIGURE G-13: Screen showing inserted pictures

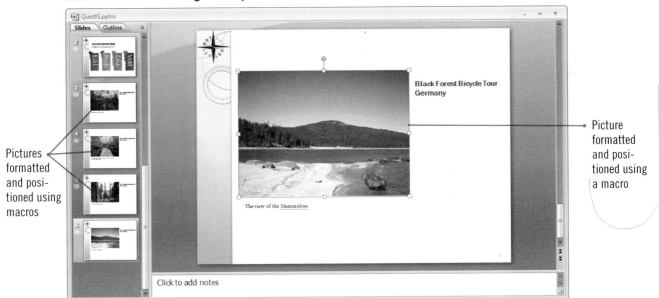

## Macro security

There are certain risks involved when you enable macros on your computer. The macros used in this lesson are simple commands that automate the size reduction and relative position of picture on a slide; however, hackers can introduce harmful viruses or other malicious programs into your computer using macros. By default, PowerPoint disables macros when you open a presentation file that includes macros to prevent possible damage to your computer. To understand PowerPoint's security settings and how PowerPoint checks for harmful macros, click the Macro Security button on the Developer tab or click the Office button, click PowerPoint Options, then click Trust Center. The bottom line with macros is if you can't trust the source of the macro, do not enable it.

# Adding Action Buttons

An action button is an interactive button that you create from the Shapes gallery to perform a specific task. For example, you can create an action button to play a movie or a sound, or to hyperlink to another slide in your presentation. Action buttons can also hyperlink to an Internet address on the Web, a different presentation, or another file created in another program. You can also run a macro or another program using an action button. Action buttons are commonly used in self-running presentations and presentations published on the Web. ▨▨▨ You finish working on this presentation by adding action buttons to each slide, which will allow you to move from slide to slide and back to the first slide.

## STEPS

1. **Click Slide 1 in the Slides tab, then click the Home tab on the Ribbon, if it is not already selected**

   Slide 1 appears in the Slide pane.

2. **Click the Shapes button in the Drawing group, click Action Button: Forward or Next in the Action Buttons section, press and hold [Shift], refer to Figure G-14 as you drag to create a button, then release [Shift]**

   A small action button appears on the slide and the Action Settings dialog box opens.

3. **Make sure Next Slide is selected in the Hyperlink to list, then click OK**

   The dialog box closes.

4. **Click the Drawing Tools Format tab on the Ribbon, click the More button ⬇ in the Shape Styles group, then click Subtle Effect – Dark 1 in the first column**

   The action button is easier to see.

5. **Drag the action button to the bottom of the slide under the left edge of the table**

6. **Click the Home tab on the Ribbon, click the Copy button ▨ in the Clipboard group, click Slide 2 in the Slides pane, then click the Paste button in the Clipboard group**

   An exact copy of the action button is placed on the slide.

7. **Paste a copy of the action button on Slides 3, 4, and 5, click Slide 6 in the Slides tab, click the Shapes button in the Drawing group, then click Action Button: Home in the Action Buttons section**

   The action button is copied onto slides 1–5 of the presentation. You selected the Home Action button.

8. **Drag an action button about the same size as the first action button below the image on Slide 6, click OK, click the Drawing Tools Format tab on the Ribbon, click ⬇ in the Shape Styles group, then click Subtle Effect – Dark 1**

   This new action button is formatted the same as the other action buttons. Compare your screen to Figure G-15.

9. **Click the Slide Show button ▨ on the status bar, click the Home action button, then click the action buttons to move from slide to slide, then press [Esc] to end the slide show**

   The pointer changes to 👆 when you click each action button.

10. **Save your changes, click ▨, then click Close**

FIGURE G-14: New action button

Action button

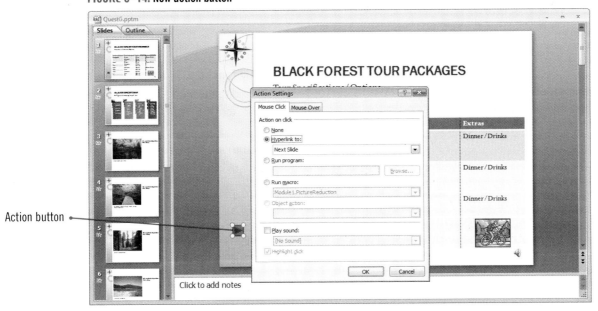

FIGURE G-15: Last slide showing Home action button

Home action button

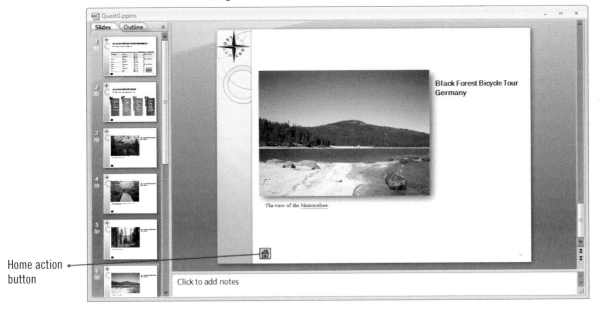

## The compatibility checker

In order to make certain that your PowerPoint 2007 presentation will open and function properly in an earlier version of PowerPoint, you need to run the Compatibility Checker. The Compatibility Checker analyzes your presentation and finds potential problems between your PowerPoint 2007 presentation and earlier versions of PowerPoint. After you run the Compatibility Checker, a report is created that identifies features you have used in your presentation that will be lost or degraded by saving your presentation in an earlier file format. For example, SmartArt graphics can't be edited in previous versions of PowerPoint. To run the Compatibility Checker, click the Office button, point to Prepare, then click Run Compatibility Checker.

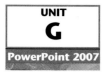

# Inserting a Hyperlink

Often you will want to view a document that either won't fit on the slide or is too detailed for your presentation. In these cases, you can insert a hyperlink, a specially formatted word, phrase, graphic, or drawn object that you click during your slide show to "jump to," or display, another slide in your current presentation; another PowerPoint presentation; a Word, Excel, or Access file; or a Web page on the Internet. Inserting a hyperlink is similar to linking because you can change the object in the source program after you click the hyperlink. ⬛⬛ You add two hyperlinks to the primary presentation you have been working on for Ellen that will provide access to more detail on the Black Forest bicycle tour.

1. **Open the presentation** PPT G-10.pptx **from the drive and folder where you store your Data Files, save the presentation as** QuestGFinal, **click the** View tab **on the Ribbon, then click the** Arrange All button **in the Window group**

2. **Click** Slide 12 **in the Slides tab, select** Biking Austria **in the table, click the** Insert tab **on the Ribbon, then click the** Hyperlink button **in the Links group**

   The Insert Hyperlink dialog box opens. The Existing File or Web Page button is selected in the Link to: pane, and the Current Folder button is selected in the Look in page.

3. **Locate the file** PPT G-11.docx **from the drive and folder where you store your Data Files, click** OK, **then click in a blank area of the slide**

   Now that you have made "Biking Austria" a hyperlink to the file PPT G-11.docx, the text formatting changes to a green color, the hyperlink color for this presentation's theme, and is underlined. It's important to test any hyperlink you create.

4. **Click the** Slide Show button 🖵 **on the status bar, point to** Biking Austria **to see the pointer change to** 👆, **then click** Biking Austria

   Microsoft Word opens, and the Word document containing a detailed description of the Biking Austria tour appears, as shown in Figure G-16.

5. **Click the** down scroll arrow **and read the document, then click the Word window** Close button ⊠

   The PowerPoint slide reappears in Slide Show view. The hyperlink is now an olive green, the color for followed hyperlinks in this theme, indicating that the hyperlink has been used or viewed.

6. **Press [Esc] to end the slide show, right-click the** Information action button **in the Black Forest Tour cell of the table, click** Hyperlink, **click the** Hyperlink to option button, **click the** Hyperlink to list arrow, **click the** down scroll arrow, **then click** Other PowerPoint Presentation

   The Hyperlink to Other PowerPoint Presentation dialog box opens.

7. **Locate the file** PPT G-12.pptx **from the drive and folder where you store your Data Files, then click** OK

   The Hyperlink to Slide dialog box opens. You can choose which slide of the presentation you want to link to.

8. **Click** OK **to link to Slide 1, click** OK **to close the Action Settings dialog box, click** 🖵, **click the** Information action button, **click through the presentation using the action buttons, press [Esc] to end the slide show, then press [Esc] again**

   The slide show ends. Both hyperlinks work correctly.

9. **Add your name to the Slide footer, save your changes, then click the** Slide Sorter button 🏁

   Compare your screen to Figure G-17.

10. **Print the outline and the slides, close the presentation, then exit PowerPoint**

**FIGURE G-16:** Linked Word document

Document in Microsoft Word →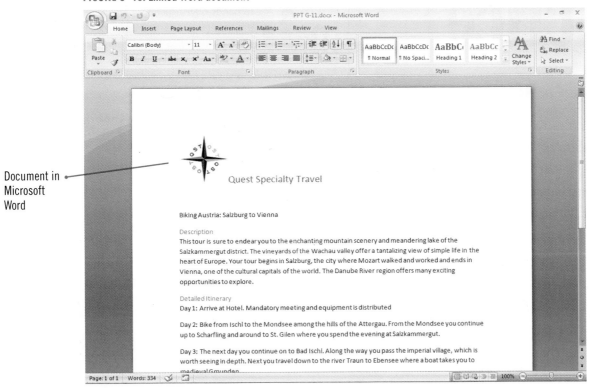

**FIGURE G-17:** Final presentation in Slide Sorter view

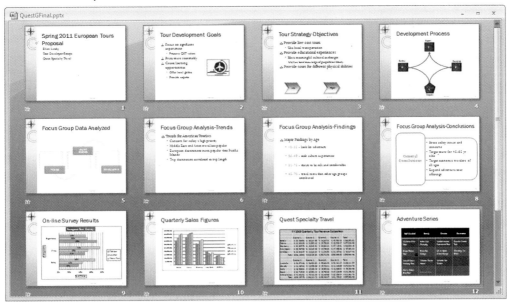

## Changing PowerPoint options

You can customize your installation of PowerPoint by changing various settings and preferences. To change PowerPoint settings, click the Office button, then click PowerPoint Options to open the PowerPoint Options dialog box. In the dialog box there are eight sections identified by a word in the left pane, which offer you ways to customize PowerPoint. For example, the Popular area includes options for viewing the Mini toolbar, enabling Live Preview, and showing the Developer tab on the Ribbon.

# Practice

If you have a SAM user profile, you may have access to hands-on instruction, practice, and assessment of the skills covered in this unit. Log in to your SAM account (http://sam2007.course.com/) to launch any assigned training activities or exams that relate to the skills covered in this unit.

## ▼ CONCEPTS REVIEW

**Label each element of the PowerPoint window shown in Figure G-18.**

FIGURE G-18

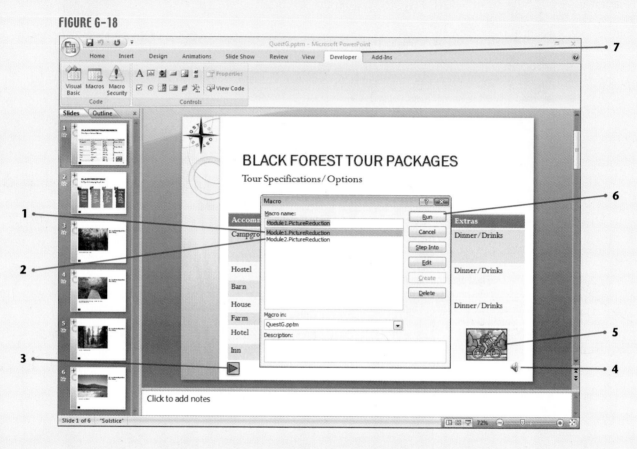

**Match each of the terms with the statement that best describes its function.**

8. Clip Organizer
9. Macro-enabled presentation
10. Animation
11. Movie
12. Action button
13. Hyperlink

a. Multiple images that move when you run a slide show
b. A file with the .pptm file extension
c. A specially formatted word or graphic that you can click to jump to another document
d. An interactive shape that performs a specific task when clicked
e. A folder that stores media clips on the computer
f. Live action captured in digital format by a camera

**Select the best answer from the list of choices.**

**14.** **A recording of an action that automates a task best describes which of the following:**
    **a.** Hyperlink                        **c.** Macro
    **b.** Action button                   **d.** Movie

**15.** **Which of the following combines content with an illustrative diagram?**
    **a.** SmartArt                         **c.** Hyperlink
    **b.** Action button                   **d.** Table

**16.** **Which statement best describes a hyperlink?**
    **a.** A type of animation
    **b.** Another name for a macro
    **c.** A button used in a table to start a slide show
    **d.** A specially formatted shape that is clicked to display an Excel file

**17.** **What is a GIF file?**
    **a.** A movie                          **c.** A sound
    **b.** An animation                   **d.** A hyperlink

# ▼ SKILLS REVIEW

**1. Create custom tables.**

    **a.** Start PowerPoint, open the presentation PPT G-13.pptm from the drive and folder where you store your Data Files, then save it as **Cheese Cooperative**.

    **b.** Go to Slide 5, select the table, click the Table Tools Design tab, click the More button in the Table Styles group, then click the Light Style 2 – Accent 1 in the Light section in the second row.

    **c.** Click the Pen Weight button in the Draw Borders group, select a solid line style, select 2¼ pt, then apply the new line style to the bottom horizontal cell border in the first row.

    **d.** Apply the 2¼-pt line style to the vertical border lines between the cells in the first row, then click the Draw Table button.

    **e.** Open the Table Tools Layout tab, select the table, click the Cell Margins button in the Alignment group, then click Wide.

    **f.** Click anywhere in the upper-left cell, click the Select button in the Table group, click Select Row, then click the Center button in the Alignment group.

    **g.** Click anywhere in the bottom row, click the Insert Below button in the Rows & Columns group, click the left cell, type **Bleu de Gex**, press [Tab], type **Bethmale**, press [Tab], type **Agour Ossau-Iraty**.

    **h.** Save your changes.

**2. Design a SmartArt graphic.**

    **a.** Go to Slide 4, click the SmartArt graphic, then click the SmartArt Tools Design tab.

    **b.** Click the More button in the Layouts group, then click Vertical Picture Accent List in the third row.

    **c.** Open the Text Pane if necessary, click the Add Shape button list arrow in the Create Graphic group, then click Add Shape After.

    **d.** Type **Production**, press [Enter], click the Demote button in the Create Graphic group, type **Cow cheese 1.66 million tons**, press [Enter], type **Goat cheese 0.68 million tons**, press [Enter], type **Ewe cheese 0.52 million tons**.

    **e.** Close the Text Pane, click the Change Colors button in the SmartArt Styles group, then click Gradient Range – Accent 2 in the Accent 2 section.

    **f.** Resize and reposition the SmartArt graphic so it is centered on the slide, then save your changes.

**3. Format a SmartArt graphic.**

    **a.** Click the SmartArt Tools Format tab, click the top circle shape in the graphic, then click the Smaller button in the Shapes group twice.

    **b.** Following the instructions in the step above, decrease the size of the other two circle shapes.

    **c.** Click the picture icon in the bottom circle shape, then locate and insert the file PPT G-14.jpg from the drive and folder where you store your Data Files.

    **d.** Follow the above instructions and insert the file PPT G-14.jpg to the other two circle shapes.

    **e.** Save your changes.

**4. Insert an animation.**

    **a.** Go to Slide 7, then open the Clip Art task pane.

    **b.** Insert an animated GIF file of your choosing on the slide. Type the word **email** to search for an appropriate animated GIF.

    **c.** Resize and reposition the GIF file as necessary.

    **d.** Click the Contrast button in the Adjust group, then click +30%.

    **e.** Preview the animation in Slide Show view, then save your presentation.

**5. Insert a sound.**

    **a.** Go to Slide 2.

    **b.** Click the Insert tab, click the Sound button list arrow in the Media Clips group, then click Sound from File.

    **c.** Locate and insert the sound file PPT G-15.wav from the drive and folder where you store your Data Files. Set the sound to play when clicked.

    **d.** Drag the sound icon to the right side of the graphic of France.

    **e.** Click the Sound Tools Options tab on the Ribbon, click the Slide Show Volume button in the Sound Options group, then click Low.

    **f.** Click the Loop Until Stopped check box in the Sound Options group, click the Preview button in the Play group, then save your presentation.

**6. Use macros.**

    **a.** Go to Slide 6, click the Office button, click PowerPoint Options, then add the Developer tab to the Ribbon.

    **b.** Click the Insert tab on the Ribbon, click the Picture button in the Illustrations group, then locate and insert the file PPT G-16.jpg from the drive and folder where you store your Data Files.

    **c.** Click the Developer tab, click the Macros button in the Code group, then click Run in the Macro dialog box. Click OK to run the macro, if necessary.

    **d.** Click the Picture Tools Format tab on the Ribbon, click the More button in the Picture Styles group, then click Soft Edge Rectangle in the top row.

    **e.** Remove the Developer tab from the Ribbon.

**7. Add action buttons.**

    **a.** Go to Slide 1, click the Shapes button in the Drawing group, then click Action Button: Forward or Next.

    **b.** Draw a small button, click OK in the Action Settings dialog box, then position the button in the lower-left corner of the slide.

    **c.** Click the Drawing Tools Format tab on the Ribbon, click the More button in the Shape Styles group, then click Intense Effect – Accent 5 in the bottom row.

    **d.** Copy the action button to Slides 2–7.

    **e.** Go to Slide 8, click the Shapes button, click Action Button: Beginning, draw a small button, then click OK.

    **f.** Click Slide 7, click the action button, click the Format Painter button in the Clipboard group, click Slide 8, then click the action button.

    **g.** Position the button in the lower-left corner of the slide.

    **h.** Run the slide show from Slide 1 and test the action buttons, then save your work.

## ▼ SKILLS REVIEW (CONTINUED)

**8. Insert a hyperlink.**

a. Go to Slide 6, then select the words Maria McNibs in the text object.

b. Click the Insert tab on the Ribbon, click the Hyperlink button in the Links group, locate the file PPT G-17.docx from the drive and folder where you store your Data Files, then click OK.

c. Click in the notes pane, then type **The hyperlink links to Maria's cheese review of the 2010 Camembert**.

d. Open Slide Show view, click the hyperlink, read the review, then click the Word window Close button.

**FIGURE G-19**

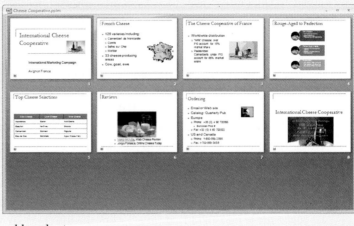

e. Press [Esc], then add your name as a footer to notes and handouts.

f. Run the spell checker, view the presentation in Slide Show view. Make any necessary changes. The completed presentation is shown in Figure G-19.

g. Print the slides as Notes Pages, then save and close the presentation.

## ▼ INDEPENDENT CHALLENGE 1

Tounger Engineering is a mechanical and industrial design company that specializes in designing manufacturing plants around the world. As a company financial analyst, you need to investigate and report on a possible contract to design and build a large manufacturing plant in China.

a. Open the file PPT G-18.pptx, then save it as **Chinese Plant**.

b. On Slide 3, apply the table style Medium Style 3 – Accent 3, then draw a dotted line down the center of the table using the Pen Style button.

c. Click in the top row of the table, insert a row above the top row, type **Line Item** in the left cell, then type **Budget** in the right cell.

d. Click the Overhead/Benefits cell, split the cell into two columns and one row, then move the word Benefits to the new cell and delete the slash.

e. Create a new SmartArt graphic on Slide 4 using the following process information: **Planning and Design**; **Site Acquisition and Preparation**; **Underground Construction**; **Above-ground Construction**; and **Final Building**.

f. Change the colors of the graphic to a colorful theme, then apply an intense SmartArt Style effect.

g. Change the shape of at least one shape in the SmartArt graphic using the Change Shape button, then click the Right to Left button in the Create Graphic group on the SmartArt Tools Design tab.

h. Add your name as a footer to the notes and handouts, then save your changes.

**Advanced Challenge Exercise**

- Create a new slide using the Title and Content slide layout, type **Project Organization** in the title placeholder, then create an organizational chart SmartArt graphic.
- Fill the text boxes with the following job titles: **Project Manager**; **Administrator**; **Project Foreman**; **Design Manager**; and **Project Coordinator**.
- Click the top shape, click the Layout button in the Create Graphic group, then click Right Hanging.
- Format the graphic by adding a new style and color theme, make any other necessary changes, then save the presentation as **Chinese Plant ACE**.

i. View the presentation in Slide Show view, print the presentation as handouts (two slides per page), then close the presentation and exit PowerPoint.

**PowerPoint 2007**

# ▼ INDEPENDENT CHALLENGE 2

You are the director of operations at The Fisher Group, a large investment banking firm in New York. Fisher is considering merging with DuPont Financial Services, a smaller investment company in Miami, to form the 8th largest financial institution in the United States. As the director of operations, you need to present some financial projections regarding the merger to a special committee formed by The Fisher Group to study the proposed merger.

**a.** Open the file PPT G-19.pptx from the drive and folder where you store your Data Files, then save it as **Merger**.

**b.** Format the table on Slide 3 as directed in the following steps: (1) apply a table style from the Light Style 2 styles section of the Table Styles gallery; (2) draw three 1½-pt dotted vertical cell separator lines in the table; and (3) click the Total Row check box and the Last Column check box in the Table Style Options group.

**c.** Convert the text on Slide 5 to a SmartArt graphic using one of the List layouts.

**d.** Format the SmartArt graphic by: (1) applying an Accent 2 color theme, (2) changing the SmartArt style to Subtle Effect, (3) deleting the empty shape, and (4) applying a fill using the Shape Fill button in the Shape Styles group.

**e.** Insert an animation on Slide 3. Use the word **profits** to search for an appropriate animated GIF.

**f.** Select the word DuPont on Slide 2, click the Insert tab on the Ribbon, click the Hyperlink button in the Links group, locate the file PPT G-20.pptx from the drive and folder where you store your Data Files, then click OK.

**g.** Add your name as a footer to the notes and the handouts, save your changes, then view the presentation in Slide Show view. Be sure to click the hyperlink on Slide 2.

**h.** Print the final slide presentation as handouts (four per page), then close the presentation and exit PowerPoint.

# ▼ INDEPENDENT CHALLENGE 3

You have been recently hired at AsiaWorld Inc., a U.S. company that exports goods and services to companies in all parts of Asia, including Japan, Hong Kong, China, and the Philippines. One of your new responsibilities is to prepare short presentations on different subjects for use on the company Web site using data provided to you by others in the company.

**a.** Open the file PPT G-21.pptx from the drive and folder where you store your Data Files, then save it as **AsiaWorld**.

**b.** Add a design theme, background shading, or other objects to make your presentation look professional.

**c.** Convert the text on Slide 3 to a SmartArt graphic, then format the graphic using any of the formatting commands available.

**d.** Insert an appropriate animation on the last slide of the presentation.

**e.** Insert a sound on Slide 2. Use the word **harbor** to search for an appropriate sound.

**f.** Create, format, and position Forward action buttons on Slides 1–5.

**g.** Create, format, and position a Home action button on Slide 6.

**h.** Create, format, and position Back action buttons on Slides 2–6.

**Advanced Challenge Exercise**

- Go to Slide 1.
- Insert a CD of your choice into the CD drive of your computer, click the Insert tab on the Ribbon, then click the Sound button list arrow.
- Click Play CD Audio Track, select the start track, select the end track, set any other options you feel are necessary, then click OK.
- Click Automatically, click the sound icon if necessary, click the Play Track list arrow in the Set Up group, click Play across slides, then click the Slide Show button on the status bar.
- Press [Esc] when finished.

**i.** Add your name as a footer to the slides and notes and handouts, save your changes, then print the final slide presentation.

**j.** View the presentation in Slide Show view, then exit PowerPoint.

# ▼ REAL LIFE INDEPENDENT CHALLENGE

One of the assignments in your business course at the university is to give a 15 minute presentation on any subject to the class. The goal of the assignment is for you to persuade the class (and your instructor) to make an informed decision about the subject you are presenting based on your ability to communicate the facts. You decide to create a presentation using pictures and other media to play in the background while you give your presentation.

To develop the content of this presentation:

- Choose your own subject matter, for example, a favorite hobby or sport.
- Use your own media clips (pictures, sounds, or movies) on your computer. If you don't have your own media clips, you can search the Clip Organizer for appropriate clips.

**a.** Open the file PPT G-22.pptm from the drive and folder where you store your Data Files, then save it as **Business 410**. The file PPT G-22.pptm has no content, but is macro-enabled.

**b.** Add your name, the date, and the slide number as the footer on all slides, except the title slide.

**c.** Decide on a presentation subject, then think about what results you want to see and what information you will need to create the slide presentation.

**d.** Insert one picture (your own or one from the Clip Organizer) on each slide, then run the available macro for each picture.

**e.** Insert one or more appropriate sounds from your computer or the Clip Organizer.

**f.** Insert one or more appropriate animations or movies from your computer or the Clip Organizer.

**g.** Give each slide a title and add main text where appropriate. Create additional slides as necessary.

**h.** Apply an appropriate design theme.

**i.** Spell check the presentation, view the final presentation in Slide Show view, save the final version, then print the slides as handouts. See Figure G-20.

**j.** Close the presentation, then exit PowerPoint.

**FIGURE G-20**

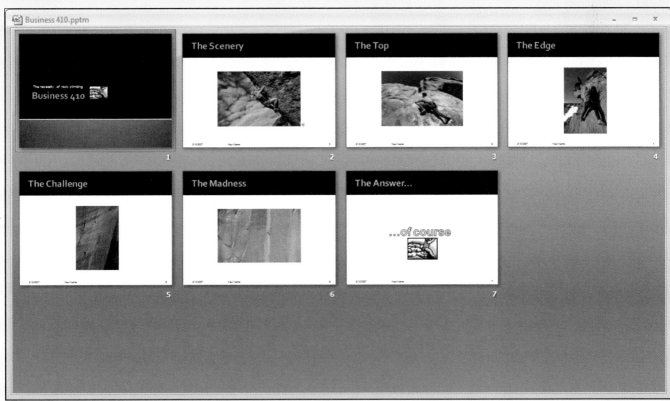

# ▼ VISUAL WORKSHOP

Create a slide that looks like the example in Figure G-21. The SmartArt is created using the Horizontal Bullet List layout with the Polished style and the colored Fill – Accent 1 color. Save the presentation as **California**. Add your name as a footer on the slide, then save and print the slide.

**FIGURE G-21**

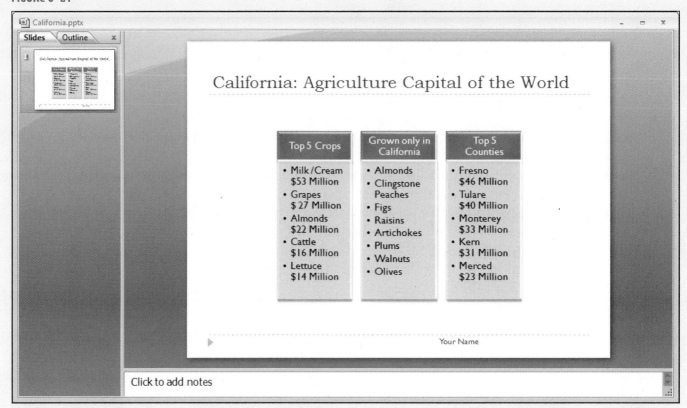

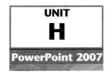

# Using Advanced Features

**Files You Will Need**

PPT H-1.pptx
PPT H-2.pptx
PPT H-3.pptx
PPT H-4.jpg
PPT H-5.jpg
PPT H-6.jpg
PPT H-7.jpg
PPT H-8.jpg
PPT H-9.pptx
PPT H-10.pptx
PPT H-11.jpg
PPT H-12.jpg
PPT H-13.jpg
PPT H-14.jpg
PPT H-15.jpg
PPT H-16.jpg
PPT H-17.pptx
PPT H-18.pptx
PPT H-19.jpg
Pacific Theme.thmx

After your work on a presentation is complete, PowerPoint provides you with several options for preparing and distributing your final presentation. For example, you can send the presentation out for review and receive comments, package it to be used on another computer, or save it for viewing on the Web. At this stage in the process you can also create customized slide shows and use advanced options to set up a slide show. You have finished working on the content for the Quest Specialty Travel (QST) presentation that Ellen Latsky will use in an upcoming meeting. Now you need to send the presentation to Ellen so she can review it before you leave work for the weekend. You create a custom slide show, change slide show options, prepare the presentation for distribution, save it for viewing on the Web, then package the presentation. You end your day by having a little fun and creating a photo album of your trip to Ireland.

**OBJECTIVES**

Use templates and add comments

Send and review a presentation

Use advanced slide show options

Create a custom show

Prepare a presentation for
    distribution

Save a presentation for the Web

Package a presentation

Create a photo album

# Using Templates and Adding Comments

PowerPoint 2007 offers you a variety of ways to create a presentation including beginning with a blank presentation, a theme, a template, or an existing presentation. Occasionally you may need a little help starting a new presentation. Looking through the templates in the New Presentation dialog box may provide just the inspiration you need to begin. PowerPoint divides the templates into two sections: Templates and Microsoft Office Online. The templates in the Templates section are installed on your computer and include the blank presentation, installed themes, and installed templates. The templates in the Microsoft Office Online section are designed for many different purposes and have professional layouts; you can download them from Microsoft Office Web site. ▰▰▰▰▰ You need to review available PowerPoint templates that could be used to display pictures of upcoming tour specials for the company Web site.

## STEPS

1. **Start PowerPoint, click the Office button 🗔, then click New**
   The New Presentation dialog box opens. The Blank Presentation icon is selected in the center pane at the top of the dialog box by default.

2. **Click Installed Themes in the left pane, scroll through the themes, then click Installed Templates in the left pane**
   All of these themes and templates are installed on your computer and are available for you to use. The themes you see are the same themes you can access from the Design tab on the PowerPoint Ribbon. Each template comes with sample content including graphics and text. Themes do not have sample content.

3. **Make sure that Classic Photo Album is selected, click Create, click the Save button 🖫 on the Quick Access toolbar, then save the file as Sample Album to the drive and folder where you store your Data Files**
   A new presentation with seven slides appears in the program window.

4. **Click the View tab on the Ribbon, click the Arrange All button in the Window group, click the Review tab on the Ribbon, then click the New Comment button in the Comments group**
   A new comment box appears next to the review comment thumbnail on the slide, as shown in Figure H-1.

**QUICK TIP**

You can copy the text of a comment to the slide by clicking the review comment thumbnail, then dragging the comment text to the slide.

5. **Type Ellen, is this sample photo album what you had in mind?, click Slide 5 in the Slides tab, click the New Comment button in the Comments group, then type This layout would work well for us., then click in a blank area of the slide**
   A new comment appears on Slide 5.

6. **Drag the review comment thumbnail so it is positioned over the left photograph, then click the Edit Comment button in the Comments group**
   The comment box opens and is ready to be modified.

7. **Type I like this picture style., then click the Previous button in the Comments group**
   The first comment on Slide 1 appears.

8. **Click the Show Markup button in the Comments group, then click the Show Markup button again**
   The Show Markup button is a toggle button, which alternates between showing and hiding comments.

9. **Click the Save button 🖫 on the Quick Access toolbar**
   After you save the presentation, the review comment thumbnail changes to A1, as shown in Figure H-2, identifying the comment as being made by the author of the presentation.

**FIGURE H-1:** Slide with new comment

Review comment thumbnail

User name appears here

New comment box

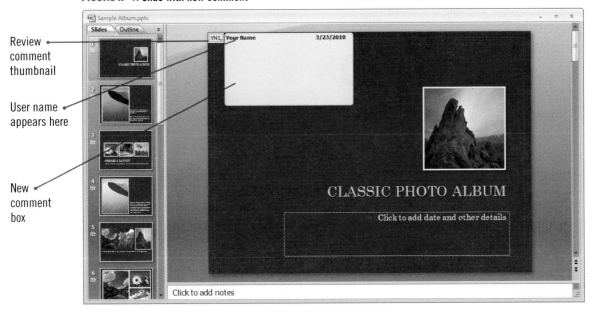

**FIGURE H-2:** Slide with completed comment

Review comment thumbnail after you save the file

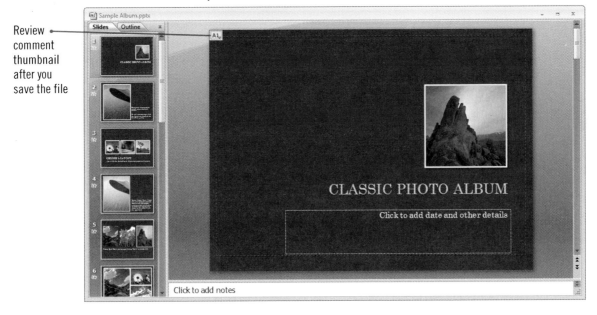

## Creating a document workspace

You may be in a work environment where you work with several people who all collaborate on the same presentation. Instead of trying to manage different versions of the presentation as it passes from person to person, you can set up a document library on a Document Workspace Web site, where everyone involved with the presentation has access to the same file. A Document Workspace Web site is created on the Microsoft Windows SharePoint Services Web site, where you need permission to create a shared document library. Files located in this shared document library can be created, managed, and updated by anyone who has access to the site. One way to create a Document Workspace Web site is to click the Office button, click Publish, then click Create Document Workspace. Follow the directions in the Document Management task pane.

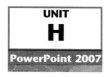
# Sending and Reviewing a Presentation

When you finish creating a presentation, it is often helpful to have others look over the content for accuracy and clarity. When you are not in the same location as the reviewers, you can e-mail the presentation file. If you have Microsoft Outlook on your computer, you can open Outlook directly from PowerPoint and send a presentation file as an attachment in an e-mail. A reviewer can open the presentation on their computer, make changes and comments, and then e-mail it back to you. ▓▓▓▓ Use Outlook to send your presentation to Ellen to get her comments and then open the reviewed presentation.

## STEPS

**TROUBLE**

If Outlook is not configured to send and receive e-mail on your computer, you will get a warning dialog box that the action cannot be completed. Click OK, then skip Steps 2–3.

1. **Click the Office button 🔘, point to Send, then click E-mail**

   Microsoft Outlook opens in a new window. The subject line is filled in for you and the Sample Album presentation is automatically attached to the e-mail. If you don't have Outlook installed on your computer, you will not be able to e-mail your presentation.

2. **Click the To text box, type your e-mail address, click in the message body window, then type Please review and get back to me. Thanks.**

   The e-mail is ready to send. Compare your screen to Figure H-3.

3. **Click the Send button, click 🔘, then click Close**

   Outlook sends the e-mail message with the attached presentation file, and the Outlook window closes. By clicking Close, the presentation closes, but PowerPoint remains open.

**QUICK TIP**

If the presentation you are sending for review includes linked files, you need to attach the linked files to your e-mail message or change the linked files to embedded objects.

4. **Open the presentation PPT H-1.pptx from the drive and folder where you store your Data Files, save the presentation as Sample Album Reviewed, click the View tab on the Ribbon, then click the Arrange All button in the Window group**

5. **Click the Review tab on the Ribbon, then click the review comment thumbnail in the upper-left corner of Slide 1**

   A small comment box opens.

6. **Click the Next button in the Comments group, read the comment, continue to click the Next button until you reach the comment on Slide 7, then click the Previous button in the Comments group**

   The previous comment on Slide 5 opens again.

7. **Click the Delete button list arrow in the Comments group, then click the Delete All Markup on the Current Slide button in the Comments group**

   The comments on Slide 5 are deleted. Compare your screen to Figure H-4.

8. **Click the Slide Sorter button 🔲 on the status bar, click the Home tab on the Ribbon, click the Select button in the Editing group, then click Select All**

   All of the slides are selected in Slide Sorter view.

9. **Click the Animations tab on the Ribbon, click the No Transition option in the Transition to This Slide group, double-click Slide 1, then save your work**

   All of the transitions are removed from the presentation.

10. **Click the Office button 🔘, then click Close**

FIGURE H-3: Outlook window

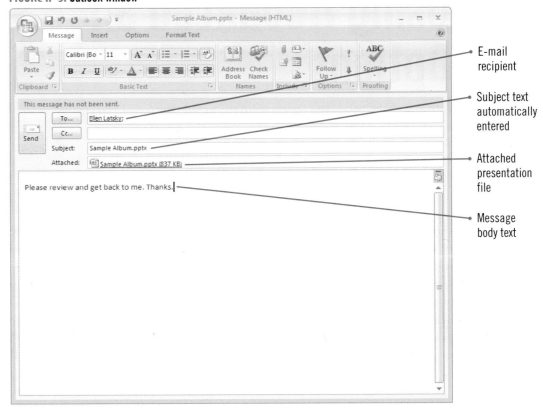

- E-mail recipient
- Subject text automatically entered
- Attached presentation file
- Message body text

FIGURE H-4: Slide with removed comments

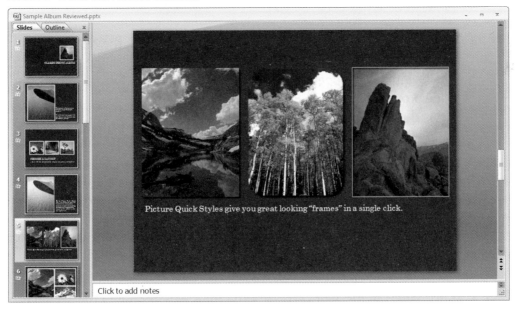

## Using PowerPoint's proofing tools

Along with the spell checker, PowerPoint has a research feature and a language feature that can help you in the development of your presentation. The research feature contains several tools which can help you research topics through encyclopedias and Internet sites, look up words using one of three different thesauruses, and translate words using 14 different languages. If you are working with text that is a different language than the default PowerPoint language (English), the language feature allows you to identify selected text in a presentation with its correct language. To access PowerPoint's proofing tools, click the Review tab on the Ribbon, then click a button in the Proofing group.

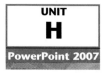
# Using Advanced Slide Show Options

With PowerPoint, you can create a self-running slide show that plays on its own. For example, you can set up a presentation so viewers can watch a slide show on a stand-alone computer, called a **kiosk**, at a convention, mall, or some other public place. You can also create a self-running presentation on a CD or DVD for others to watch. You have a number of options when designing a self-running presentation; for example, you can include hyperlinks or action buttons to assist your audience as they move through the presentation. You can also add a synchronized voice that narrates the presentation and set either manual or automatic slide timings. You prepare the presentation so it can be self-running.

## STEPS

1. **Open the presentation** PPT H-2.pptx **from the drive and folder where you store your Data Files, save the presentation as** QuestH, **click the** View tab **on the Ribbon, then click the** Arrange All button **in the Window group**

2. **Click the** Slide Show tab **on the Ribbon, click the** Set Up Slide Show button **in the Set Up group, then click the** Browsed at a kiosk (full screen) option button **in the Show type section of the Set Up Show dialog box**
   The Set Up Show dialog box has options you can set to specify how the show will run.

3. **Make sure the** All option button **is selected in the Show slides section, then make sure the** Using timings, if present option button **is selected in the Advance slides section**
   These settings include all the slides in the presentation and enable PowerPoint to advance the slides at time intervals you set. See Figure H-5.

4. **Click** OK, **click the** Animations tab **on the Ribbon, click the** Automatically After check box **in the Transition to This Slide group to select it, click the** Automatically After up arrow **until** 00:05 **appears, then click the** Apply To All button **in the Transition to This Slide group**
   Each slide in the presentation now has a slide timing of 5 seconds.

5. **Click the** Slide Show button ☑ **on the status bar, view the show, let it start again, press** [Esc], **then click the** Slide Show tab **on the Ribbon**
   PowerPoint advances the slides automatically at five-second intervals, or faster if someone advances the slide manually. After the last slide, the slide show starts over because the kiosk slide show option loops the presentation until someone presses [Esc].

6. **Click the** Set Up Slide Show button, **click the** Presented by a speaker (full screen) option button, **then click** OK
   The slide show options are back to their default settings.

7. **Click** Slide 1 **in the Slides tab, click the** Hide Slide button **in the Set Up group, click the** From Beginning button **in the Start Slide Show group, then press** [Esc]
   The slide show begins with Slide 2. Notice that Slide 1 in the Slides tab is dimmed and has a hidden slide icon on its number indicating it is hidden, as shown in Figure H-6.

8. **Right-click** Slide 1 **in the Slides tab, then click** Hide Slide **in the shortcut menu**
   The hidden slide icon is removed.

9. **Save your changes**

**FIGURE H-5:** Set Up Show dialog box

**FIGURE H-6:** Figure showing hidden slide

Hidden slide icon

Hidden slide

## Using Presenter view

Presenter view is a special view that permits you to run a presentation through two monitors; one monitor that you see on your computer and a second monitor that your audience views. Running a presentation through two monitors provides you more control over your presentation, allowing you to click thumbnails of slides to jump to specific slides and run other programs, if necessary. Presenter view is designed with large icons, buttons, and other tools, which help you easily navigate through a presentation. Speaker notes are large and easy to read for the presenter. To use this feature, your computer must have multiple monitor capacity and you need to turn on multiple monitor support and Presenter view. To turn on multiple monitor support, click the Use Presenter View check box in the Monitors group on the Slide Show tab and follow the instructions.

# Creating a Custom Show

A custom show gives you the ability to adapt a presentation for use in different circumstances or with different audiences. For example, you might have a 25-slide presentation that you show to new customers, but only 12 of those slides are necessary for existing customers to view. PowerPoint provides two types of custom shows: basic and hyperlinked. A basic custom show is a separate presentation or a presentation that includes slides from the original presentation. A hyperlinked custom show is a separate (secondary) presentation that is linked to a primary custom show. 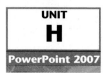 You have been asked to create a version of the presentation for a staff meeting, so you create a custom slide show containing only the slides appropriate for that audience.

## STEPS

1. **Click the** Slide Show **tab on the Ribbon, click the** Custom Slide Show button **in the Start Slide Show group, click** Custom Shows, **then click** New
   The Define Custom Show dialog box opens. The slides that are in your current presentation are listed in the Slides in presentation list box.

2. **Press and hold [Ctrl], click** Slide 1, **click** Slides 6-8, **click** Slides 12-16, **release [Ctrl], then click** Add
   The nine slides you selected move to the Slides in custom show list box, indicating that they will be included in the new presentation. See Figure H-7.

3. **Click** 5. Adventure Series **in the Slides in custom show list, then click the** Slide Order up arrow button **until the Adventure Series slide is at the top of the Slides in custom show list**
   The slide moves to the top of the list. You can arrange the slides in any order in your custom show using the Slide order up and down arrows.

4. **Click** 2. Spring 2011 European Tours Proposal, **click** Remove, **drag to select the existing text in the Slide show name text box, type** Brief Presentation, **then click** OK
   The Custom Shows dialog box lists your custom presentation. The custom show is not saved as a separate slide show on your computer even though you assigned it a new name. To view a custom slide show, you must first open the presentation you used to create the custom show in Slide Show view. You then can open the custom show from the Custom Shows dialog box.

QUICK TIP
To print a custom show, click the Office button, click Print, click the Custom Show option button in the Print range section, select the custom show you want in the Custom Show list box, set any other printing preferences, then click OK.

5. **Click** Show, **view the** Brief Presentation **slide show, then press [Esc] to end the slide show**
   The slides in the custom show appear in the order you set in the Define Custom Show dialog box. At the end of the slide show, you return to the presentation in Normal view.

6. **Click the** Slide Show button ⬚ **on the status bar, right-click the screen, point to** Custom Show, **then click** Brief Presentation, **as shown in Figure H-8**
   The Brief Presentation custom show appears in Slide Show view.

7. **Press [Esc] at the end of the slide show, then save your changes**

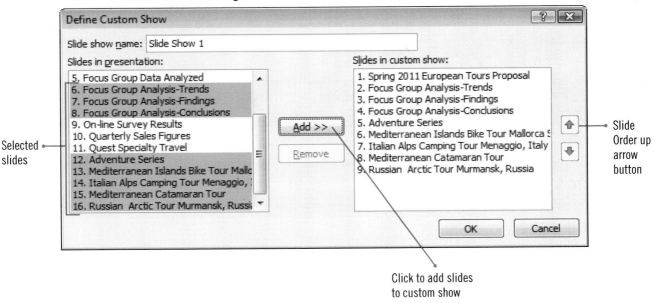

## Link to a custom slide show

You can use action buttons to switch from the "parent" show to the custom show. Click the Shapes button in the Drawing group on the Home tab, then click an action button. Draw an action button on the slide. Click the Hyperlink to list arrow, click Custom Show, click the custom show you want to link, then click OK. Now when you run a slide show you can click the action button you created to run the custom show. You can also create an interactive table of contents using custom shows. Create your table of contents entries on a slide, then hyperlink each entry to the section it refers to using a custom show for each section.

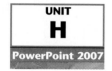

# Preparing a Presentation for Distribution

Reviewing and preparing your presentation before you share it with others can be an essential step, especially with so many security issues on the Internet today. One way to help secure your PowerPoint presentation is to set a security password, so only authorized people can view or modify its content. If you plan to open a presentation in an earlier version of PowerPoint, it is a good idea to determine if the presentation is compatible. Some features in PowerPoint 2007, such as SmartArt graphics, are not compatible in earlier versions of PowerPoint. ████ Ellen wants you to learn about PowerPoint's security and compatibility features so you can use them on presentations and other documents.

## STEPS

1. **Click Slide 1 in the Slides tab, click the Office button 🗔, point to Prepare, then click Encrypt Document**
   The Encrypt Document dialog box opens.

2. **Type 123abc**
   As you type the password, solid black symbols appear in the text box and make the password unreadable. If anyone is looking while you type, this helps protect your privacy. Protecting a file is part of the **encryption**. See Figure H-9.

> **TROUBLE**
> If you mistype the password in the Confirm Password dialog box, an alert dialog box opens.

3. **Click OK to open the Confirm Password dialog box, type 123abc as shown in Figure H-10, then click OK**
   The presentation is now set with a password. Once the presentation is closed, this password must be entered in a Password dialog box to open the presentation.

4. **Click 🗔, click Close, click Yes to save changes, then open QuestH from the drive and folder where you store you Data Files.**
   The Password dialog box opens.

> **QUICK TIP**
> To set other password options, open the Save As dialog box, click Tools, then click General Options.

5. **Type 123abc, then click OK**
   The presentation opens. Be aware that if you don't remember your password, there is no way to retrieve it from the presentation or from Microsoft.

6. **Click 🗔, point to Prepare, click Encrypt Document, select the password, press [Delete], then click OK**
   The password is removed and is no longer needed to open the presentation.

7. **Click 🗔, point to Prepare, click Run Compatibility Checker**
   The Compatibility Checker analyzes the presentation, then the Microsoft Office PowerPoint Compatibility Checker dialog box opens, as shown in Figure H-11. Each item in the dialog box represents a feature that is not supported in earlier versions of PowerPoint. This means that if you try to run this presentation using an earlier version of PowerPoint, the items listed will function in a limited capacity or not at all.

8. **Click the down scroll arrow, read all of the items in the dialog box, click OK, add your name to the Notes and Handouts footer, then click the Slide Sorter button 🗔 on the status bar**
   The dialog box closes. Compare your screen to Figure H-12.

9. **Save your work, then print the Handouts (4 slides per page)**

**FIGURE H-9:** Encrypt Document dialog box

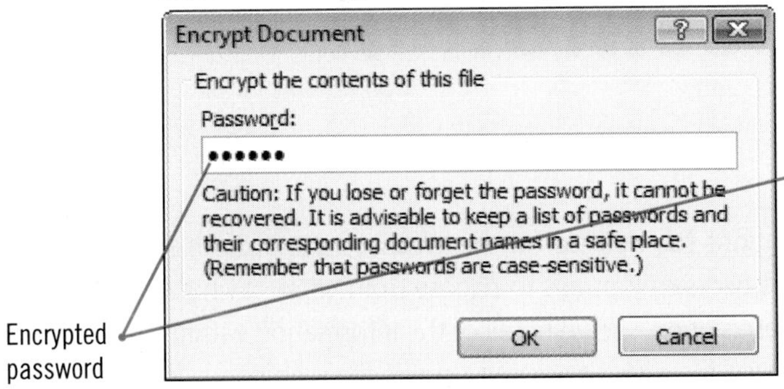

**FIGURE H-10:** Confirm Password dialog box

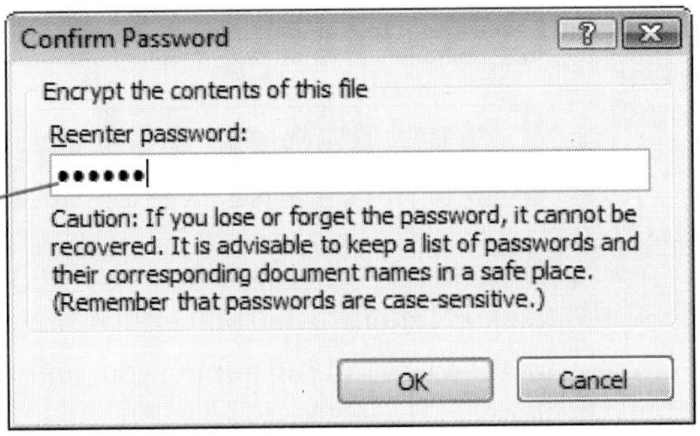

Encrypted password

**FIGURE H-11:** Compatibility Checker dialog box

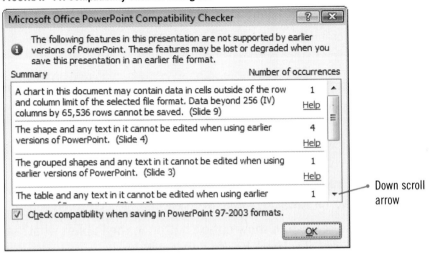

Down scroll arrow

**FIGURE H-12:** Final presentation in Slide Sorter view

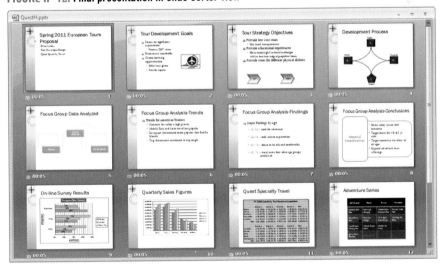

## Creating a strong password

Creating a strong password is a vital part of securing your presentations, other sensitive documents, Internet accounts, and personal information. The strongest password is a random complex string of lowercase and uppercase characters and numbers. For example, the password used in this lesson, 123abc, is a weak password. Though it has both numbers and lowercase letters, it is an easy sequential password that someone could guess. Here are some simple guidelines to making a good password: (1) make the password long, 8 or more characters, (2) use a wide variety of uppercase and lowercase letters, symbols, and numbers, (3) if possible use words or phrases that you can remember that are difficult for others to guess, (4) keep your password secret and never reveal it in an e-mail, and (5) regularly change your password.

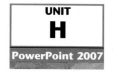

# Saving a Presentation for the Web

You can use PowerPoint to create presentations for viewing on the Web by saving the file in Hypertext Markup Language (HTML) format. You have two save options to choose from when saving a presentation for the Web. You can publish your entire presentation, including all of the information within the presentation and supporting documents, such as linked files, which creates a single file Web page. The other publishing option is to create a presentation as a Web page, which creates a separate folder that contains all supporting files, such as bullets, pictures, background objects, and linked files. Once your presentation is published to a computer that hosts Web pages called a **Web server**, others can view (but not change) the presentation on the Web. ▰▰▰▰ You want to publish the custom show version of the Spring 2011 European Tours Proposal presentation to be viewed on the company Web site.

## STEPS

1. **Click the** Office button 🏢, **click** Save As, **click the** Save as type list arrow, **then click** Web Page (*.htm;*.html)

   The Save As dialog box opens. As soon as you select the Web page file type, the Publish button appears in the Save As dialog box.

2. **Select the filename in the File name text box, type** Webpres, **then click** Publish

   The Publish as Web Page dialog box opens.

3. **Click the** Custom show option button **in the Publish what? section, then click the** Display speaker notes check box **to deselect it**

4. **In the Browser support section, click the** All browsers listed above (creates larger files) option button

   You want to make sure most browsers can view the HTML file you publish. At the bottom of the dialog box, notice that the default filename for the HTML file you are creating is the same as the presentation filename and that it will be saved to the same folder in which the presentation is stored.

5. **Click the** Change button **in the Publish a copy as section**

   The Set Page Title dialog box opens. The title displayed in this dialog box appears in the title bar of your Internet browser window.

6. **Type** QST 2011 European Tours, **click** OK, **then click the** Open published Web page in browser check box **to select it, if it is not already selected**

   The page title changes to the new title. See Figure H-13.

7. **Click** Publish, **click the** security bar **in the Internet Explorer window if it appears, click** Allow Blocked Content, **then click** Yes **in the Security Warning dialog box**

   PowerPoint creates a copy of your presentation in HTML format and opens the published presentation in your default Internet browser. Your screen should look similar to Figure H-14, which shows the presentation in Internet Explorer 7. The slide titles on the left are hyperlinks to each slide.

8. **Click each** slide title hyperlink **in the left pane of the screen to see each presentation slide in the browser**

   You can also click the Slide Show button or the Next Slide and Previous Slide buttons at the bottom of the browser screen to view the presentation slides.

9. **Close your browser window, save your work, then close the presentation**

   Your original presentation closes but PowerPoint remains open.

**FIGURE H-13:** Publish as Web Page dialog box

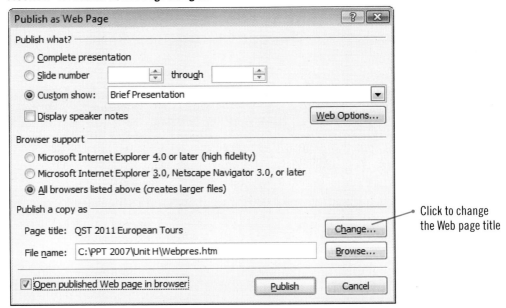

Click to change the Web page title

**FIGURE H-14:** Internet Explorer window displaying Web presentation

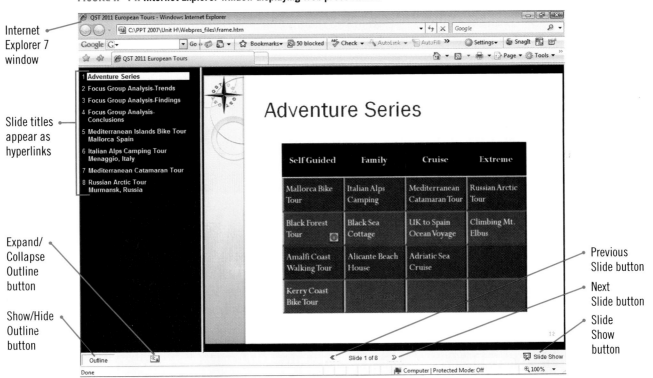

Internet Explorer 7 window

Slide titles appear as hyperlinks

Expand/Collapse Outline button

Show/Hide Outline button

Previous Slide button

Next Slide button

Slide Show button

## Publish slides to a Slide Library

If your computer is connected to a network server running Office SharePoint Server 2007 software, you can store slides in a folder called a **Slide Library** for others to access, modify, and use. Using a Slide Library, others can make changes to your slides and you in turn can track and review all changes and have access to the latest version of your slides. To publish slides from PowerPoint 2007 to a Slide Library (after a Slide Library is created on a server), click the Office button, point to Publish, then click Publish Slides. The Publish Slides command only appears if you are connected to an Office SharePoint Server 2007 server. To add slides to your presentation from a Slide Library, click the Home tab, click the New Slide button arrow, then click Reuse Slides. Select the slides you want to insert into your presentation using the Reuse Slides task pane.

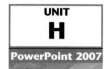

# Packaging a Presentation

When you need to distribute one or more presentations or present a slide show using another Windows computer, you can package (or copy) your presentation to a CD, DVD, a network folder, or a local computer hard drive. To package the files you'll need to run a slide show on another computer (including your presentation, embedded and linked objects, and fonts), you'll use the Package for CD feature. Before you package a presentation, it is a good idea to inspect the presentation for hidden or personal data that may be inappropriate for others to view. The PowerPoint Viewer is included by default with a packaged presentation. The PowerPoint Viewer is a program that allows you to view a presentation in Slide Show view on a computer that does not have PowerPoint installed. You package a version of the European Tours Presentation using the Package to CD feature so Ellen can present it at an off-site meeting. You package the presentation to a new folder that you create on your computer's hard drive.

## STEPS

1. **Open the presentation PPT H-3.pptx from the drive and folder where you store your Data Files, then save the presentation as Packaged Presentation**

**QUICK TIP**

If you want to package more than one presentation, click the Add Files button in the Package for CD dialog box, select the files, then click Add.

2. **Click the Office button ⊞, point to Publish, click Package for CD, then click OK to ensure the files are compatible with the PowerPoint Viewer if necessary**
   The Package for CD dialog box opens.

3. **Click the Options button in the dialog box**
   The Options dialog box opens.

4. **Click the Embedded TrueType fonts check box, then click the Inspect presentations for inappropriate or private information check box**
   Embedding TrueType fonts with the packaged presentation ensures that all of your fonts display properly on another computer. See Figure H-15.

5. **Click OK, click the Copy to Folder button, then type Spring 2011 Packaged Pres**
   The Copy to Folder dialog box opens and you create a new folder for the packaged presentation.

6. **Click the Browse button to open the Choose Location dialog box, locate the drive and folder where you store your Data Files, then click Select**
   Compare the Copy to Folder dialog box on your screen to Figure H-16.

7. **Click OK, click Yes to include linked files in the package, click the Off-Slide Content check box in the Document Inspector dialog box, click Inspect, then click Close**
   PowerPoint packages the presentation to the folder you created and displays the Package for CD dialog box.

8. **Click Close to close the Package for CD dialog box, open Windows Explorer, navigate to the Spring 2011 Packaged Pres folder, then view the folder contents**
   Compare your screen to Figure H-17. All the files you need to run the presentation are in this folder, including the linked files.

9. **Close the Windows Explorer window, then close the presentation**

FIGURE H-15: Options dialog box

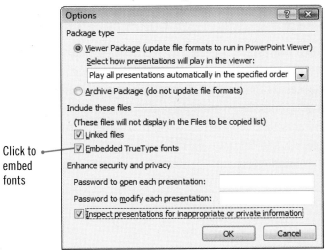

Click to embed fonts

FIGURE H-16: Package for CD dialog box

Click to add additional PowerPoint files to be packaged

FIGURE H-17: Windows Explorer window showing the packaged files

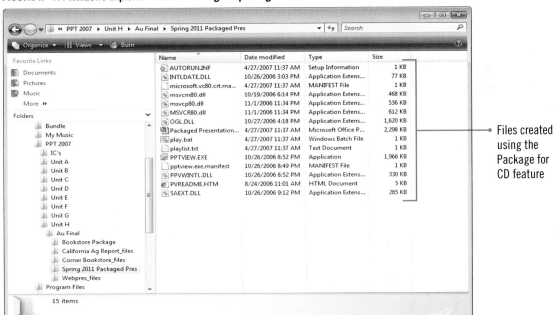

Files created using the Package for CD feature

## Using the Microsoft PowerPoint Viewer

The Microsoft PowerPoint Viewer is a program used to show a presentation on a computer that doesn't have PowerPoint installed. The PowerPoint Viewer is a free program distributed by Microsoft from the Office Web site. The PowerPoint Viewer is included by default when you package a presentation. To view a presentation slide show using the PowerPoint Viewer, open the Microsoft Office PowerPoint Viewer dialog box by double-clicking the PPTVIEW.EXE file, then select the presentation you want to view. If you have a presentation that is only going to be shown as a slide show, you can save it with a special PowerPoint show file format (.ppsx), which opens the presentation up in Slide Show view instead of Normal view.

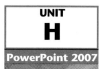
# Creating a Photo Album

A **PowerPoint photo album** is a special presentation designed specifically to display photographs. You can add pictures to a photo album from your hard drive, digital camera, scanner, or Web camera. As with any presentation, you can customize the layout of a photo album presentation by adding title text to slides, applying frames around the pictures, and applying a design template. You can also format the pictures of the photo album by adding a caption, converting the pictures to black and white, rotating them, and changing their brightness and contrast. ▄▟▛▜ You have a little extra time at the end of your day, so you decide to use PowerPoint to create a photo album of a recent trip to Ireland.

**STEPS**

1. **Click the** Insert tab **on the Ribbon, then click the** Photo Album button **in the** Illustrations group
   The Photo Album dialog box opens.

2. **Click** File/Disk, **select the file** PPT H-4.jpg **from the drive and folder where you store your Data Files, then click** Insert
   The photograph appears in the Preview box and is listed in the Pictures in album list, as shown in Figure H-18. The buttons below the Preview box allow you to rotate the photo or change its contrast or brightness.

3. **Click** File/Disk, **click the file** PPT H-5.jpg, **press and hold** [Shift], **click the file** PPT H-8.jpg, **release** [Shift], **then click** Insert
   Four more photographs appear in the dialog box. One photo is out of order.

4. **Make sure** PPT H-8.jpg **is selected in the Pictures in album list, click the** up arrow button **below the list once, then click** Create
   A new presentation opens. PowerPoint creates a title slide along with a slide for each photograph that you inserted. The computer user name appears in the subtitle text box by default.

**QUICK TIP**

If you want others to have access to your photo album on the Web, you can save the photo album presentation as a Web page.

5. **Save the presentation as** Ireland Trip **to the drive and folder where you store your Data Files, change the slide title to** Ireland Trip, **click the** Photo Album button list arrow **in the** Illustrations group, **then click** Edit Photo Album
   The Edit Photo Album dialog box opens. You can use this dialog box to format the photographs and slide layout of your photo album presentation.

6. **Click** PPT H-4.jpg **in the Pictures in album list, press and hold** [Shift], **click** PPT H-7.jpg, **release** [Shift], **click the** Picture layout list arrow **in the** Album Layout section, **click** 1 picture with title, **click the** Frame shape list arrow, **click** Center Shadow Rectangle, **then click** Update
   All of the slides now have a title text placeholder, and the photographs are formatted with a shadow.

7. **Click** Slide 5 **in the Slides tab, click the** title placeholder, **type** Why did I get shaved first?, **enter your own title text on the other four slides, then click the** Slide Sorter button 🔲 **on the status bar**
   Compare your screen to Figure H-19.

**QUICK TIP**

To show a slide show in a different screen resolution, click the Slide Show tab, click the Resolution list arrow, then choose a resolution setting.

8. **Click** Slide 1, **click the** Slide Show button 🖵 **on the status bar, advance through the slides, then double-click** Slide 1
   All of the slides now have a title.

9. **Add your name to the notes and handouts header, then print Handouts (1 per page)**

10. **Save your changes, close the presentation, then exit PowerPoint**

**FIGURE H-18:** Photo Album dialog box

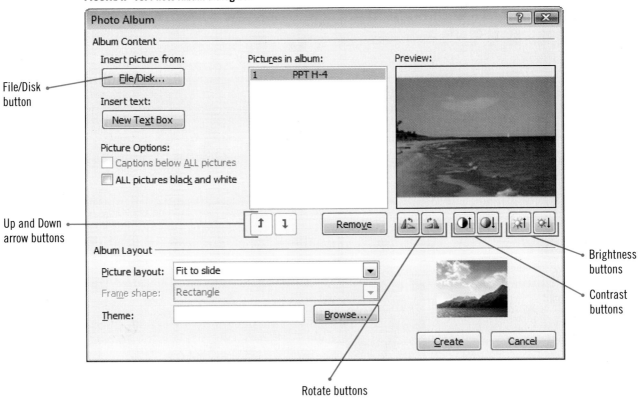

File/Disk button

Up and Down arrow buttons

Brightness buttons

Contrast buttons

Rotate buttons

**FIGURE H-19:** Completed photo album presentation

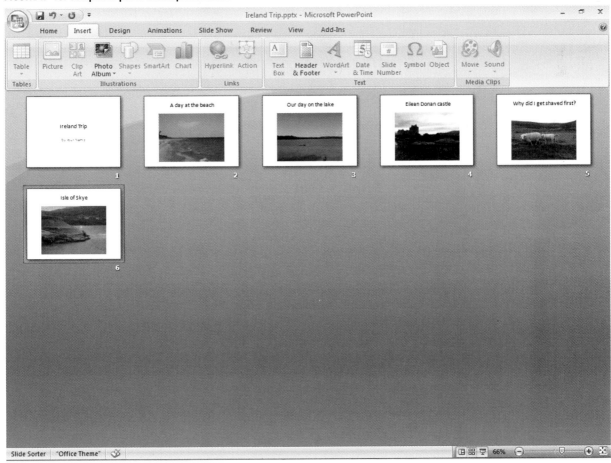

# Practice

If you have a SAM user profile, you may have access to hands-on instruction, practice, and assessment of the skills covered in this unit. Log in to your SAM account (http://sam2007.course.com/) to launch any assigned training activities or exams that relate to the skills covered in this unit.

## ▼ CONCEPTS REVIEW

**Label each element of the PowerPoint window shown in Figure H-20.**

FIGURE H-20

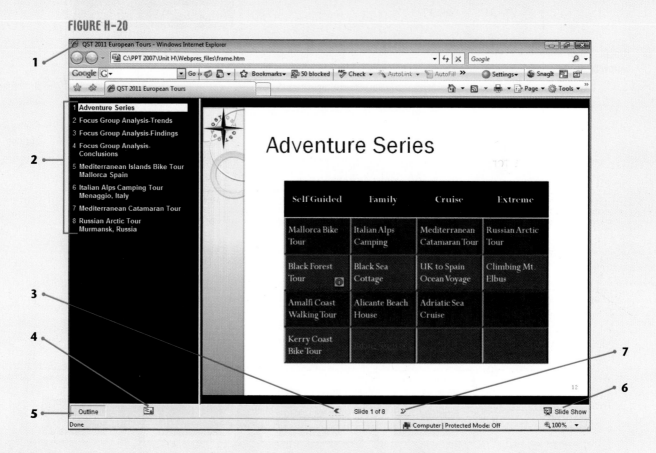

**Match each term with the statement that best describes its function.**

8. Kiosk

9. Packaged presentation

10. Web server

11. Slide Library

12. Custom show

a. A stand-alone computer that can run a slide show without user intervention

b. A host computer where you can only view a presentation

c. A presentation you can open on a computer that does not have PowerPoint installed

d. A special slide show created from selected slides in a presentation

e. A folder that stores slides for others to access and modify

**Select the best answer from the list of choices.**

13. **Which of the following statements is *not* true about a presentation set to run at a kiosk?**

a. The presentation loops continuously.

b. The presentation works best with manual slide timings.

c. You can use action buttons to progress through the slides.

d. You don't have to be present to run the slide show.

14. **Which view allows you to view a presentation using two monitors?**
    a. Theater View
    b. Multiple Monitor View
    c. Slide Show View
    d. Presenter View

15. **What is a basic custom show?**
    a. A separate presentation that is linked to a primary custom show
    b. A presentation copied to a CD to be used on another computer
    c. A presentation that includes slides from the original presentation
    d. A photo album presentation

16. **What does the PowerPoint Viewer allow you to do?**
    a. View a presentation on the Web
    b. View and participate in an online meeting
    c. View a presentation in Slide Show view on any compatible computer
    d. View a presentation in all four views at the same time

17. **The _____ identifies features that will not work in earlier versions of PowerPoint.**
    a. PowerPoint Viewer
    b. Web server
    c. Document Inspector
    d. Compatibility Checker

18. **When you save a presentation in Hypertext Markup Language, you are saving it to be used on _____.**
    a. a Slide Library
    b. a custom show
    c. the Web
    d. a kiosk

19. **When you type a password in the password text box, the text _____.**
    a. Changes to small black symbols.
    b. Is transparent.
    c. Moves to a special folder.
    d. Converts to random symbols.

20. **What is the primary purpose of packaging a presentation?**
    a. To distribute it
    b. To create a backup copy of it
    c. To be able to post it to a Web server
    d. To see it in a Slide Library

# ▼ SKILLS REVIEW

1. **Use templates and add comments.**
   a. Start PowerPoint, click the Office button, click New, click Installed Templates, click Contemporary Photo Album, then click Create.
   b. Save the presentation as **Contemporary Album** to the drive and folder where you store your Data Files.
   c. Click the Review tab on the Ribbon, click the New Comment button, type **What do you think of this slide layout?**, then go to Slide 3.
   d. Add a new comment, type **This is an interesting photo layout.**, click the Previous button, then click the Edit Comment button.
   e. Type **I like it.**, then save your work.

2. **Send and review a presentation.**

   **a.** Click the Office button, point to Send, then click E-mail.

   **b.** Get approval and direction from your instructor before you send this e-mail to a colleague or friend, then close the presentation.

   **c.** Open the file PPT H-9.pptx from the drive and folder where you store your Data Files, then save it as **Reviewed Contemporary Album**.

   **d.** Click the Review tab, click the top-left review comment thumbnail, click the Next button, read the comment, then click the Next button until you read all the comments.

   **e.** Click the Previous button, click the Delete button arrow, then click Delete All Markup on the Current Slide.

   **f.** Save your changes, then close the presentation.

3. **Use advanced slide show options.**

   **a.** Open the file PPT H-10.pptx from the drive and folder where you store your Data Files, then save it as **Corner Bookstore**.

   **b.** Click the Slide Show tab, click the Set Up Slide Show button, then set up a slide show that will be browsed at a kiosk, using automatic slide timings.

   **c.** Set a slide timing of 4 seconds to each slide, run the slide show all the way through once, then press [Esc] to end the slide show.

   **d.** Set the slide show to run using manual slide timings and presented by a speaker.

   **e.** Run through the slide show from Slide 1 using the action buttons at the bottom of the slides. Move forward and backward through the presentation, watching the animation effects as they appear.

   **f.** Hide Slide 5, run through the slide show, then unhide Slide 5.

   **g.** When you have finished viewing the slide show, reset the slide timings to automatic, then save your changes.

4. **Create a custom show.**

   **a.** Create a custom show called **Goals** which includes Slides 2, 3, 4, and 5.

   **b.** Move Slide 3 Performance Series above Slide 2 Lecture Series.

   **c.** View the show from within the Custom Shows dialog box, then press [Esc] to end the slide show.

   **d.** Go to Slide 1, begin the slide show, then, when Slide 1 appears, go to the Goals custom show.

   **e.** View the custom slide show, return to Normal view, then save your changes.

5. **Prepare a presentation for distribution.**

   **a.** Click the Office button, point to Prepare, then open the Encrypt Document dialog box.

   **b.** Type **12345**, then type the same password in the Confirm Password dialog box.

   **c.** Close the presentation, save your changes, open the presentation, then type **12345** as the password in the Password dialog box.

   **d.** Open the Encrypt Document dialog box again, then delete the password.

   **e.** Click the Office button, point to Prepare, open the Compatibility Checker, read the information, then close the dialog box.

   **f.** Save your work, then add your name to the notes and handouts footer. The completed presentation is shown in Figure H-21.

   **g.** Print the slides in the presentation as Handouts (2 slides per page.)

FIGURE H-21

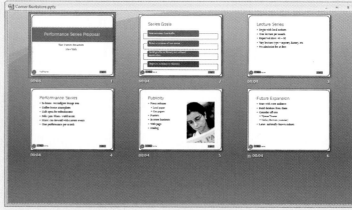

6. **Save a presentation for the Web.**

   **a.** Click the Office button, click Save As, click the Save as type list arrow, then select Web Page.

   **b.** Click the Publish button, and make sure that speaker notes do not display and all browsers are supported.

   **c.** Change the page title to **Corner Bookstore Presentation**, then click Publish.

# ▼ SKILLS REVIEW (CONTINUED)

**d.** View the presentation in your browser using the hyperlinks in the left pane, the Next Slide and Previous Slide buttons, and the action buttons on the slides.

**e.** Close your browser, then save your work.

**7. Package a presentation.**

**a.** Click the Office button, point to Publish, then open the Package for CD dialog box.

**b.** Open the Options dialog box, embed TrueType fonts and inspect the presentation for appropriate content. Click OK.

**c.** Click the Copy to Folder button, create a folder where you store your Data Files with the name **Bookstore Package**, then package the presentation.

**d.** Run the Document Inspector, close the Document Inspector dialog box, then close the Package for CD dialog box.

**e.** Open Windows Explorer, view the contents of the Bookstore Package folder, then close the Windows Explorer window.

**f.** Save and close the presentation.

**8. Create a photo album.**

**a.** Create a photo album presentation, then from the drive and folder where you store your Data Files, insert the files PPT H-11.jpg, PPT H-12.jpg, PPT H-13.jpg, PPT H-14.jpg, PPT H-15.jpg, and PPT H-16.jpg.

**b.** Move picture PPT H-16.jpg so it is second in the list, move PPT H-14.jpg so it is last in the list, create the photo album, then save it as **Africa 2011** to the drive and folder where you store your Data Files.

**c.** Change the title on the title slide to **Africa 2011**, then type your name in the subtitle text box.

**d.** Open the Edit Photo Album dialog box, change the picture layout to 2 pictures with title, change the frame shape to a simple black frame, then update the presentation.

**e.** Provide a title for rest of the slides, add your name as a footer to the slides, then save your changes.

**f.** Print the slides of the presentation, then exit PowerPoint.

# ▼ INDEPENDENT CHALLENGE 1

You work for Pacific Island Tours, an international tour company that provides specialty tours to destinations throughout Asia and the Pacific. You have to develop presentations that the sales force can use to highlight different tours at conferences and meetings.

To complete the presentation, you need to create at least two of your own slides. Assume that Pacific Island Tours has a special (20% off regular price) on tours to Fiji and the Cook Islands during the spring of 2011. Also assume that Pacific Island Tours offers tour packages to the Philippines, Japan, Australia, and New Zealand.

**a.** Start PowerPoint, open the presentation PPT H-17.pptx, then save it as **Pacific Tours** to the drive and folder where you store your Data Files.

**b.** Open the Review tab on the Ribbon, use the Next button to view each comment, read the comment, then delete the last comment on the Departing Cities slide.

**c.** Use the Previous button to move back to slides that have comments and write a response comment to each of the original comments.

**d.** Use the Compatibility Checker on the presentation.

**e.** Use the information provided above to help you develop additional content for two new slides.

**f.** Insert at least three different media clips (pictures, animations, movies, clip art, or sounds). Use clips from PowerPoint or from other approved legal media sources.

**g.** Apply slide transitions, timings, and animations to all the slides in the presentation.

**h.** Apply a saved design theme. On the Design tab, click the More button in the Themes group, click Browse for Themes, then apply the Pacific Theme.thmx theme from the drive and folder where you store your Data Files.

**i.** Convert the text on Slide 2 to a SmartArt diagram, then format the diagram using the techniques you learned in this book.

**j.** Use the Compatibility Checker again on the presentation. Note any differences.

**k.** View the presentation in Slide Show view.

**l.** Add your name as a footer on all notes and handouts. Print the presentation as handouts (2 per page), close the presentation, then exit PowerPoint.

# ▼ INDEPENDENT CHALLENGE 2

You work in Sacramento, California at the State Agricultural Statistics Agency. Part of your job is to compile agricultural information gathered from the counties of California and create presentations that display the data for public viewing. You are currently working on a summary presentation that will be made public on the agency Web site.

a. Start PowerPoint, open the presentation PPT H-18.pptx, then save it as **Ag Report** to the drive and folder where you store your Data Files.

b. Convert the information on Slide 5 to a SmartArt diagram using one of the List layouts. Use a layout that includes pictures and insert the file PPT H-19.jpg from the drive and folder where you store your Data Files to the SmartArt graphic.

c. Format the SmartArt diagram using the commands on the SmartArt Tools Design and Format tabs.

d. Format the table on Slide 4. Change the table layout so the table displays the information properly, split the Cattle and Calves cell into two cells, then format the table.

e. Create a custom slide show that displays four slides.

f. Insert appropriate media clips on at least two slides.

g. Save the presentation in HTML format for the Web, save it as **California Ag Report**, preview the presentation as a Web page in your browser, then close your browser.

## Advanced Challenge Exercise (Internet connection and instructor approval required)

■ Write at least two comments in the presentation, then send the presentation as an e-mail attachment to another student in your class.

■ The reviewing student should create and insert their own comments, then send it back to you.

■ Once you get the presentation back, review the comments.

h. Save the presentation, then view the presentation in Slide Show view.

i. Add your name as a footer on all notes and handouts. Print the presentation as handouts (2 per page), close the presentation, then exit PowerPoint.

# ▼ INDEPENDENT CHALLENGE 3

You are the assistant director of operations at NorthWest Cargo Inc., an international marine shipping company based in Seattle, Washington. NorthWest Cargo handles 65 percent of all the trade between Asia, the Middle East, and the West Coast of the United States. You need to give a quarterly presentation to the company's operations committee outlining the type and amount of trade NorthWest Cargo handled during the previous quarter.

Plan a presentation with at least six slides that details the type of goods NorthWest Cargo carries. Create your own content, but assume the following:

• NorthWest Cargo hauls automobiles from Tokyo to San Francisco. Northwest can usually haul between 2800 and 3500 automobiles in a quarter.

• NorthWest Cargo hauls large tractor equipment and parts made by Caterpillar Tractor and John Deere Tractor from the United States.

• NorthWest Cargo hauls common household goods that include electronic equipment, appliances, toys, and furniture.

• NorthWest Cargo owns five cargo ships that can operate simultaneously. All five ships were in operation during the last quarter.

• NorthWest Cargo hauled a total of 1.8 million tons during the last quarter.

a. Start PowerPoint, create a new presentation based on a template or theme in the New Presentation dialog box, then save it as **Cargo Report**.

b. Use the assumptions provided to help develop the content for your presentation. If you have Internet access, use the Internet to research the shipping business.

# ▼ INDEPENDENT CHALLENGE 3 (CONTINUED)

    **c.** Use at least two different media clips to enhance your presentation.

    **d.** Set transitions and animations, and rehearse slide timings.

    **e.** View the presentation in Slide Show view.

### Advanced Challenge Exercise

    ■ Select one word and translate it to French using the Translate button in the Proofing group on the Review tab.

    ■ Select one word, use the Thesaurus button in the Proofing group to find a different word, then apply the word.

    **f.** Save your work, then add your name as a footer on all notes and handouts.

    **g.** Print the final slide presentation as handouts (2 per page), close the presentation, then exit PowerPoint.

# ▼ REAL LIFE INDEPENDENT CHALLENGE

Your assignment for your cultural history class is to create a photo album based on your personal life and family history. You must use your own pictures of past and present family members, pets, a family home, a family business, or any other type of family activity that help tell the story of your personal family life and history.

    **a.** Start PowerPoint,create a photo album presentation, insert your pictures to the presentation, then save it as **My Photo Album** to the drive and folder where you store your Data Files.

    **b.** Add your name to the title slide and as the footer on the handouts.

    **c.** Use the Edit Photo Album dialog box to format the pictures.

    **d.** Spell check the presentation, then view the final presentation in Slide Show view.

    **e.** Save the final version, print the slides, close the presentation, then exit PowerPoint. See Figure H-22.

**FIGURE H-22**

# ▼ VISUAL WORKSHOP

Create the slide shown in Figure H-23. Save the presentation as **Western Forests**. The SmartArt is a Vertical Box List layout. Convert the shapes in the SmartArt graphic to the Snip Diagonal Corner Rectangle shape, then apply the Cartoon SmartArt Style. Add your name to the slide footer, then print the slide of the presentation.

**FIGURE H-23**

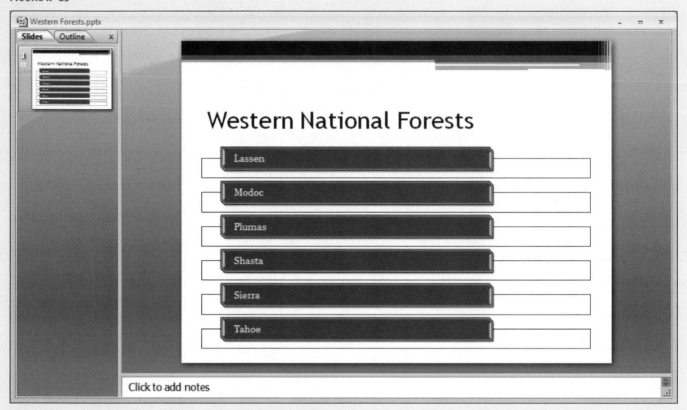

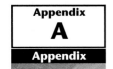
# Restoring Defaults in Windows Vista and Disabling and Enabling Windows Aero

**Files You
Will Need:**

No files needed.

Windows Vista is the most recent version of the Windows operating system. An operating system controls the way you work with your computer, supervises running programs, and provides tools for completing your computing tasks. After surveying millions of computer users, Microsoft incorporated their suggestions to make Windows Vista secure, reliable, and easy to use. In fact, Windows Vista is considered the most secure version of Windows yet. Other improvements include a powerful new search feature that lets you quickly search for files and programs from the Start menu and most windows, tools that simplify accessing the Internet, especially with a wireless connection, and multimedia programs that let you enjoy, share, and organize music, photos, and recorded TV. Finally, Windows Vista offers lots of visual appeal with its transparent, three-dimensional design in the Aero experience. This appendix explains how to make sure you are using the Windows Vista default settings for appearance, personalization, security, hardware, and sound and to enable and disable Windows Aero. For more information on Windows Aero, go to *www.microsoft.com/windowsvista/experiences/aero.mspx.*

**OBJECTIVES**

Restore the defaults in the Appearance and Personalization section

Restore the defaults in the Security section

Restore the defaults in the Hardware and Sound section

Disable Windows Aero

Enable Windows Aero

# Restoring the Defaults in the Appearance and Personalization Section

*The following instructions require a default Windows Vista Ultimate installation and the student logged in with an Administrator account. All of the following settings can be changed by accessing the Control Panel.*

**STEPS**

- To restore the defaults in the Personalization section
  1. Click Start, and then click Control Panel. Click Appearance and Personalization, click Personalization, and then compare your screen to Figure A-1
  2. In the Personalization window, click Windows Color and Appearance, select the Default color, and then click OK
  3. In the Personalization window, click Mouse Pointers. In the Mouse Properties dialog box, on the Pointers tab, select Windows Aero (system scheme) in the Scheme drop-down list, and then click OK
  4. In the Personalization window, click Theme. Select Windows Vista from the Theme drop-down list, and then click OK
  5. In the Personalization window, click Display Settings. In the Display Settings dialog box, drag the Resolution bar to 1024 by 768 pixels, and then click OK

FIGURE A-1

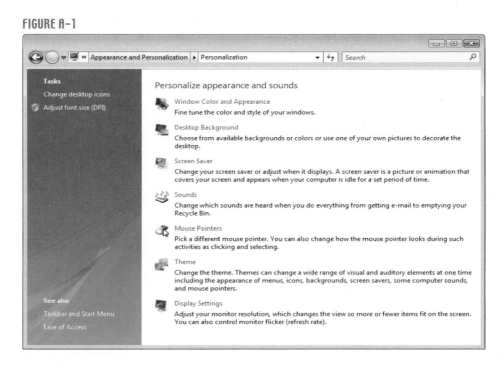

- To restore the defaults in the Taskbar and Start Menu section
  1. Click Start, and then click Control Panel. Click Appearance and Personalization, click Taskbar and Start Menu, and then compare your screen to Figure A-2
  2. In the Taskbar and Start Menu Properties dialog box, on the Taskbar tab, click to select all checkboxes except for "Auto-hide the taskbar"
  3. On the Start Menu tab, click to select the Start menu radio button and check all items in the Privacy section
  4. In the System icons section on the Notification Area tab, click to select all of the checkboxes except for "Power"
  5. On the Toolbars tab, click to select Quick Launch, none of the other items should be checked
  6. Click OK to close the Taskbar and Start Menu Properties dialog box

- To restore the defaults in the Folder Options section
  1. Click Start, and then click Control Panel. Click Appearance and Personalization, click Folder Options, and then compare your screen to Figure A-3
  2. In the Folder Options dialog box, on the General tab, click to select Show preview and filters in the Tasks section, click to select Open each folder in the same window in the Browse folders section, and click to select Double-click to open an item (single-click to select) in the Click items as follows section
  3. On the View tab, click the Reset Folders button, and then click Yes in the Folder views dialog box. Then click the Restore Defaults button
  4. On the Search tab, click the Restore Defaults button
  5. Click OK to close the Folder Options dialog box

- To restore the defaults in the Windows Sidebar Properties section
  1. Click Start, and then click Control Panel. Click Appearance and Personalization, click Windows Sidebar Properties, and then compare your screen to Figure A-4
  2. In the Windows Sidebar Properties dialog box, on the Sidebar tab, click to select Start Sidebar when Windows starts. In the Arrangement section, click to select Right, and then click to select 1 in the Display Sidebar on monitor drop-down list
  3. Click OK to close the Windows Sidebar Properties dialog box

FIGURE A-3

FIGURE A-4

FIGURE A-2

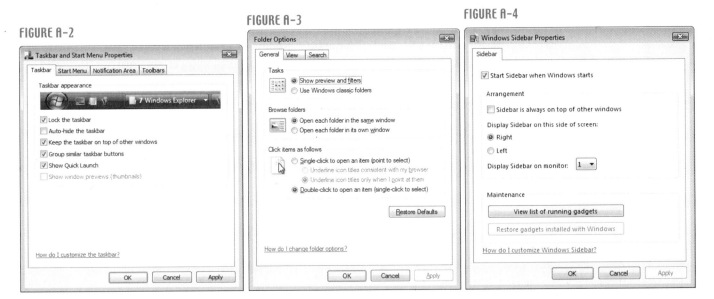

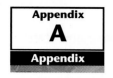
# Restoring the Defaults in the Security Section

*The following instructions require a default Windows Vista Ultimate installation and the student logged in with an Administrator account. All of the following settings can be changed by accessing the Control Panel.*

- To restore the defaults in the Windows Firewall section

  1. Click Start, and then click Control Panel. Click Security, click Windows Firewall, and then compare your screen to Figure A-5

  2. In the Windows Firewall dialog box, click Change settings. If the User Account Control dialog box appears, click Continue

  3. In the Windows Firewall Settings dialog box, click the Advanced tab. Click Restore Defaults, then click Yes in the Restore Defaults Confirmation dialog box

  4. Click OK to close the Windows Firewall Settings dialog box, and then close the Windows Firewall window

- To restore the defaults in the Internet Options section

  1. Click Start, and then click Control Panel. Click Security, click Internet Options, and then compare your screen to Figure A-6

  2. In the Internet Properties dialog box, on the General tab, click the Use default button. Click the Settings button in the Tabs section, and then click the Restore defaults button in the Tabbed Browsing Settings dialog box. Click OK to close the Tabbed Browsing Settings dialog box

  3. On the Security tab of the Internet Properties dialog box, click to uncheck the Enable Protected Mode checkbox, if necessary. Click the Default level button in the Security level for this zone section. If possible, click the Reset all zones to default level button

  4. On the Programs tab, click the Make default button in the Default web browser button for Internet Explorer, if possible. If Office is installed, Microsoft Office Word should be selected in the HTML editor drop-down list

  5. On the Advanced tab, click the Restore advanced settings button in the Settings section. Click the Reset button in the Reset Internet Explorer settings section, and then click Reset in the Reset Internet Explorer Settings dialog box

  6. Click Close to close the Reset Internet Explorer Settings dialog box, and then click OK to close the Internet Properties dialog box

FIGURE A-5

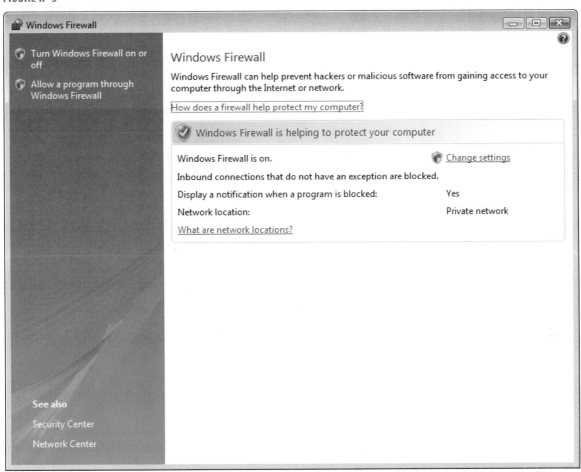

FIGURE A-6

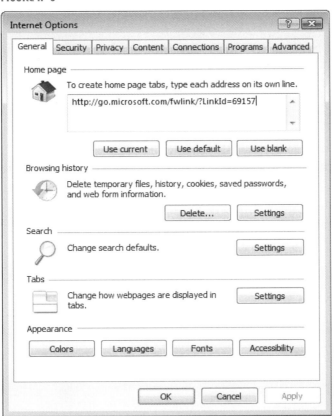

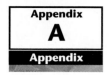

# Restoring the Defaults in the Hardware and Sound Section

*The following instructions require a default Windows Vista Ultimate installation and the student logged in with an Administrator account. All of the following settings can be changed by accessing the Control Panel.*

**STEPS**

- To restore the defaults in the Autoplay section
    1. Click Start, and then click Control Panel. Click Hardware and Sound, click Autoplay, and then compare your screen to Figure A-7. Scroll down and click the Reset all defaults button in the Devices section at the bottom of the window, and then click Save

- To restore the defaults in the Sound section
    1. Click Start, and then click Control Panel. Click Hardware and Sound, click Sound, and then compare your screen to Figure A-8
    2. In the Sound dialog box, on the Sounds tab, select Windows Default from the Sound Scheme drop-down list, and then click OK

- To restore the defaults in the Mouse section
    1. Click Start, and then click Control Panel. Click Hardware and Sound, click Mouse, and then compare your screen to Figure A-9
    2. In the Mouse Properties dialog box, on the Pointers tab, select Windows Aero (system scheme) from the Scheme drop-down list
    3. Click OK to close the Mouse Properties dialog box

## FIGURE A-7

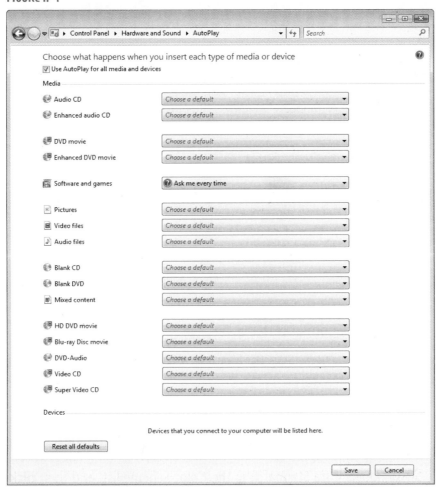

## FIGURE A-8

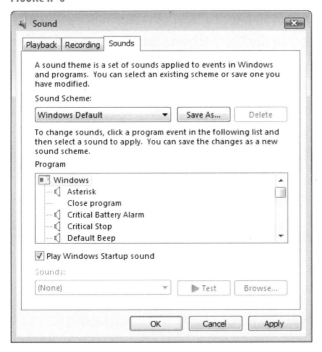

## FIGURE A-9

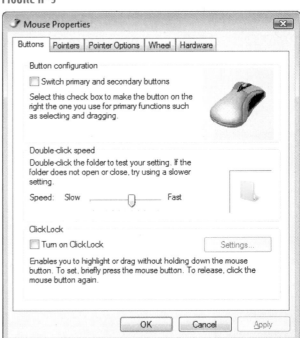

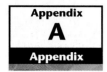
# Disabling and Enabling Windows Aero

Unlike prior versions of Windows, Windows Vista provides two distinct user interface experiences: a "basic" experience for entry-level systems and more visually dynamic experience called Windows Aero. Both offer a new and intuitive navigation experience that helps you more easily find and organize your applications and files, but Aero goes further by delivering a truly next-generation desktop experience.

Windows Aero builds on the basic Windows Vista user experience and offers Microsoft's best-designed, highest-performing desktop experience. Using Aero requires a PC with compatible graphics adapter and running a Premium or Business edition of Windows Vista.

*The following instructions require a computer capable of running Windows Aero, with a default Windows Vista Ultimate installation and student logged in with an Administrator account.*

## STEPS

- **To Disable Windows Aero**

*We recommend that students using this book disable Windows Aero and restore their operating systems default settings (instructions to follow).*

1. **Right-click the desktop, select** Personalize, **and then compare your screen in Figure A-10. Select** Window Color and Appearance, **and then select** Open classic appeareance properties for more color options. **In Appearance Settings dialog box, on the Appearance tab, select any non-Aero scheme (such as** Windows Vista Basic **or** Windows Vista Standard) **in the Color Scheme list, and then click OK. Figure A-11 compares Windows Aero to other color schemes. Note that this book uses Windows Vista Basic as the color scheme**

- **To Enable Windows Aero**

1. **Right-click the desktop, and then select** Personalize. **Select** Window Color and Appearance, **then select** Windows Aero **in the Color scheme list, and then click OK in the Appearance Settings dialog box**

FIGURE A-10

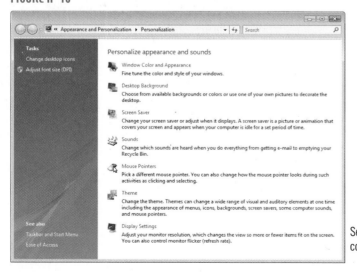

Select other color schemes

FIGURE A-11

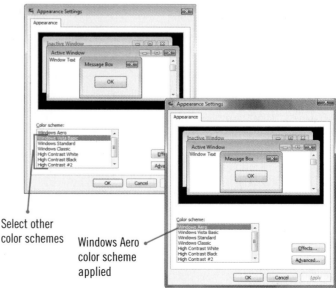

Windows Aero color scheme applied

# Glossary

**Action button** An interactive button that you click in Slide Show view to perform an activity, such as advancing to the next slide.

**Active** The currently available document, program, or object; on the taskbar, the button of the active document is appears in a darker shade while the buttons of other open documents are dimmed.

**Active cell** A selected cell in an Excel worksheet.

**Adjustment handle** A small yellow diamond that changes the appearance of an object's most prominent feature.

**Align** To place objects' edges or centers on the same plane.

**Animation** The illusion of making a static object appear to move. Some graphics such as an animated .gif (Graphics Interchange Format) file has motion when you run the slide show.

**Animation tag** Identifies the order an object is animated on a slide during a slide show.

**Annotate** A freehand drawing on the screen made by using the Annotation tool. You can annotate only in Slide Show view.

**Axis label** Text in a worksheet that identifies data.

**Background** The area behind the text and graphics on a slide.

**Background graphic** An object placed on the slide master.

**Backward-compatible** Software feature that enables documents saved in an older version of a program to be opened in a newer version of the program.

**bmp** The file extension for the bitmap graphics file format.

**Bullet** A small graphic symbol, usually a round or square dot, often used to identify items in a list.

**Category axis** The horizontal axis in a chart.

**Cell** The intersection of a column and row in a worksheet, datasheet, or table.

**Chart** A graphical representation of numerical data from a worksheet. Types include 2-D and 3-D column, bar, pie, area, and line charts.

**Clip art** Predesigned graphic images you can insert in any document or presentation to enhance its appearance.

**Clip Organizer** A library of art, pictures, sounds, video clips, and animations that all Office applications share.

**Clipboard** Temporary storage area in Windows.

**Column heading** The gray box containing the column letter at the top of the column in a worksheet.

**Comment** A note you attach to a slide.

**Compatible** The capability of different programs to work together and exchange data.

**Compatibility Checker** Finds potential compatibility issues between a PowerPoint 2007 presentation and earlier versions of PowerPoint.

**Content placeholder** A placeholder that is used to enter text or objects such as clip art, charts, or pictures.

**Contextual tab** Tab on the Ribbon that appears when needed to complete a specific task; for example, if you select a chart on a PowerPoint slide, three contextual Chart Tool tabs (Design, Layout, and Format) appear.

**Crop** To hide part of an object, such as clip art using the Cropping tool or to delete a part of a picture.

**Data series** A column or row in a datasheet.

**Data series marker** A graphical representation of a data series, such as a bar or column.

**Destination file** The file an object is embedded into, such as a presentation.

**Dialog box** A window that opens when a program needs more information to carry out a command.

**Dialog box launcher** An icon available in many groups on the Ribbon that you can click to open a dialog box or task pane, offering an alternative way to choose commands.

**Digital Signature** A way to authenticate a presentation file using computer cryptography. A digital signature is not visible in a presentation.

**Distribute** To evenly divide the space horizontally or vertically between objects relative to each other or the slide edges.

**Document Inspector** A PowerPoint feature that examines a presentation for hidden data or personal information.

**Document window** Workspace in the program window that displays the current presentation or document.

**Embedded object** An object that is created in one application and inserted into another. Embedded objects remain connected to the original program file in which they were created for easy editing.

**Error bars** Identify potential error amounts relative to each data marker in a data series.

**Exception** A Formatting change that differs from the slide master.

**File** The presentation you create using PowerPoint. An electronic collection of stored data that has a unique name, distinguishing it from other files.

**File format** A file type, such as .pptx, .bmp, .jpg, or .gif.

**Fixed layout format** A specific file format that locks the file from future change.

**Folder** A subdivision of a disk that works like a filing system to help you organize files.

**Gif** The file extension for the graphics interchange format.

**Group** To combine multiple objects into one object on a slide

**Group (Ribbon)** A set of like commands on each tab of the Ribbon.

**Handout master** The master view for printing handouts.

**Hanging indent** The first line of a paragraph begins to the left of all subsequent lines of text.

**Hyperlink** An object or link (a filename, word, phrase, or graphic) that, when clicked, "jumps to" another location in the current file or opens another PowerPoint presentation, a Word, Excel, or Access file, or an address on the World Wide Web.

**Jpg** The file extension for the JPEG (Joint Photographic Experts Group) File Interchange Format.

**Indent levels** Text levels in the master text placeholder. Each level is indented a certain amount from the left margin, and you control their placement by dragging indent markers on the ruler.

**Indent markers** Small markers (two triangles and one square) on the horizontal ruler that indicate the indent settings for the selected text.

**Insertion point** A blinking vertical line that indicates where the next character will appear when text is entered in a text placeholder in PowerPoint.

**Integrate** To incorporate a document and parts of a document created in one program into another program; for example, to incorporate an Excel chart into a PowerPoint slide, or an Access table into a Word document.

**Interface** The look and feel of a program; for example, the appearance of commands and the way they are organized in the program window.

**Kiosk** A freestanding computer used to display information, usually in a public area.

**Launch** To open or start a program on your computer.

**Leading** The spacing between lines of text in a text object within the same paragraph.

**Legend** Names in the top row of a worksheet that provides information about the data.

**Link** A connection between a source file and a destination file, which when the source file is updated, the destination file can also be updated. Can also refer to a *Hyperlink*.

**Live Preview** A feature that lets you point to a choice in a gallery or palette and see the results in the document or on the slide before you apply the change.

**Macro** An action or a set of actions that you use to automate tasks.

**Major gridlines** Identify major units on a chart axis and are identified by tick marks.

**Margin** The distance between the edge of the text and the edge of the text box.

**Masters** One of three views that stores information about the presentation theme, fonts, placeholders, and other background objects. The three views are Slide Master view, Handout Master view, and Notes Master view.

**Master view** A specific view in a presentation that stores information about font styles, text placeholders, and color scheme. There are three master views: Slide Master view, Handout Master view, and Notes Master view.

**Metadata** Another name for document properties that includes the author name, the document subject, the document title, and other personal information.

**Microsoft Graph** A program that creates a chart to graphically depict numerical information when you don't have access to Microsoft Excel.

**Mini toolbar** A small toolbar that appears next to selected text.

**Minor gridlines** Identify minor units on a chart axis.

**Movie** Live action captured in digital format by a movie camera.

**Normal view** A presentation view that divides the presentation window into three sections: Slides or Outline tab, Slide pane, and Notes pane.

**Notes master**  The master view for Notes Page view.

**Notes Page view**  A presentation view that displays a reduced image of the current slide above a large text box where you can type notes.

**Notes pane**  The area in Normal view that shows speaker notes for the current slide; also in Notes Page view, the area below the slide image that contains speaker notes.

**O**bject  An item you place or draw on a slide that can be modified. Objects include drawn lines and shapes, text, clip art, imported pictures, and charts.

**Online collaboration**  The ability to incorporate feedback or share information across the Internet or a company network or intranet.

**Organization chart**  A diagram of connected boxes that shows reporting structure in a company or organization.

**Outline tab**  The section in Normal view that displays your presentation text in the form of an outline, without graphics.

**P**ane  A section of the PowerPoint window, such as the Slide or Notes pane.

**Paragraph spacing**  The space before and after paragraph text.

**Photo album**  A type of presentation that displays photographs.

**Picture**  A digital photograph, piece of line art, or clip art that is created in another program and is inserted into PowerPoint.

**Placeholder**  A dashed line box where you place text or objects.

**PowerPoint Viewer**  A special application designed to run a PowerPoint slide show on any compatible computer that does not have PowerPoint installed.

**PowerPoint window**  A window that contains the running PowerPoint application. The PowerPoint window includes the Ribbon, the panes, and Presentation window.

**Program tab**  Single tab on the Ribbon specific to a particular view, such as Print Preview.

**Presentation software**  A software program used to organize and present information.

**Presenter view**  A special view that permits you to run a presentation through two monitors.

**Preview**  Prior to printing, to see onscreen exactly how the printed presentation will look.

**Publish**  To save a version of a presentation in HTML format. You can save the HTML files to a disk or save them directly to an intranet or Web server.

**Q**uick Access toolbar  A small customizable toolbar at the top of the PowerPoint window that contains buttons for commonly used Office commands such as Save and Undo.

**Quick Style**  Determines how fonts, colors, and effects of the theme are combined and which color, font, and effect is dominant. A quick style can be applied to Smart Art, shapes, or text

**R**ead-only  A file that can't be edited or modified.

**Ribbon**  A wide (toolbar-like) band that runs across the PowerPoint window that organizes primary commands into tabs and groups.

**Rotate handle**  A green circular handle at the top of a selected object that you can drag to rotate the selected object.

**Row heading**  The gray box containing the row number to the left of the row in a worksheet.

**S**cale  To change the size of a graphic to a specific percentage of its original size.

**Screen capture**  A snapshot of your screen, as if you took a picture of it with a camera, which you can paste into a document or presentation.

**Scroll**  To use the scroll bars or arrow keys to display different parts of a PowerPoint window.

**Selection box**  A dashed border that appears around a text object or placeholder, indicating that it is ready to accept text.

**Series in Columns**  The information in the columns of a worksheet that are on the Value axis; the row labels are on the Category axis.

**Series in Rows**  The information in the rows of a worksheet that are on the Value axis; the column labels are on the Category axis.

**Sizing handles**  The small circles and squares that appear around a selected object. Dragging a sizing handle resizes the object.

**Slide layout**  This determines how all of the elements on a slide are arranged, including text and content placeholders.

**Slide Library**  A folder where you store presentation slides for others to access, modify, or use.

**Slide pane**  The section of Normal view that contains the current slide.

**Slide Show view**  A view that shows a presentation as an electronic slide show; each slide fills the screen.

**Slide Sorter view**  A view that displays a thumbnail of all slides in the order in which they appear in your presentation; used to rearrange slides and slide transitions.

**Slides tab**  The section in Normal View that displays the slides of your presentation as small thumbnails.

**Slide timing**  The amount of time a slide is visible on the screen during a slide show.

**Slide transition**  The special effect that moves one slide off the screen and the next slide on the screen during a slide show. Each slide can have its own transition effect.

**SmartArt**  A professional quality graphic diagram that visually illustrates text.

**SmartArt Style**  A pre-set combination of formatting options that follows the design theme that you can apply to a SmartArt graphic.

**SmartArt text pane**  A small text pane attached to a SmartArt graphic where you can enter and edit text.

**Source program**  The program in which a file was created.

**Source file** Where an object you create with the source program is saved.

**Status bar** The bar at the bottom of the PowerPoint window that contains messages about what you are doing and seeing in PowerPoint, such as the current slide number or the current theme.

**Subtitle text placeholder** A box on the title slide reserved for subpoint text.

**Suite** A group of programs that are bundled together and share a similar interface, making it easy to transfer skills and program content among them.

**Tab** A set of commands on the Ribbon related to a common set of tasks or features. Tabs are further organized into groups of related commands.

**Tab selector** Cycles through the tab alignment options.

**Task pane** A separate pane that contains sets of menus, lists, options, and hyperlinks such as the Custom Animation task pane that are used to customize objects.

**Template** A type of presentation that contains custom design information made to the slide master, slide layouts, and theme.

**Text label** A text box you create using the Text Box button, where the text does not automatically wrap inside the box. Text box text does not appear in the Outline tab.

**Text placeholder** A box with a dotted border and text that you replace with your own text.

**Theme** Predesigned combinations of colors, fonts, effects, and formatting attributes you can apply to a presentation or any document in any Office program.

**Theme colors** The set of 12 coordinated colors that make up a PowerPoint presentation; a color scheme assigns colors for text, lines, fills, accents, hyperlinks, and background.

**Thumbnail** A small image of a slide. Thumbnails are visible on the Slides tab and in Slide Sorter view.

**Tick mark** A small line of measurement that intersects an axis and identifies the categories, values or series of a chart.

**Timing** *See* slide timing.

**Title** The first line or heading on a slide.

**Title bar** Area at the top of every program window that displays the document and program name.

**Title placeholder** A box on a slide reserved for the title of a presentation or slide.

**Title slide** The first slide in a presentation.

**Trendline** A graphical representation of an upward or downward trend.

**User interface** A collective term for all the ways you interact with a software program.

**Value axis** The vertical axis in a chart.

**View** A way of displaying a presentation, such as Normal view, Notes Page view, Slide Sorter view, and Slide Show view. Also, display settings that show or hide selected elements of a document in the document window, to make it easier to focus on a certain task, such as formatting or reading text.

**View Shortcuts** The buttons at the bottom of the PowerPoint window that you click to switch among views.

**Web server** A computer that hosts Web pages.

**Window** A rectangular area of the screen where you view and work on the open file.

**Word processing box** A text box you create using the Text Box button, where the text automatically wraps inside the box.

**WordArt** A set of decorative styles or text effects that is applied to text.

**Worksheet** The document in Excel that stores data in cells. Used to create a chart in PowerPoint.

**Zoom slider** A feature that allows you to change the zoom percentage of a slide. Located in the status bar.

**Zooming in** A feature that makes a document appear bigger but shows less of it on screen at once; does not affect actual document size.

**Zooming out** A feature that shows more of a document on screen at once but at a reduced size; does not affect actual document size.

# Index

## ►A

.accdb file extension, OFF 8
accent colors, PPT 77
Access, OFF 2, OFF 3
action buttons, PPT 158–159
active program, OFF 4
adjustment handles, PPT 34, PPT 35
advanced formatting, PPT 122
   tools, PPT 100–101
advancing slide shows, PPT 14
aligning objects, PPT 36, PPT 37
animation, PPT 16, PPT 17
   charts, PPT 130–131
   customizing effects, PPT 102–103
   inserting in presentations, PPT 152–153
   slides, PPT 88–89
   timings, PPT 103
Animation tags, PPT 88, PPT 89
annotating slides, PPT 78, PPT 79
area charts, PPT 59
arrows in dialog boxes, OFF 10
Aspect theme, OFF 7
audience
   audience impact from visual presentations, PPT 87
   planning presentations, PPT 4
axes, charts, PPT 60, PPT 61
axis labels, PPT 58

## ►B

background color, PPT 77
background graphics, PPT 76
background styles, slides, PPT 76–77
backward compatibility, OFF 11
bar charts, PPT 59
black and white presentations, PPT 7
bubble charts, PPT 59
bullets
   default, resetting to, PPT 106
   picture, inserting, PPT 106, PPT 107
buttons, action, PPT 158–159

## ►C

category axis, PPT 60, PPT 61
CDs, playing music from, PPT 155
cells, charts, PPT 58
Center-aligned tab marker, PPT 109
charts, PPT 121–137
   animation, PPT 130–131
   cells, PPT 58
   creating using Excel from PowerPoint, PPT 122, PPT 123
   editing data, PPT 60, PPT 61
   embedding, PPT 122, PPT 132–133
   entering data, PPT 60, PPT 61
   formatting elements, PPT 128–129
   inserting in presentations, PPT 58–59
   layout, PPT 122, PPT 124, PPT 125, PPT 126–127
   linking, PPT 122
   organizational, PPT 149
   saving as templates, PPT 125
   styles, PPT 122, PPT 124, PPT 125
   types, PPT 59
   worksheets, PPT 58
clip art
   Clip Organizer, PPT 52
   finding online, PPT 53
   inserting, PPT 11
   inserting in presentations, PPT 52–53
   scaling, PPT 52
Clip Organizer, PPT 52, PPT 152
Clipboard. See also Office Clipboard
   screen captures, OFF 13
colors
   hyperlinks, PPT 77
   theme, PPT 76, PPT 77
column(s)
   data series in, PPT 61
   text boxes, PPT 101
column charts, PPT 59
column headings, charts, PPT 58, PPT 59
commands, groups, OFF 6
comments, PPT 170, PPT 171
compatibility
   backward, OFF 11
   programs, OFF 2
Compatibility Checker, PPT 159
Compatibility Checker dialog box, PPT 178, PPT 179
Compatibility mode, OFF 11
compression, pictures, PPT 55
Compression Settings dialog box, PPT 55
computer, preparing for presentations, PPT 83
Confirm Password dialog box, PPT 178, PPT 179
connector tools, PPT 98–99
content placeholders, PPT 10, PPT 11
contextual tabs, program windows, OFF 6
copying and pasting, Office Clipboard, OFF 9
copying shapes, PPT 34, PPT 35
copyright, PPT 5
correcting errors, Undo button, OFF 6
cropping pictures, PPT 54, PPT 55
custom shows, PPT 176–177
   links to, PPT 177
   printing, PPT 175
custom tables, creating, PPT 146–147
customizing
   animation effects, PPT 102–103
   PowerPoint installation, PPT 161
   Quick Access toolbar, OFF 7

   slide layouts, PPT 104–105
   themes, PPT 13

## ►D

data series
   charts, PPT 58
   in rows vs. columns, PPT 61
   worksheets, PPT 123
data series markers, PPT 123
   charts, PPT 58, PPT 59
databases, file extension, OFF 8
dates, slide headers and footers, PPT 38, PPT 39
Decimal-aligned tab marker, PPT 109
destination file, PPT 132
dialog box(es). See also specific dialog boxes
   arrows, OFF 10
   ellipsis, OFF 10
dialog box launcher, OFF 6, OFF 7
digital signatures, PPT 85
distribution, preparing presentations for, PPT 178
document(s)
   file extension, OFF 8
   previewing, OFF 12, OFF 13
   printing, OFF 12, OFF 13
Document Inspector, PPT 84–85
Document Recovery task pane, OFF 15
document window, OFF 6, OFF 7
Document Workspace Web site, PPT 171
.docx files, OFF 8
   inserting in presentations, PPT 50–51
doughnut charts, PPT 59
drawing
   freeform shapes, PPT 99
   SmartArt graphics, PPT 148–149
   tables, PPT 147

## ►E

editing
   chart data, PPT 60, PPT 61
   shapes, PPT 34, PPT 35
ellipsis, OFF 10
e-mailing presentations, PPT 57
embedded objects, PPT 58
embedding
   charts, PPT 122
   Excel charts in slides, PPT 132–133
   linking versus, PPT 135
   worksheets in slides, PPT 133
Encrypt Document dialog box, PPT 178, PPT 179
error bars, PPT 122, PPT 123
Excel, OFF 2, OFF 3
   creating charts using, from PowerPoint, PPT 122
exceptions, Slide Master, PPT 107
exiting programs, OFF 4, OFF 5

### ▶ F

file(s)
  creating, OFF 8, OFF 9
  opening, OFF 10, OFF 11
  read-only, PPT 84
  recovering, OFF 15
  saving, OFF 8, OFF 9, OFF 10, OFF 11
file extensions, Office programs, OFF 8
filenames, Office programs, OFF 8
fills color, PPT 77
First line indent marker, PPT 109
Fit slide to current window button, PPT 6
fixed layout format, PPT 129
fonts
  replacing, PPT 29
  saving with presentation, PPT 9
  theme, PPT 12
footers, slides, PPT 38–39
formatting
  advanced, PPT 100–101, PPT 122
  chart elements, PPT 128–129
  charts, PPT 122
  master text, PPT 106–107
  SmartArt graphics, PPT 150–151
  text, PPT 28–29
formatting tools, advanced, PPT 100–101
freeform shapes, drawing, PPT 99

### ▶ G

GIF files, PPT 152
graph charts, inserting, PPT 11
graphics
  saving slides as, PPT 63
  SmartArt. See SmartArt graphics
Graphics Interchange Format (GIF) files, PPT 152
grayscale presentations, PPT 7
gridlines
  major, PPT 126
  minor, PPT 126, PPT 127
grouping objects, PPT 36, PPT 37
groups, PPT 6, PPT 7
  commands, OFF 6

### ▶ H

handouts, PPT 112, PPT 113
  creating in Word, PPT 113
  preparing for presentations, PPT 83
Hanging indent marker, PPT 109
header(s), slides, PPT 38–39
Header and Footer dialog box, PPT 38, PPT 39
Help system, OFF 14–15
.htm files, inserting in presentations, PPT 50–51
HTML format documents, inserting in presentations, PPT 50–51
hyperlinks
  colors, PPT 77
  inserting, PPT 160–161

### ▶ I

indent(s), master text, PPT 108–109
indent levels, PPT 108, PPT 109
indent markers, PPT 108, PPT 109
Insert Chart dialog box, PPT 58, PPT 59

inspecting presentations, PPT 84–85
integration, OFF 2
interfaces, OFF 2

### ▶ K

kiosks, PPT 174

### ▶ L

labels, charts, PPT 58
launching programs, OFF 4, OFF 5
layout
  charts, PPT 122, PPT 124, PPT 125, PPT 126–127
  Slide Master, restoring, PPT 105
  slides, custom, PPT 104–105
leading, PPT 110
Left indent marker, PPT 109
Left-aligned tab marker, PPT 109
legends, charts, PPT 58
lighting, preparing for presentations, PPT 83
line charts, PPT 59
line spacing, PPT 110, PPT 111
linking
  charts, PPT 122
  to custom shows, PPT 177
  embedding versus, PPT 135
  updating linked Excel worksheets, PPT 136–137
  worksheets to slides, PPT 134–135
Live Preview feature, OFF 6

### ▶ M

macros, PPT 156–157
  security, PPT 157
major gridlines, PPT 126
margins, PPT 110, PPT 111
master(s), PPT 74–75
  custom slide layouts, PPT 75
Master Layout dialog box, PPT 105
master text
  formatting, PPT 106–107
  indents, PPT 108–109
message
  evaluating presentations, PPT 4
  planning presentations, PPT 4
metadata, PPT 84
Microsoft Graph, PPT 58
Microsoft Office Online Web site, templates, PPT 65
Microsoft PowerPoint Viewer, PPT 183
minor gridlines, PPT 126, PPT 127
mouse pointer, OFF 7
movie(s), inserting in presentations, PPT 153
movie clips, inserting, PPT 11
moving
  shapes, PPT 33
  text between text objects, PPT 56
multiple themes, applying to same presentation, PPT 12
music, playing from CDs, PPT 155

### ▶ N

Normal view, PPT 6, PPT 7, PPT 15
  Slide Sorter view, PPT 15
notes, PPT 3
  adding to slides, PPT 39
  audience handouts, PPT 3

online meeting, PPT 3
  printing, PPT 39
notes masters, PPT 112, PPT 113
Notes Page view, PPT 15

### ▶ O

objects, PPT 8, PPT 35
  aligning, PPT 36, PPT 37
  distributing, PPT 37
  embedded, PPT 58
  grouping, PPT 36, PPT 37
Office 2007, OFF 1–15
  benefits, OFF 1
  component programs, OFF 2, OFF 3. See also specific programs
Office Clipboard, OFF 9
online collaboration, OFF 2
Open dialog box, OFF 10, OFF 11
  options, OFF 10
opening files, OFF 10, OFF 11
Options dialog box, PPT 182, PPT 183
organizational charts, PPT 149
outline pages, PPT 3
Outline tab, PPT 6, PPT 7
  entering text, PPT 26–27
Outlook window, PPT 172, PPT 173
overheads, PPT 3
  printing, PPT 16

### ▶ P

Package for CD dialog box, PPT 182, PPT 183
packaging presentations, PPT 182–183
page setup, changing, PPT 151
panes, Normal view, PPT 6, PPT 7
paragraph spacing, PPT 110, PPT 111
passwords, PPT 178, PPT 179
  strong, PPT 179
Paste Special command, PPT 137
PDF format, saving files, PPT 129
permissions, setting, PPT 27
photo album(s), PPT 184–185
Photo Album dialog box, PPT 184, PPT 185
pictures, PPT 54–55
  compression, PPT 55
  cropping, PPT 54, PPT 55
  inserting, PPT 11
pie charts, PPT 59
placeholders
  content, PPT 10, PPT 11
  text, PPT 8, PPT 9
plain text format documents, inserting in presentations, PPT 50–51
planning presentations, PPT 4–5
PowerPoint, OFF 2, OFF 3
  checking versions, PPT 159
  uses, PPT 2, PPT 3
  versions, PPT 84
PowerPoint photo albums, PPT 184–185
PowerPoint window, PPT 6–7
.pptx file extension, OFF 8
presentation(s). See also slide(s)
  adding slides, PPT 10–11
  aligning and grouping objects, PPT 36–37
  animation, PPT 16, PPT 17, PPT 82–83, PPT 152–153
  black and white, PPT 7

charts, PPT 58–61
checklist for preparing, PPT 83
clip art, PPT 52–53
converting text to SmartArt, PPT 30–31
custom shows, PPT 176–177
design themes, PPT 12–13
e-mailing, PPT 57
entering slide text, PPT 8–9
entering text in Outline tab, PPT 26–27
evaluating, PPT 86–87
file extension, OFF 8
formatting text, PPT 28–29
grayscale, PPT 7
inserting movies, PPT 153
inspecting, PPT 84–85
location of file, PPT 83
masters, PPT 74–75
on-screen, PPT 3
packaging, PPT 182–183
permissions, PPT 27
pictures, PPT 54–55
planning, PPT 4–5
preparing for distribution, PPT 178
printing, PPT 16–17
reviewing, PPT 172, PPT 173
saving fonts with, PPT 9
saving for Web, PPT 180–181
self-running, PPT 174, PPT 175
sending, PPT 172, PPT 173
shapes, PPT 32–35
signing digitally, PPT 85
slide headers and footers, PPT 38–39
slide show timings, PPT 80, PPT 81
slide show transitions, PPT 80, PPT 81
Slide Show view, PPT 78, PPT 79
slides from other presentations, inserting, PPT 51
sound, PPT 154–155
spell checking, PPT 40–41
tables, PPT 62–63
templates, PPT 88–89
text boxes, PPT 56
text from Word, inserting, PPT 50–51
views, PPT 14–15
WordArt, PPT 64–65
presentation software, PPT 2. *See also* PowerPoint
Presenter view, PPT 175
previewing documents, OFF 12, OFF 13
Print dialog box, OFF 12, OFF 13, PPT 16, PPT 17
Print Preview, PPT 16, PPT 17
printing
   custom shows, PPT 175
   documents, OFF 12, OFF 13
   notes, PPT 39
   overheads, PPT 16
   presentations, PPT 16–17
programs. *See also* specific programs
   active, OFF 4
   compatibility, OFF 2
   exiting, OFF 4, OFF 5
   source, PPT 132
   starting, OFF 4, OFF 5
   switching between, OFF 5
projection devices, preparing for presentations, PPT 83
proofing tools, PPT 173
Publish as Web Page dialog box, PPT 180, PPT 181
publishing slides to Slide Libraries, PPT 181

**Q**

Quick Access toolbar, PPT 6, PPT 7
   customizing, OFF 7
   program windows, OFF 7
Quick print button, PPT 16
Quick Styles, PPT 32

**R**

radar charts, PPT 59
read-only files, PPT 84
Recent Documents list, OFF 10
recovering files, OFF 15
rehearsal, slide shows, PPT 83
Rehearsal toolbar, PPT 81
rehearsing slide show timings, PPT 81
Research task pane, PPT 127
resizing shapes, PPT 33
reviewing presentations, PPT 172, PPT 173
Ribbon, PPT 6, PPT 7
   program windows, OFF 6, OFF 7
Rich Text Format documents, inserting in
   presentations, PPT 50–51
Right-aligned tab marker, PPT 109
room lighting, preparing for presentations, PPT 83
rotate handles, PPT 34, PPT 35
row headings in charts, PPT 58, PPT 59
rows, data series in, PPT 61
.rtf files, inserting in presentations, PPT 50–51

**S**

Save As dialog box, OFF 8, OFF 9, OFF 10, OFF 11
saving
   files. *See* saving files
   fonts with presentation, PPT 9
   slides as graphics, PPT 63
saving files, OFF 8, OFF 9, OFF 10, OFF 11
   PDF and XPS file formats, PPT 129
   presentations for Web, PPT 180–181
scaling clip art, PPT 52
scatter charts, PPT 59
screen captures, OFF 13
ScreenTips, OFF 7, OFF 14
security
   macros, PPT 157
   passwords, PPT 178, PPT 179
sending presentations, PPT 172, PPT 173
Set Up Show dialog box, PPT 174, PPT 175
shadows color, PPT 77
shapes
   connecting, PPT 98–99
   duplicating, PPT 34, PPT 35
   editing, PPT 34, PPT 35
   freeform, drawing, PPT 99
   inserting, PPT 32, PPT 33
   modifying, PPT 32, PPT 33
   moving, PPT 33
   resizing, PPT 33
shortcut keys, moving between programs, OFF 5
signatures, digital, PPT 85
sizing handles, PPT 32, PPT 33, PPT 34, PPT 35
slide(s)
   adding to presentation, PPT 10–11
   annotating, PPT 78, PPT 79

background styles, PPT 76–77
embedding Excel charts, PPT 132–133
embedding worksheets, PPT 133
headers and footers, PPT 38–39
linking worksheets, PPT 134–135
notes, PPT 39
from other presentations, inserting, PPT 51
publishing to Slide Libraries, PPT 181
saving as graphics, PPT 63
slide layouts, PPT 10
slide layouts masters, custom, PPT 75
Slide Libraries, publishing slides to, PPT 181
Slide Master
   exceptions, PPT 107
   restoring layout, PPT 105
Slide Master view, PPT 74, PPT 75
slide orientation, changing, PPT 151
Slide pane, PPT 6, PPT 7
slide show(s)
   advancing, PPT 14
   rehearsing, PPT 83
   timings, PPT 80, PPT 81
   transitions, PPT 80, PPT 81
   voice narrations, PPT 131
Slide Show view, PPT 15, PPT 78, PPT 79
   keyboard controls, PPT 78, PPT 79
slide timings, PPT 80, PPT 81
   rehearsing, PPT 81
slide transitions, PPT 80, PPT 81
Slides tab, PPT 6, PPT 7
SmartArt graphics
   choosing, PPT 31
   converting text to, PPT 30–31
   drawing, PPT 148–149
   formatting, PPT 150–151
   inserting, PPT 11
SmartArt Styles, PPT 30
sound, inserting in presentations, PPT 154–155
source file, PPT 132
source program, PPT 132
spacing, text, PPT 110, PPT 111
spell checking, PPT 40–41
   as you type, PPT 41
Spelling dialog box, PPT 40, PPT 41
Start menu, OFF 4, OFF 5
starting programs, OFF 4, OFF 5
status bar, PPT 6, PPT 7
stock charts, PPT 59
strong passwords, PPT 179
styles, charts, PPT 122, PPT 124, PPT 125
subtitle text placeholder, PPT 8, PPT 9
suites, OFF 2
surface charts, PPT 59
Switch Row/Column command, PPT 60, PPT 61
switching
   between programs, OFF 5
   between views, PPT 14
Symbol dialog box, PPT 106, PPT 107

**T**

tab(s), PPT 6, PPT 7
   contextual, OFF 6
   program windows, OFF 7
tab markers, PPT 108, PPT 109
tab selector, PPT 108

**tables**
  custom, creating, PPT 146–147
  drawing, PPT 147
  inserting, PPT 11
  inserting in presentations, PPT 62–63
**templates**, PPT 88–89, PPT 170
  Microsoft Office Online Web site, PPT 65
  PowerPoint, installed, PPT 65
  saving charts as, PPT 125
**text**
  converting to SmartArt, PPT 30–31
  entering in Outline tab, PPT 26–27
  formatting, PPT 28–29
  moving between text objects, PPT 56
  replacing, PPT 29
  Word, inserting in presentations, PPT 50–51
  WordArt, PPT 64–65
**text and lines color**, PPT 77
**text boxes**, PPT 56–57
  columns, PPT 101
**text objects**, adjusting, PPT 110–111
**text placeholders**, PPT 8, PPT 9
**text spacing**, PPT 110, PPT 111
**theme colors**, PPT 76, PPT 77
**theme effects**, PPT 12
**theme fonts**, PPT 12

**themes**, PPT 12–13
  customizing, PPT 13
  multiple, applying to same presentation, PPT 12
  from other presentations, applying, PPT 89
**thumbnails**, PPT 6
**tick marks**, PPT 122, PPT 123
**timings**, animation, PPT 103
**title bar**, program windows, OFF 6, OFF 7
**title text color**, PPT 77
**title text placeholder**, PPT 8, PPT 9
**trendlines**, PPT 122
**.txt files**, inserting in presentations, PPT 50–51

**►U**

**Undo button**, OFF 6
**updating linked Excel worksheets**, PPT 136–137
**user interface**, OFF 6–7

**►V**

**value axis**, PPT 60, PPT 61
**video clips**, inserting, PPT 11
**view(s)**, PPT 6, PPT 7, PPT 14–15. *See also* specific views
  switching between, PPT 14
**View Shortcuts**, PPT 6, PPT 7
**Visual Basic window**, PPT 156, PPT 157

**►W**

**Web servers**, PPT 180
**Word**, OFF 2, OFF 3
  inserting text in presentations, PPT 50–51
**WordArt**, PPT 64–65
**workbooks**, file extension, OFF 8
**worksheets**
  charts, PPT 58
  data series, PPT 123
  embedding in slides, PPT 133
  linked, updating, PPT 136–137
  linking to slides, PPT 134–135
**World Wide Web**, saving presentations for,
  PPT 180–181

**►X**

**.xisx file extension**, OFF 8
**XPS format**, saving files, PPT 129
**XY charts**, PPT 59

**►Z**

**Zoom button**, OFF 12, OFF 13
**Zoom slider**, PPT 6, PPT 7
  program windows, OFF 7
**zooming in**, OFF 12, OFF 13
**zooming out**, OFF 12, OFF 13